The Condor Years

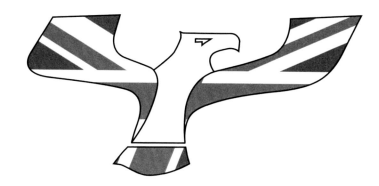

The Condor Years

A Panorama of British Cycling 1945-2000

Peter Whitfield

Foreword by
Alf Engers

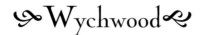

Published in 2005 by

Wychwood
Tachbrook House
Charlbury
Oxfordshire

In association with

Condor Cycles
51 Gray's Inn Road
London WC1

ISBN: 0 9514838 9 7

Text copyright: Peter Whitfield
Design: Kim Alexandra/Wychwood Studio

All rights reserved

Contents

Foreword by Alf Engers

My mother once said to me "You like your sport, don't you son?" I thought at the time Sport! It's not a sport, it's a way of life.

Newcomers to cycling are probably unaware of the comparatively recent history of the sport. Around the turn of the century, cycling was the pastime of the well-off middle classes, because bikes were very expensive things. Let's not forget that the present motor show actually started as a cycle show. Gradually over the years bikes became more affordable and more popular, and so cycling acquired its cloth-cap image with the public at large. But even before this competitive cycle racing was born. One testament to this is the Bidlake Memorial on what was the old Great North Road. The war of course stopped most cycle races, but for time-trialling at least, rather like the first sub four-minute mile for runners, history was made when two unbelievable riders beat the hour for 25 miles on the same day. This then became the benchmark for cyclists to aim for. Around this time also the sport's three governing bodies came into conflict. Two of them - the National Cyclists' Union and the British League of Racing Cyclists - came head to head over road-racing. The N.C.U. promoted mainly circuit races on disused aerodromes like Matching Green, Stapleford Tawney and Dunmow, which for the most part had fallen into disrepair, full of potholes and grit. These are now private flying clubs.

As a fourteen-year-old I watched one of these races, massed-starts as they were called, but as yet there were no junior races, and you had to be sixteen. What could I do? The answer came to me in a flash: Lie about my age, which I duly did. This of course became complicated, and eventually I had to lose two years. The B.L.R.C. promoted races on the open road. Your club had to be affiliated to the League to compete in League races, and clubs could not be affiliated to both bodies. This prompted riders including myself to join clubs "second claim". In many ways some people considered the League to be the more progressive of the two bodies, and of course there was great rivalry between the two. Training groups would pass each other, and a shout of "Up the League" would go up; in return a shout of "Fuck the League" was the reply. In this war the R.T.T.C. would always be in the background. This writer believes that some officials still dress in black alpaca jackets. Matters came to a head when the U.C.I. insisted that British cycling had to be recognised, and they would only accept one governing body, so the British Cycling Federation was born.

Thinking back to my early cycling days, the thing that stood out was the camaraderie that prevailed among clubmen. In the 1950s a group of fifty riders trained - or should I say raced - around Regent's Park outer circle in London. Could you imagine that today? I vividly remember notices in the cafes in the surrounding area saying "No cyclists served". Yes I'm afraid there was a rowdy element in those days. You had to have your spare tubular wrapped in a plastic ice-cream sign, the type that used to hang outside confectioners' shops; I wonder how many were lost to cyclists.

As a young boy I was fascinated by the whole cycling scene and around this time I joined my first club, the Barnet, and was privileged to be taken to see various national championships, including the national 25. I was gobsmacked to see two brothers, the Higginson twins, compete. These two brothers - of whom Stan had previously won the national 25 and held competition record with a ride of 56 minutes - rode like I had never seen anybody ride before. They sat perfectly still, not any movement in the upper body, and it was obvious from the look of concentration on their faces that they were oblivious to everything. Also they rode in straight lines, cutting all the corners. I decided there and then that I would emulate them. This was to get me suspended in the future, more than I ever imagined.

In many things the first time for everything is the most memorable, and for me my first race captured the atmosphere of the 1950s. I rode my first 25 on a course called the F4A just outside Barnet on what was then the old North Road. The event HQ was an infamous transport cafe called "The Beacon" that had a heavy smell of embrocation in the air. The clink-clink of shoe plates seemed to be amplified to a very nervous thirteen-year-old. I rode on gears, which was said at the time to be three minutes slower than fixed - how times have changed! Having finished my first 25 in a time of 1:12, I felt pleased with myself because at last I was a cycle racer. I played a new record on the jukebox - Elvis Presley's "Heartbreak Hotel" - more than once.

For me at this stage my ambition was to beat the hour, probably goaded on by a remark by a cycling uncle as I looked at his wooden sprint wheels: "Beat the hour son, no you'll never do that". Years later on a misty morning on the 32nd course (the E1) I achieved my ambition at last. I took comfort in the fact that I had done my best, and there and then looked to the future, little knowing what lay ahead for me.

The writer of this book is a dedicated cycling enthusiast and he has gone a long way to capturing the atmosphere of years gone by. Nostalgic maybe, but I hope that readers will enjoy this book, and continue to enjoy cycling as much as I have.

Don't forget it's only a sport - or is it?

Alf Engers

March 2005

condor /ˈkɒndɔː/ *n.* E17. [Sp. *cóndor* f. Quechua *kuntur*.] Either of two very large vultures, *Vultur gryphus*, native to the Andes of S. America (more fully *Andean condor*), and *Gymnogyps californianus*, of the mountains of California (more fully *Californian condor*).

Preface

I would guess that during the fifty years covered by this book, at least 100,000 bike races have taken place in Britain, contested by a similar number of riders. In this book I have described or mentioned only a few hundred of these races, and only a few hundred individual riders. I am painfully aware how compressed this book is, and how many good riders and important events don't even get a mention. Nevertheless I believe that a book of this kind is long overdue, a book that brings together some memories of the riders who have been outstanding in British cycle sport since the end of the Second World War. I see it as a kind of antidote to all the books about the Tour de France which keep appearing year after year. The Tour is all very well in its own way, but it inhabits a different world altogether from the bike racing that takes place here each weekend, and British cycling too has a story which deserves to be told. I also wanted to explore some of the wider changes in the world of cycling - the way our changing lifestyles and ideas have altered our approach to sport. Like most other sports, cycling has evolved with the sociey around it, and in many ways the history of cycling over the last fifty years has held up a mirror to our changing lives.

I see the history of Condor Cycles as a window on the sport as a whole. Condor was founded just after the war, a small business building quality bikes and supplying equipment to club cyclists, one of hundreds of such shops all over the country. Since then almost all these small frame-builders have gone, yet Condor has survived, continually up-dating its models, maintaining its commitment to the sport, and building its own niche at the heart of cycling. They provide a great link with the past, and my narrative moves continually between their story and the wider history of British cycling. The intriguing thing is the way that Condor's history has reflected so many of the forces that have shaped the sport: dedication to the craft of frame-building, supporting races with service cars, sponsoring both professional teams and amateur clubs, suffering when cycling was in decline, and profiting when it came back into vogue, developing cycling's image through the media, responding to changes in fashion but always hanging on to its own identity.

There are several things this book could not do without being two or three times as long as it is. The inside story of what really went on in the big races, the politics of the governing bodies, the huge commercial changes in the bike industry - these things are hugely important, but they would need to be written by someone who lived through them on the inside, and they would each fill several books of their own. Instead I have tried to trace the overall pattern of bike racing in this country, how much it has changed under the impact of internationalism, commercialism and the application of science - both to training and to the bike itself. Like so much else in modern life, cycling has become more serious, more calculated, more technical and more expensive; in other words it has become professionalised, and I have tried to show how it was pushed inevitably in that direction.

But the real aim of the book was to focus on the riders, to show how they fulfilled their ambitions, or how their dreams were dispelled. It is true that riders are like actors on a stage: behind them lie scores of other poeple - writers, directors, designers and so on - whom we never see but who create the setting in which the actors can shine. In the sport of cycling there exists a whole network of figures in the industry, in the clubs, in the race managements, in the governing bodies, in the media, who all create the context in which bike racing takes place. But it is obviously the riders who count the most. If all these other people vanished tomorrow, then the day after that a group of cyclists would be meeting somewhere and saying Let's put on a race this weekend. This is the great thing about cycling, that it is about participation, it comes from within ourselves and expresses something that cannot be expressed in any other way, and in spite of all the changes described in this book, I like to believe that there is something essentially unchanging about this sport. So it is really for all the riders of today and yesterday that this book has been written, as a greeting and as a celebration.

I have talked to a number of great riders while I was writing this book, and I would like to thank the following for giving me their time: Sid Barras, Dave Bonner, Ray Booty, Ian Cammish, Bob Downs, Alf Engers, Alf Howling, Steve Joughin, Colin Lewis, Dave Lloyd, Bob Maitland, Hugh Porter, John Pritchard, Martyn Roach, Eileen Sheridan, Dennis Tarr and John Woodburn. I have also been helped by several other people with expert knowledge of the history of the sport: Robin Hatherell, Phil Heaton, Phil Liggett, Dave Orford, Jock Shaw and Len Unwin. Orford is the expert on the era of the independents, while Shaw knows more than anyone else about the history of Scottish cycling. I must emphasise however that none of these people are responsible for the ideas or opinions put forward in this book, nor are they in any way to blame for any mistakes that I have made.

Many of the pictures in this book have never been published before. Condor Cycles have a photo archive of their own which I have used extensively. I am grateful to the staff of *Cycling* for allowing me access to their huge collection of pictures, and above all to Ron Good for permitting me to select from the thousands of marvellous photographs which he has taken over the last fifty years. I have also used a number of pictures from Jock Wadley's *Sporting Cyclist* and from its successor, *International Cycle Sport.* I have made efforts to trace the originators of all photographs, but I apologise if any copyrights have been inadvertently breached.

Alf. Engers is obviously the ideal person to write the foreword to this book. He is a legend in the sport, in fact I think he may be the only rider who features in all three chapters. He started cycling as a kid in post-war London, he was riding through all the changes of the 50s, 60s and 70s, and he set one of the greatest time-trialling records in history when he was approaching forty. Always a joker, he nevertheless had a single-minded determination to be the best. His cycling career was 99% talent and another 99% dedication. Like Condor Cycles, he is a great link with the past, and we are delighted that he is associated with this book.

A final word of thanks to Monty and Grant Young, who have helped this book to develop over the past year. They agreed with me that a book like this was needed, and they accepted from the outset that it was not to be a narrow company history, but that it must tell the Condor story within the framework of British cycling as a whole. Their generosity has enabled the book to be published, and I hope it does justice to their part in the history of the sport.

Chapter One

Tradition and Conflict, 1945-1960

1948

London, 1948: a different world from ours, a world which now appears to us in shades of black, white and grey, like the photographs and the films of the period. The aftermath of war was everywhere. London, like many other British cities, was still partly in ruins, with bomb-sites around every street corner. Even the rebuilding of the Houses of Parliament after the 1941 air-raids, had only just begun. Food rationing was still the curse of every-day life, and was even increasing: bread, never rationed in the war itself, was now on the list, and to save on petrol imports, all non-essential "pleasure motoring" had been forbid-den. Currency restrictions made foreign travel virtually impossible, so that even the newly-married Princess Elizabeth and her husband, Prince Philip, had spent their honeymoon at home in Hampshire. German prisoners of war, among them Field Marshall von Rundstedt, last commander-in-chief of Hitler's armies, were still being held in British camps. Collaborators were still being shot in Paris, and in Germany itself the trial of war criminals continued. Nor was there much peace between the victorious allies: tensions with Russia over control of Berlin were so bad as to threaten a new war in Europe. The dissolution of the British Empire had commenced in the previous year, when Indian inde-pendence had arrived amid bloodshed and near-civil war. Thousands of British troops still remained in India, while in Palestine the birth of another nation - the State of Israel - involved British personnel in daily scenes of violence and terrorism.

It was an era of austerity, but also a time of tremendous hope, for the Britain that was emerging painfully from the shadows of the war was a new Britain. Virtually bank-rupt with war-debts, the nation was nevertheless attempting to restructure its entire social life: coal mining, power generation, railways, docks, road transport, and even the Bank of England, were all nationalised, while the drive to replace the thousands of homes destroyed in the war had begun. Shortages and strikes however remained endless, and the weather seemed to conspire against us, with a series of bitter, snow-bound winters. In July 1948 the great-est social experiment of all was launched: the National Health Service, the lynchpin of a new era of social justice. "Homes, health, educa-tion, social security - these are your birthright", ran the slogan, but no one yet knew if or when these experi-ments would yield results, or what kind of society would emerge. Social planning was taking physical shape too, with the unveiling of plans for the first new towns which were to offer escape from London's bomb-

Kids racing their bikes on the bomb-sites of post-war London.

In 1948 the Olympics came to London with a small programme of events at Herne Hill and a road race at Windsor. Reg Harris won two silver medals on the track; he had been expected to take gold.

sites and prefabs: Crawley, Basildon and Stevenage were the first. The era of cars, credit and consumerism lay still in the future: although the number of cars produced in the UK topped three quarters of a million, many of them were destined for export, and at the first post-war Motor Show at Earl's Court, those admiring the Humbers, Rileys, Wolseleys and Daimlers were still very much the elite. Looking back, it now seems to us an era of tremendous austerity, a time *before* everything: before television, before motorways, before credit cards, before foreign holidays, before supermarkets, before rock music, before the permissive society, and before the electronics revolution.

Yet life moved on, as it always must, at work and at play, in the factory and the office, in the cinema and the dance-hall, the football ground and the cycling club. The one thing never rationed was tobacco: the British consumed 100,000 tons of it in 1948. Everybody smoked, from the King downwards: statesmen, soldiers, actors, doctors, miners, bankers, shopkeepers, everybody; sportsmen and athletes smoked, although some of them gave it up during hard training; even the cycling weeklies carried cigarette advertisements. The British people would need their new health service. That summer the Australians were in England for the first post-war Ashes series, and a nineteen-year-old player, Malcolm Hilton, became England's hero when he took Bradman's wicket twice in one match. The Aussies easily won the series, despite the batting power of Dennis Compton - "no rationing during a Compton innings" cried the press - but Bradman would retire at the end of the year. At the end of July however, all other sports were eclipsed by the London Olympic Games, which took place during scorching summer weather. The press delighted most of all in the running of "the flying housewife", Holland's Fanny Blankers-Koen, who took four gold medals on the Wembley track, including a narrow victory in the sprint hurdles final over Britain's Maureen Gardner. The modest thirty-year-old Dutch woman was hailed as the female Jesse Owens, while on the same track, Emil Zatopek first revealed his greatness as a distance runner to an international audience.

But the Olympics was not only about running: across London at the Herne Hill stadium, four cycling gold medals were to be awarded, and all English hopes were on Reg Harris, the reigning world amateur sprint champion. Harris would go on to become the most famous British cyclist of his generation, winning several more world championships, but in 1948 he had to settle for the silver medal, beaten by the eighteen-year old Italian, Mario Ghella. In the tandem sprint too he took silver, partnered by Alan Bannister. There was huge controversy surrounding Harris's performance, for he had been expelled from the team just days before his ride. His offence was absenting himself from the Olympic team headquarters, in an effort to escape the stifling heat of London. He was reinstated after an appeal, but Britain's cyclists were furious at this cavalier treatment of their star rider, and they had little doubt that Harris had been demoralised and cheated out of gold.

In fact a serious car accident earlier in the year meant that Harris was far from his best form. Harris was not the only cyclist in the spotlight however: in the Olympic road race in Windsor Great Park, Bob Maitland of Solihull, an outstanding young roadman and time-triallist, was highly fancied for the gold medal. On the day, Maitland finished a fine sixth place in the front group, just seconds behind the winner, Jean Bayaert of France. Before the Games the NCU, the sport's governing body in Britain, had declared aggressively that "Not a single cycling gold medal would be allowed

Monty Young (right) with friends at the Paddington Track, late 40s.

to leave these shores." In the event they all did, for there were no British winners; but the programme was smaller then – no individual pursuit, no points race, no paced event, and no women's events at all.

Just a few months before these Games took place, an east London teenager had left his job as a cabinet-maker, and had tentatively entered the bike trade, little knowing that he was embarking on a fifty-year career which would place him at the centre of British cycling, in which he would design and build a range of outstanding racing bikes for a whole generation of British riders. Monty Young was born in Stoke Newington in the summer of 1930. His father was a tailor while his mother ran a sweet shop. If you believe in inheritance, he gained from his parents the twin legacies of craftsmanship and dedication to hard work. Evacuated from London during the war at the age of ten, his schooling ended at fourteen, and he went to work as an apprentice cabinet-maker in one of the scores of Jewish workshops which thronged that area of London. Like most kids he had a bike, but the sport which captured his attention even more was weightlifting, at which he became outstanding, and would undoubtedly have reached an international standard had he not devoted so much time to his business. His first exposure to serious cycling came through his friendship with a near neighbour, Harry Rensch of Paris Cycles in Stoke Newington. In the late forties Paris sponsored one of the first commercial racing teams, and Monty would often go out with Rensch in his service van to watch the weekend's racing. He also took part in regular training and racing sessions at the old Paddington track.

The first great turning-point in Monty's life came when Walter Conway, who was soon to marry Monty's older sister, started a new venture. Wally was versatile businessman, who had secured the London agency for Triumph Cycles of Coventry, and had found a central shop premises at number 90 Gray's Inn Road to run it from. This agency meant not only retailing Triumph bikes, but supplying them to other shops throughout the London area. Wally was the admin man, and he badly needed a good mechanic to handle the bikes themselves, a role which he offered to his future brother-in-law. Monty seized

Monty takes the strain: weightlifting was his first sporting passion

the opportunity and in 1948 their small shop became Triumph House, and they were in business. With his craftsman's skill, Monty swiftly taught himself everything about bike mechanics, including both frame-building and wheel-building, at which he became unrivalled. Triumph (originally linked to the motor-cycle manufacturer, but by then a separate business) had recently opened a new factory in Coventry, where they turned out their massed-produced workaday bikes, heavy single-gear machines always painted black, which were a far cry from the gleaming hand-built lightweights which Monty would soon be designing. The business went well from the first, and soon Monty's family helped him to buy into an equal partnership with Conway. A second shop was quickly opened at 211 Ball's Pond Road, equipped with a workshop where the earliest Condor frames would be built. In a sense, the creation of this business was a small part of the reconstruction of post-war Britain, while its subsequent development would mirror many of the changes in fortune of the British cycle industry as a whole.

From the outset Monty's ambition was to do more than sell Triumph roadsters: he wanted to enter the sphere of cycle sport, and to build fine lightweight machines like those he had seen used by Harry Rensch's Paris team. He and Conway planned to produce their own frames, hand-built and meticulously designed, aimed at the top end of the sports market. Conway was a possible name for the new marque, or Conway and Young, but these were somehow lacking in impact, in appeal to the imagination. They wanted something that suggested speed and power, something visual and unique. A bird was an obvious image for a speeding cycle, but Eagle already existed as Coventry Eagle (and Falcon would soon be born too). It was the first syllable of Conway's name which gave the clue: *Condor*. The Condor is one of the largest birds in the world, with a wing-span measuring up to ten feet, native to the high Andes Mountains, whose peoples regarded the bird as a majestic natural symbol, which they embodied in their myths and rituals. The very word condor has a very unusual history: it is the Spanish version of the Quechua Indian name for the bird – *kuntur* – and is thus one of the very few words in English derived from the ancient language of the Incas. The concept was exactly right, and an artist was commissioned to produce a number of crests showing the bird spreading its powerful wings. From this design badges were pressed out by the well-known firm of Markovits, and in the autumn of 1948 Condor Cycles was born and the first Condor bikes were sold. Monty had secured a year's deferment of his National Service, but in 1949 he had reluc-tantly to leave his new profession, and his two years in the army took him to North Africa. Here he joined the famous Buckshee Wheelers, which spread throughout the British forces in the Middle East, and whose reunion events continued long after the war. No frames were built during Monty's absence, but the Condor story would resume in 1951. In many people's eyes, Gray's Inn Road, on the fringe of the City of London, was not an obvious choice of location for a bike shop: it was seen as a business district rather than a residential or retail one. But the critics forgot that around half a million people worked within fifteen minutes' walk of Condor, and all these people had lunch hours when they were free to shop. Nor was the area as dead at the weekends as might be imagined: just around the corner at Holborn Circus was Gamage's legendary department store, the poor man's Harrods, selling everything from cars to kittens, and a mecca for Saturday shoppers. Gamage's is long gone, but retailing in and around the City has never stopped growing, and lunchtime in the Condor shop is always bedlam.

A very early Condor track frame, built by Monty in 1952.

The Cycling Scene

What was the cycling scene in the late forties which Monty Young had entered? In the post-war years the bike industry was undoubtedly an attractive field in which to invest. Bikes were relatively low-tech engineering, whose components could be produced by many factories in the Midlands, and there was a huge pent-up demand among consumers for their own cheap form of transport, while serious cyclists were numbered in their hundreds of thousand. Perhaps surprisingly, the war had never entirely killed off cycle racing. In 1939 there had been more than 600 time trials, but even in 1940 and 1941 over 200 time trials were run at distances from 10 to 100 miles. It was only the 12 hour and 24 hour events that were found to be impractical during the war years. The BAR competition however was suspended until 1944, when a special short-distance version was run, over 25, 50 and 100 miles, won by Londoner Albert Derbyshire at an average speed of 23.5 mph. It was in 1944 too that the R.T.T.C. first designated national championships at the time trialling distances, although not yet at 24 hours. The absence of championships before that date perhaps explains some of the glamour which attached to certain events such as the Comet 25, the Charlotteville 50 or the Bath Road 100, events which functioned almost as unofficial championships in the 1930s. Even road record breaking continued during the war, with Marguerite Wilson the great star, in some ways the forerunner of Eileen Sheridan, setting several new R.R.A. records between 1939 and 1942 - her Land's End to John O'Groats record was actually completed on 3 September 1939, in the first blacked-out night of the war. The war undoubtedly disrupted many careers - Harris for example spent two gruelling years in North Africa and was badly wounded - but evidently there were still enough able-bodied men at home in reserved occupations to sustain the sport.

Monty Young and Wally Conway outside the first Condor shop at 90 Gray's Inn Road. They are preparing for a weekend refit, hence the less than brilliant window display.

It was in 1942-3 that Ernest Strevens founded the V.T.T.A. (Veterans' Time-Trialling Association) and devised the form of veterans time-trialling which we still use, with its structure of age-related standards, which was to give new incentive to thousands of older riders.

By the summer of 1945 with the war over, more serious than a lack of riders was the lack of machines. Engineering companies large and small had been diverted to war work for almost six years, and new bikes of any kind, not just racers, were at a premium. The Sunbeam Company ran a series of press ads explaining "It takes skilled engineers to win a war -that's why Sunbeams are in short supply". The Raleigh factory had been making munitions, and even the Claud Butler workshop in South London was building parts for weapons instead of bikes. In the first full year after the war, the UK bicycle industry was restored and turned out four million machines, although these were basic roadsters, and half of them were destined for export.

Yet even those basic roadsters were badly needed, for this was an era when working people in their millions depended on bicycles for their everyday transport. It was this everyday use which underpinned the sport, introducing each new generation to the personal freedom that comes with cycling, and it explains why cycling was above all a working-class sport. The bicycle meant escape: escape from routine work, from dead-end neighbourhoods, from boring companions, from family conflicts, even from the anxiety of poverty and want. People rode everywhere – to the factory or the office, to the shops, to the pub, to the football match, even to weddings and funerals. A survey in 1947 revealed that there were 14 million bicycles in use in Britain, while other figures for the same year showed that no less 69,000 were stolen. Utility cycling bred the desire for pleasure cycling - on country roads and at weekends - and this in turn bred the urge to race. Club cyclists covered huge distances during their weekend runs: Eileen Sheridan recalled her early cycling experiences in the mid 1940s, riding over 100 miles from Coventry to west Wales on a Saturday, sleeping in youth hostels, and then returning on the Sunday. This was done regularly, and these long steady-state rides formed the training base from which club riders progressed confidently to 100-mile or 12-hour or 24-hour time trials. It was virtually unknown for a cyclist to own a car, and the only way to reach an event was to ride out to it. It was quite normal for the time-triallist to cycle anything up to 100 miles on a Saturday, sleep in digs or camp near the start, race on the Sunday morning, another 100 miles perhaps, and then cycle stoically home again in the afternoon. These immense distances fostered the belief that stamina and staying power were the essentials of cycling. Only a handful of dedicated short-distance riders went out to train specifically for speed, and even to them, talk about pulse rates, aerobic thresholds or training levels would have been a totally unknown language. In a sense, most riders then did not train in order to race: instead their racing was simply an extension of their leisure riding. Providing bed and breakfast for cyclists was a minor industry: race entry forms in those days asked if accommodation was required, and if so the event secretary would arrange it. Near many of the time-trial courses lived a now-vanished breed of landladies who accepted the duty of cooking breakfast at 5 a.m. for six, eight or even ten racing men at a time.

These long hours spent together on the roads, in cheap lodgings or in youth hostels, fostered many deep friendships and a form of communal club-life very different from that of today. The cycling club was obviously central to the lives of thousands of hard-working people: their winter evenings and their summer weekends revolved around riding or socialising with other riders. It was a sub-culture from an age before television, before car travel, before exotic holidays abroad. The Sunday morning time-trial was an opportunity for a whole weekend away with the club. The highpoint of the club year came in the annual dinner around Christmas time, dining, dancing, speech-making and prize-giving, celebrating the identity of the club as a vital component in people's lives. The fundamental appeal of this serious recreational cycling was undoubtedly escape. The majority of club cyclists lived in the big towns and cities, and on each weekend or summer holiday, the bicycle provided their means to escape into the countryside, to the villages, hills or moorlands which were so utterly different from their everyday environment. The cycling press fed this sense of escape by presenting each week a stream of enticing touring articles describing the South Downs, the Cotswolds, the Welsh Hills or the Yorkshire Dales. These articles, well-written and evocative, with their grey, misty photographs or the fine pencil drawings by Frank Patterson, presented images of an idyllic England - full of tranquil lanes, wooded riversides, old bridges, historic inns, wild hills and moorlands - which was waiting for the cyclist to discover. Perhaps not everyone relished the communal rituals of club-life, but then as now, cycling catered for the loner too.

Albert Derbyshire, BAR winner in 1944, 1946 and 1947.

For lack of anything better, many riders raced on the same machines that they toured on - virtually roadster frames, converted by the addition of lighter wheels and drop handlebars. Those who demanded something better, and who could afford it, went to one of the many small custom frame-builders - in London Claud Butler, E.G.Bates, Freddie Grubb, Hobbs of Barbican, Paris or Hetchins, while in the north of England there was Harry Quinn, Mercian, Jack Taylor and many others. Claud Butler was the best-known simply because Claud himself was a showman who promoted himself endlessly, although he himself probably never built a frame, and many people regarded him as a bit of a fraud. His regular press advertisements, accompanied by pictures of himself, read like personal messages from "good old Claud" to club-folk everywhere, urging them to call at his shop for personal advice, get their orders in early for their new frames, take advantage of his credit terms, and above all

*Claud Butler,
self-promoting king of
the lightweight frame-
builders from the 1930s
to the 1950s.*

come to his annual Christmas gala. This was a huge affair, attended by a couple of thousand cyclists, a combined cabaret, dinner and dance which was one of the highlights of the winter season. Claud at one time had five shops in London, he employed many fine frame-builders such as George Stratton, and he sponsored or helped a number of leading riders, Reg Harris among them. But all his flair did not prevent him running into bankruptcy in 1956 – his principal creditor was the Inland Revenue to whom he owed £15,000 in unpaid purchase tax. After an attempted re-launch by Claud himself, the famous Butler name was bought by Holdsworth and then acquired by Falcon and applied to a range of lower quality machines. Lightweight tubing for these frame-builders had been unobtainable during the war, but by 1946 Reynolds 531 was back on the market. Purchase tax was levied on complete bikes, but not on frames or parts bought separately, so this was an added reason for enthusiasts to build their own bikes rather than buy off-the-peg machines. All these lightweight firms were dependent on the skill of their builders, perhaps a couple of dozen men in the whole of London, who worked behind the scenes, unseen by the public. They kept their trade secrets to themselves, but there is no doubt that a certain amount of branding went on, and that all kinds of tricks and disguises were used. Talk to one of these men today and they will admit that all was not what it seemed in the hand-built frame world.

Some of these small builders tried to catch the public eye with novel and startling frame designs: the Baines "Flying Gate", the Paris "Galibier", the Bates diadrant fork model, the curly Hetchins, the Thanet "Silverlight", or Joe Cook's "Imperial Petrel", made famous by Basil Francis. Why were these bizarre designs brought out? Their builders made strong claims for their engineering superiority: they were stronger, lighter, more responsive, more rigid and so on, but in reality it was a marketing gimmick, the creation of a brand image that was unique and unmistakable. Part of their motive lay in the strict amateur code of the day, imposed by the sport's controlling bodies, which forbade riders from advertising. This extended to any press photographs in which a manufacturer's name might be read on the bike's frame, and it was to get around this rule that many frame-builders produced their unconventional designs, designs which no photographic trick could disguise.

The quest for innovation or gimmicks has always been part of cycling, and it was there in the 1940s too. There was the puncture which repaired itself; there was the flywheel mounted beside the chain-wheel, which was claimed to smooth out power delivery; there was the rear derailleur which was moved by a lever on the chainstay and which actually shifted the wheel in the frame while the bike was in motion; there was the three-speed fixed wheel; there was the wooden bicycle from Italy, made of laminated ash, like a ski; and there was even a design for a hydraulic-drive bicycle, which did away entirely with chain and cogs. Yet all these experiments and gimmicks could not shake the doctrine that all serious training and racing must be done on a fixed wheel: everyone time-trialled on a fixed wheel, even in 24-hour events. This was partly because the gears at that time did not work brilliantly, nor were the ratios particularly wide. Above all, the wisdom of the past argued that the concentration required for racing only came with a fixed wheel; even continental road racing had only recently made the transition to gears. But a great break with time-trialling's past had come during the war years: in 1942 the R.T.T.C. clothing rules were amended so that, although the rider must still be clothed from the ankle to the neck, they now added the words "except that the knees may be bare" – in other words racing in shorts was permitted, and the black alpaca days were almost over – almost but not quite, for as late as 1947 and 1948, many riders still preferred their black tights. In 1950 racing jerseys with short sleeves would be permitted to replace the traditional jacket, but these jerseys too had to be black, with the exception of a small panel showing the club name.

What was the road environment for cyclists in the 1940s? Was it a golden age of empty roads and peaceful countryside? There seem to be two conflicting answers. First, the number of vehicles on the roads, at around two million, was less than a tenth of today's level. As a result, in most places outside the city centres, a busy weekday afternoon then was like a Sunday morning now; you can see this quite clearly in photographs of suburban high streets and country towns taken in the late forties. Yet the undeniable fact is that the roads were far more dangerous, for cyclists and motorists alike. During the wars years, road deaths were running at up to 9,000 per year - three times the modern figure. In 1948 this had dropped sharply to 4,500, an unplanned consequence of petrol rationing. By the early 1950s the figure had climbed back to between 6,000 and 8,000 per year, where it remained until the situation began to improve in the 1970s. When the lower traffic volumes are taken into account, this gives a death rate at least twenty times

The dream of freedom on empty roads: Rydal in a classic Patterson line-drawing. The reality was less idyllic.

higher than today's, an incredible slaughter, whose toleration by society at the time is hard to explain. In January 1949, it was officially confirmed than almost 150,000 people had been killed on Britain's roads in the previous 22 years. This is half the number of deaths suffered in World War Two by all Britain's armed services combined. The number of cyclists killed each year dropped from a high point of 1,185 in 1944, to stabilise at around 850 by 1948. This is around five times the modern death-rate for cyclists. What were the reasons for this carnage?

Firstly the roads themselves were narrower, twistier, poorly surfaced and poorly lit. Likewise the cars, although slower, were less safe: brakes, lights, tyres and steering were all fairly primitive by modern standards. During the war years there was the black-out, which caused many accidents. But most of the blame must rest with the drivers, who were inattentive, thoughtless and poorly trained. Probably the very emptiness of the roads encouraged their carelessness. Nor did society at large or the legal system foster any sense of personal responsibility among drivers. Again and again the cycling press reported cases of cyclists simply wiped out by careless motorists, some drunk and some sober, where the inquest verdict was invariably "accidental death". If a cyclist was hit by a car and injured or killed, it was, by definition, an accident, a chance that you took if you cycled on the road. There was undoubtedly an element of class bias in this situation: in the 1940s it was generally assumed that car-owners belonged to the social elite, while the cyclist was inferior and working class. Modern attitudes to safety and liability had simply not begun to emerge, and the brutal fact is that life was cheaper then. To sum up: cycling was statistically an extremely dangerous occupation, but so was any form of road use, and at the same time there was also a sense of space on the roads, which made people less conscious of the risks and less conscious of the slaughter caused by road traffic. Strangely enough, cyclists themselves were incensed when in 1945 it became compulsory to fit a rear light to bicycles. Front lights had been required for years, but the back light law was seen as a terrible infringement of civil liberties, and as contradicting the fundamental rule that drivers must always drive within the limits of their vision. The law was seen as opening the way for car drivers to injure or kill cyclists with impunity if no rear light was fitted. As with the helmet arguments of today, this was seen as shifting responsibility from the potential aggressor to the potential victim, a principal that was fundamentally unjust. For similar

The top English 25-milers sketched in 1950, including the pre-war hero, Frank Southall, the first English sub-hour man, Ralph Dougherty, and George Fell, the champion of the moment.

F.W. SOUTHALL
NORWOOD PARAGON
1·2·27 – 1·0·59.

G.H. FLEMING
BELLE VUE
1·0·58 – 1·0·16

C. CARTWRIGHT
MANCHESTER CLARIO
59·18

B.B. FRANCIS
SOLIHULL
58·49 – 58·35

R. DOUGHERTY
LEAMINGTON
1·0·35 – 59·29.

G.F. FELL
BECONTREE WH.
58·0.

RICHE

reasons there was opposition when the first cycle paths began to be laid out in the London suburbs, often beside the new by-passes: to provide special routes for cyclists was felt to be the first step in banning bicycles from normal roads.

        None of the risks however seemed to deter everyday cyclists or racing men, and with the war over there was an immediate upsurge in time-trialling, and standards improved so rapidly that there was a feast of record-breaking to come. The top short-distance man was undoubtedly Cyril Cartwright, who had set a 25 record of 59:18 in 1944. He was not the first rider to beat the magic hour barrier: this had been achieved as long ago as 1934, by the Irish rider Alo Donegan, and in England by Ralph Dougherty in 1939. Scotland too had its own sub-hour man in David Scott, who had ridden a 59.55 in 1944. Cartwright won the 25 championship in 1945 with a time of 59:44. His closest challengers were Jack Simpson and Basil Francis, neither of whom however had yet beaten the hour, which was still considered to be the feat of a superman. A fast 50 was anything under 2:10, while 4:40 would win many open 100s. The full-distance BAR was restored in 1945, and the English time-trialling world was amazed when the title was taken by a twenty-year old Scots miner, Jock Allison. Allison won the Scottish BAR too, and he remains to this day the only Scot to have won the national BAR. He was unable to repeat his achievement in the following years, when the more experienced Londoner, Albert Derbyshire re-asserted his superiority. Derbyshire was not invincible, and was occasionally beaten by the other top riders, such as Arch Harding and by Reuben Firth, Harding setting the 100 competition record at 4:17:46 in August '46. Nevertheless Derbyshire won the BAR twice, in '46 and '47, taking several national championships and competition records en route. Harding was notorious as "the smoking cyclist", his first request after a race always being for a cigarette. Harding was the archetypal clubman who later moved up the distances to become national 24-hour champion in 1961. Ten years later he was tragically killed in a hit-and-run incident almost outside his own home.

        Cartwright improved his 25 record to 59:18 in May '46, only to lose it the following month to Basil Francis, who turned in a 58:49 ride. By 1949 the 25 record had fallen to George Fell with 58.00, and in the National Championship race that year, which Fell won, no less than six riders were inside the hour. Cartwright would later win the pursuit silver medal at the World Track Championships in 1949, in the same meeting at which Harris won his first professional sprint crown, and he took the pursuit gold in the Empire Games of 1950, held in New Zealand.

        Many of these riders opened their season in March not with the hilly time-trials which we now have, but with medium gear 25's, which tested early fitness and the ability to pedal fast, and with "Roughriders" events, which took in the narrowest, twistiest back lanes, sometime unsurfaced, crossing fords and climbing short, vicious hills. Among the best known of these was the Balham Roughriders 25, run through the back-lanes of the Kent-Surrey borders. Both these types of events were extensions of normal winter riding, but rather different were the mountain time-trials over the moors of Yorkshire and Lancashire which would soon become legendary, such as the 50-mile Circuit of the Dales, which appealed to the growing number of massed-start riders who raced on gears, rather than to the traditional time-triallists.

        In May 1947, another great rider of the day, George Fleming lowered his own 50 record to 2:1:32, provoking speculation about the possibility of the sub 2-hour 50, a feat which seemed fantastic at the time. In July of the same year Fleming made the dream a reality when he rode 1:59:14, and he underlined his outstanding ability by producing a sec-

George Fleming, the first man inside two hours for 50 miles in 1947.

ond sub 2-hour ride just three weeks later. Before the war, Fleming had caused a sensation by recording 57:56 for a 25 during a private ride in Ireland in 1938, a time which was viewed with disbelief by many clubmen in England, being minutes faster than the official competition record. Fleming was also a top roadman, whose career came to a very strange end: two months after making 50-mile history, he was a member of a British team which was sent to ride a stage-race in Sweden. Fleming and the others were fed with a distinctly odd milk-and-egg mixture, which had apparently soured in the heat and which made them all severely ill. A week after his return from Sweden, Fleming shocked the British cycling world by announcing that he would never race again. There were rumours that Fleming was in some kind of trouble with the N.C.U. over sponsorship, and that he retired to avoid being banned, but these stories have never been confirmed.

At the longer distances, 250 miles was the barrier which only the very best could hope to beat for the 12-hour: Cyril Hepplestone had done it in 1937, with 251.6 miles, lifted fractionally in 1945 to 251.8 by Arthur Overton, a figure which would not be bettered until 1950. In 1948 a new competition record of 454.3 miles for the 24-hour was set by Gordon Basham. There were many 24-hour events at this period - the Catford, the North Road, the Mersey, the Wessex - but only in 1948 was a National Championship at this distance instituted, and this was the event where Basham achieved his record. Many of the top 24-hour men of the time, such as Basham, S.M.Butler, S.E.Harvey or R.F.Mynott would ride two or three such events in a season. By 1949 a few riders were beginning to use gears in 12- and 24-hour races, but the fixed wheel was still the rule. That year saw the first of Ken Joy's four BAR titles, and Joy invariably raced on a fixed, indeed all his training was done on 66- or 69-inch fixed gear, and Joy was a tall, powerful figure. He had been second in the BAR the previous year to his Medway Wheelers colleague, Peter Beardsmore, and the two men were great friends and great rivals. But eyebrows were raised among the traditionalists when, in October 1949, Joy took the London-Brighton-London record which Beardsmore had set just weeks earlier: Joy had broken the unwritten rule that you did not attack a record held by your own clubmate. Joy and Beardsmore had already joined forces to form an unbeatable tandem duo, setting a tremendous 100 competition record of 3:49:35 in July 1947. This was almost 30 minutes faster than the bicycle record of the time, for the gap between tandem and solo records has steadily decreased ever since. One intriguing competition record which is now forgotten was the 200 mile event, set up in 1939 by J.Fuller, with a time of 9:49:23. No 200 mile time trials seem to have been run after the war, and the record was deleted from the R.T.T.C. lists in 1951. Another now-vanished event was the 15 mile race for women: not yet officially a championship or record distance (it became so in 1952) it was felt to be a useful intermediate distance between 10 and 25 miles, and the 40-minute barrier was a difficult but not impossible target, Eileen Sheridan was one of the few to have beaten it before 1950.

Women's time-trialling may have had fewer riders, but it was no less competitive than the men's, and these post-war years saw a continuing battle for supremacy between four or five regular rivals. There was Susie Rimmington, Stella Farrell, Joyce Dean, Janet Gregory (who would marry Ken Joy in 1952) and Eileen Sheridan, who later went on to achieve her greatest feats as a professional record-breaker. These women took turns to win National Championships and break each others' records, with Stella Farrell (nee Courtney) having perhaps the greatest number of victories. In September 1946 Stella had set an unofficial women's world hour record of 22 miles 722 yards on a track in Denmark – unofficial because there was no women's track racing at that time. Exactly one year later she set up a new women's best time for the London-Brighton-London ride, of 5:6:35 for the hilly 105 miles. Stella also claimed the London-Oxford-London record, and the longest of her RRA records, London-Portsmouth-London. However it was Joyce Dean who achieved the honour of shattering Susie Rimmington's 100 record by 17 minutes and becoming the first woman to achieve an evens 100-mile ride, with her 4:43:25 in August 1947. This was in the dedicated women-only event, the Twickenham CC Ladies 100, and that day Stella Farrell was three minutes behind her, and briefly held the competition record until Joyce finished. Some years later, in 1952, Stella rode a 100 in 4:38:28, to get within a minute of the competition record which by then had been taken by Eileen Sheridan.

In September 1949 Eileen Sheridan took the women's 12-hour record to new heights, adding 17 miles to the existing record with her 237 mile ride, a feat which provoked disbelief among many cyclists at the time. Eileen took the ladies' BAR that year and Ken Joy the men's: photographed together, Joy towered almost a foot higher than Eileen. Married with a baby son, Eileen was just five feet tall and weighed eight stone, but she pedalled fast and was gifted with enormous stamina: her 12-hour record was achieved on a 79-inch fixed. In two astonishing years, 1952-54, under contract as a professional with Hercules, she would go on to break every record in the WRRA book, from 25 to 1000 miles. Attractive, vivacious and apparently ever-smiling, Eileen was an athletic phenomenon and, to the cyclists

Ken Joy, four-times BAR champion, 1949-52, and superstar of post-war time-trialling.

Eileen Sheridan, smiling as always at the start of her great End-to-End ride of 1954; she was still smiling at the finish.

9th July 1954
Before start of
Lands End to John O'Groats

Eileen Sheridan, smiling as always at the start of her great End-to-End ride of 1954; she was still smiling at the finish.

of the fifties, a legend. In fact she was almost too perfect: she made everything she did look too easy, she never even seemed to suffer during her rides. Only when she recalled the closing stages of her 1,000-mile-record, during a third cold, sleepless night, did she reveal the extent of her exhaustion, and the hallucinations that came with sleep deprivation. It is a remarkable fact that from the 1930s onwards women's cycling has produced so many outstanding endurance athletes - Marguerite Wilson, Eileen Sheridan, Beryl Burton - long before distance running became an accepted sport for women. In their different ways all these three were oustanding personalities: Beryl Burton's achievements were probably unmatched in any sport; Eileeen's intelligence and charm made her a perfect ambassador for the sport; Marguerite Wilson, whose records Eileen beat, was a strikingly attractive woman, who had every male cyclist in England dying to know her. Many years later her admirers were shocked when it was learned that she had taken her own life.

Each year the road champions would meet – as they still do – for the RTTC gala evening, and at this period this was a truly major event, for it was a gathering of thousands at London's Albert Hall, with roller racing, music, and celebrity comperes. In fact the event became so big and at times so rowdy as to become embarrassing to the organisers, and in 1949 it was moved to a smaller venue and took place in the afternoon.

The late 40s saw relatively few tandem and trike records broken, but a few End-to-End rides deserve to be mentioned. In August 1947 Letts and Parker of the Ealing Paragon set the first tandem trike time of 2:22:41, their only mishap occurring in the first hour of their ride, when another cyclist crashed into them, flinging them into the road. The trike record of Herbert Parkes in June 1949 shows what long-distance racing was like then: Parkes had no following car, and his team of helpers kept in touch by manning public telephone boxes day and night along the route, while volunteer clubmen handed up food. Parkes's time was 3:13:3, but it was to last barely a month before Letts improved it to 3:9:27. The next year Parkes would have the last word in this dual when he took a massive nine hours from Letts's time, missing the three day barrier by just 38 minutes.

Track racing was enormously popular in this period, most major cities having at least one track, while London had Paddington as well as Herne Hill. Track racing was, and is, thrilling and accessible to spectators in a way that road racing rarely is, and the excitement of having a British world champion in Harris boosted track interest still further. From 1946 onwards whenever he rode, Harris was invariably expected to win, but he was occasionally defeated, by the London sprinter Lew Pond for example, or by his own Manchester team-mate Alan Bannister. The top pursuiters were Tommy Godwin, bronze medallist in the 1948 Olympics, and Charlie Marriner who had set a British hour record of 26 miles 838 yards which would stand for 10 years. Probably the most spectacular track events were the tandem-paced competitions of up to 50 miles, each rider using several tandems teams who rested between turns. Coordinating this kind of team riding was a major challenge, and there were frequent disasters with the change-overs and with pacers lost through exhaustion. The speed was phenomenal: in June 1949 the tandem-paced 50-mile at Herne Hill was won by Reg Waters in a time of 1:39:5. The national record for this event had been set by E.Mills in 1937 at 1:37:5. Motor paced machines were first seen at Herne Hill and other British tracks in the post-war era, although they overlapped with tandem-pacing for a number of years. The top "stayer" - as the specialist paced riders were called - was Wally Summers, sponsored by Claud Butler, and who also turned his attention to RRA record breaking and to massed-start road racing. Paced racing on the track already had a long history, for the quest for absolute speed has always had an excitement of its own. In October 1946 the press recorded the death of Bert Wills - known as "the Putney Midget" because he was just 5'1" tall - who had been a track star before the First World War. In August 1908, Wills had set a world hour record behind a motor bike on a track in Munich, covering an incredible 61 miles, 1007 yards on a gear of 163 inches.

Tandem-pacing at Herne Hill: the pacers seem to be suffering more than the man behind them.

The Massed-Start War

So the post-war years were for cycling, as for the nation as a whole, a time of tremendous reconstruction: the industry rebuilt itself, time-trialling flourished, records were falling, we had a world champion in Harris, and the Olympics came to London. But the burning issue of the day, the issue which really dominated British cycling in these years, filling the cycling press and entering into nearly every clubroom conversation, was the problem of massed-start racing. For historical reasons the form of bike racing which had developed in England since the Victorian era was the solo time-trial against the clock, whereas on continental Europe the group race to be the first over the line was the universal norm. A few British cyclists visiting France and Belgium in the 1930s brought back enthusiastic reports of "massed-start" racing, and began to ask why we too should not organise such races. The controlling bodies of British cycling, the N.C.U and the R.T.T.C. resisted these suggestions, resulting in Percy Stallard's defiant promotion of his Llangollen to Wolverhampton race in 1942, leading to the formation of the British League of Racing Cyclists, which built up a road-racing programme in the face of determined opposition by the cycling establishment. We may wonder today what was the reason for this opposition: was it mere bloody-mindedness on the part of arrogant officials who wanted no challenges to their control over their sport? Perhaps there was an element of this, and BLRC members certainly believed it. There was certainly a general feeling that the circus atmosphere which surrounded continental racing was "un-English", that it was theatrical and commercialised, and the cycling press published many articles on what it called "massed-start madness". Many of the leading figures in the B.L.R.C. were firebrands, who refused to be intimidated by the "authorities". Stallard in particular was a conscientious objector during the war, and a strong socialist, who didn't give a damn about upsetting the traditionalists. Those who had ruled cycling's governing bodies and the cycling press for years saw them as rebels.

Nevertheless there were genuine and serious reasons for being cautious about road-racing. The central problem was that the legal position of all cycle racing - and this

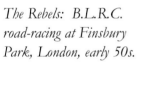

The Rebels: B.L.R.C. road-racing at Finsbury Park, London, early 50s.

included time trialling - on public roads in Britain had never really been defined. Group racing had never been forbidden by law in England, but in the late Victorian era it had been strongly opposed by the riding fraternity, who alleged that speeding cyclists disturbed their horses, and by the police; in fact the solo time-trial had evolved in the 1890s to create the legal fiction that this was not a race - that it was merely a succession of individuals riding along the highway. This strategy had succeeded, and time-trialling had established itself as a harmless, permitted form of racing. The fear now in the 1940s was that group racing - the massed-start programme which the B.L.R.C. quickly built up - would draw official attention to the sport of cycling, and result in a total ban on all road racing, including time-trials. It was for this reason that the B.L.R.C. was attacked as selfish and irresponsible by so many cyclists. This fear was strengthened by a number of statements from the Ministry of Transport in the 1940s officially discouraging massed-start racing as unsafe and disruptive to other road users, although these statements seem to have stopped short of threatening a ban on bike-racing altogether. An added reason for opposition was the British distaste for the commercialisation of the sport, which seemed inseparable from massed-start racing on the continent. Above all perhaps, there was the strongly-held view that the time-trial was the only true sporting test, and that massed-start racing involved a high degree of tactical riding and of luck, which often prevented the best man from winning. Time-trialling seemed the perfect embodiment of the amateur sporting ideal - a solitary test of will and determination, with no thought of fame or reward. This pure, idealised British amateurism seemed threatened by the whole culture of massed-start racing – foreign, brash, risky, full of intrigue, and driven by money. The attitude to commercialism was one of the fundamental cultural differences between the new League and the older governing bodies of the sport. Amateurism had been strictly enforced by the N.C.U. and the R.T.T.C. for

Ian Steel, top B.L.R.C. stage race rider, winner of the Tour of Britain and the Peace Race.

years, and no form of sponsorship or advertising had ever been sought or permitted. The League on the other hand welcomed any support and any publicity it could get. It was this approach which soon made the League and its events attractive to the cycling trade, and which created for the first time in this country a group of sponsored, semi-professional bike-racers.

These arguments were tossed backwards and forwards in the press, and among thousands of ordinary cyclists for some eight or nine years, until a truce was agreed in 1953 between the N.C.U. and the B.L.R.C., each recognising the other's role in the sport and permitting riders to cross over between the two kinds of racing. By this time the B.L.R.C.'s programme of events had become firmly established, above all the Tour of Britain, and it had become apparent that no official legal threat to bike-racing as a whole had materialised, or was likely to.

The League had a huge impact on British cycling, achieving a historic shift in the shape of bike racing in this country, and forming entirely new ambitions among the post-war generation of British cyclists. It sent British teams abroad to major events like the Peace Race. It established some classic events in the British calendar, such as the London-Holyhead, and above all the Tour of Britain, which later became the Milk Race, which in turn brought European riders to Britain. It was largely responsible for fostering an international awareness within British cycling. Yet massed-start racing has never replaced time-trialling in Britain: riders in their thousands have continued to vote with their legs and ride time-trials. The idea that time-trialling was an aberrant, second-best form of racing, accepted because there was nothing else available, is obviously untrue. One or two further inaccuracies about this conflict also need to be corrected. It has often been claimed that the cycling press refused to report B.L.R.C. events, but this is not entirely true: *Cycling's* editorial stance was definitely anti-B.L.R.C., but its reporting policy seems to have fluctuated: in some years it did indeed ignore B.L.R.C. races, while in other years it carried reasonably full reports of the major events, such as the Brighton-Glasgow stage race which was run from 1945 onwards, and which was effectively the forerunner of the Tour of Britain. *Cycling* had in fact carried a full report, with pictures, of the first, historic Stallard race in June 1942. *Cycling's* weekly rival *The Bicycle* had a much more positive attitude to the B.L.R.C. and reported its races enthusiastically. The 1953 truce between the B.L.R.C. and the N.C.U. seems to have caused a decisive shift in *Cycling's* policy, and from that year onwards the massed-start scene was fully reported, the Tour of Britain in particular becoming a major feature. The two rival magazines were to merge in June 1955. As a result of this merger one of *The Bicycle's* out-of-work journalists, Jock Wadley, decided to launch a new monthly cycling magazine which he called *The Coureur;* under its later name, *Sporting Cyclist,* it was hugely influential in stimulating British interest in European bike racing.

The N.C.U. did not outlaw massed-start racing as such, but only refused to organise it on open roads. There was in fact an extensive programme of N.C.U. massed-start racing on closed circuits – in London this meant Battersea Park or Finsbury Park, while in Manchester there was Belle Vue Park. There were also races in the grounds of country houses such as Blenheim Palace in Oxfordshire, and on police-controlled roads over War Department land in North Yorkshire. In Scotland the island of Cumbrae in the Clyde was favoured, while the classic venue was of course the Isle of Man, where the roads were devoted to bike racing for several days each June. This N.C.U. massed-start activity had been in existence since the 1930s,

Symbol of a revolution: the B.L.R.C. crest.

although it is probably true to say that it was extended under the impact of the B.L.R.C. There had been no time to organise a Manx road race in 1945, but in 1946 the race was taken by the Frenchman Baldassari, who repeated his victory in the following year. In 1948 however the race was sensationally won by a seventeen-year-old Londoner, Alan Barnes of Ealing Manor C.C., and then in 1949 it was the turn of Des Robinson (older brother of Brian) to take this, the premier massed-start race in the English calendar. In many of these races it was Bob Maitland who was the most consistent British performer, although he never crowned his efforts with outright victory. He did however win the Isle of Man time-trial several times, and also the N.C.U. massed-start championship in 1948, a race of 120 miles around the airfield at Matching Green in Essex. Continental-style racing almost came to Britain in May 1947 with a three-stage Paris to London race contested by French and British teams of thirty riders each. However, following the two massed-start stages in France, the final stage in England took the form of a time-trial from Folkestone to London, with its finish on Herne Hill track. The result was a great win for George

Commercialism in cycling: Paris Cycles of north London was one of the early team-sponsors in road-racing. Here the team poses - rather self-consciously - in a cinema foyer, to promote the 1947 film "A Boy, A Girl and a Bike", for which Paris provided the "continental" bicycle. The riders are, from left, "Stoppa" Clark, George Kessock, Karl Bloomfield and Clive Parker.

Fleming, who took the second road stage and the time-trial. Fleming was clearly enjoying the best form of his career, for this was just six weeks before he broke through the two-hour barrier for the 50. Bob Maitland was the next placed Britain in fifth place. This programme of N.C.U racing enabled Britain to enter worthwhile teams for the road races at the Olympics and World Championships.

In their battle for power, both the N.C.U. and the B.L.R.C. were capable of appalling political in-fighting. This was seen at its worst in the case of George Lander, a brilliant rider who won the 1950 Brighton-Glasgow race by a huge margin, and was set for a professional career with the Frejus team. This required him to leave the B.L.R.C. and join the N.C.U., whose licences were the only ones recognised by the U.C.I. Lander found himself trapped in the conflict between the two warring bodies: he was never granted his licence, he lost both his promised place with Frejus and his career, for he was never permitted to race in the U.K. again either, branded as a renegade by both sides. Lander, who might have been a pioneer as important as Brian Robinson, quit the sport, destroyed all his cycling materials and later took his own life. The path to the new era of road-racing in Britain was painful and difficult, and it was always the men who just wanted to race their bikes who were caught in the official cross-fire.

The massed-start revolution had a considerable impact on the bike trade in Britain, for one thing it began to break down the fixed-wheel dogma, and to spread the use of gears. Gears were obviously essential for massed-start racing, and of course they were used by all the continental riders, whose pictures were appearing more and more often in the British cycling press. The quality of the gears steadily improved, and the glamorous association of Campagnolo with Coppi's name or Simplex with Bobet's made these components highly desirable. Most short-distance time-triallists remained faithful to their fixed wheels until around 1960, but by the mid-fifties gears were widely used in the longer events and in training. In fact this development was just one aspect of a more general revolution in the British cycling trade: the move towards the import of components from France and Italy. The established British names such as Williams, Cyclo, Brampton, Baylis-Wiley, Chater-Lea, G.B., and Brooks would almost all be swept away by the fashion for European components, and their place taken by T.A., Campagnolo, Huret, Cinelli, Mafac, or Milremo. The magic word for any component in any advertisement was now "Continental". There were good design reasons to prefer some of these components: the cotterless chainset, the quick-release hub, the bar-end gear-shifters all had clear advantages, and they were made from aluminium alloy instead of steel and were therefore lighter, and they carried a glamour which British products did not.

However this fashion did not yet extend to frames, and riders remained loyal to the small craftsman frame-builders of this country, so that very few Bianchis, Bertins, or Merciers were seen on British roads. The reason for this was that British club cyclists at this time were obsessed with the geometry of the frame, and would argue endlessly over angles, tube lengths, fork rake, and bottom bracket height. These details were believed to be crucial to riding position and racing performance. The act of ordering a new frame was deeply considered: it became a kind of arcane ritual, and it required personal communication with the builder. They were therefore mystified when they discovered that top continental riders paid no attention to such things, and were content simply to order "a track frame" or "a road frame", and get on with riding it. With hindsight it is clear that, in trying to analyse the secrets of fast cycling, the British elevated one factor - frame geometry - above all others. But in fairness, it is true that little was then known of the other factors, such as aerodynamics, materials, and scientific speed training. The British attitude may also have had some social basis, in that a great many cyclists were technicians by profession: they tended to work in engineering, in draughtsmanship, in design or manufacture, and the technical language of frame geometry and construction was one that they could readily understand.

The growing attraction to continental ideas and equipment was a visible sign of a gradual sea-change in British cycling, as the sport in this country became less insular, and British cyclists found inspiration in European riders, whom they then sought to imitate. It was perhaps the first stage in what we would now call the globalisation of cycling, both in industrial and sporting terms, the first step towards the current situation where cyclists the world over want to buy and ride the machines which they see in the Tour de France. The leading designs may now originate in Italy or America, but the machines themselves can be manufactured anywhere in the world, and usually in east Asia. The impact on the British cycle industry in the 1960s of this process of internationalisation was a foretaste of what was to come in the motor bike and car industries, and indeed throughout British manufacturing in general.

It was B.L.R.C. massed-start events rather than time-trialling which provided Monty Young's first introduction to the world of racing. From the beginning, Monty and Wally Conway had worked creatively with Triumph, urging them to improve their range of bikes, brighten the designs and colours, and move towards the more sporting side of the trade. The result was the new Triumph models for clubmen launched in 1951, the "Torrington" and the "Imperial", built from Reynolds tubing, equipped with alloy components and finished in flamboyant colours. Triumph's entry into sports cycling was suf-

Monty Young as mechanic: with the Triumph team in the 1953 Tour of Britain. Stan Saunders, captain, is in the centre.

ficiently encouraging for them to take the great step of entering a trade team in the 1953 Tour of Britain. To prepare for this venture they called on Monty's frame-building skills, and in the summer of that year he worked day and night to produce a fleet of special racing frames, which were really Condors but which were branded with the Triumph name. Monty was also needed in the role of mechanic, for which he was provided with a Triumph motor-bike, specially equipped with racks to carry spare wheels and tools. On this he followed the 1953 Tour on its 14-day course, with its stages of 150 miles or more, contested by teams such as BSA, Viking, Ellis-Briggs, Wearwell and Hercules. The race was won by Gordon ("Tiny") Thomas of the BSA team, who broke away sensationally on the penultimate stage to take thirteen minutes out of the current leader, Brian Robinson, a margin which gave Thomas the final victory by five minutes. It was an important race because it also included England teams selected by the N.C.U. and it marked the truce between the N.C.U. and the B.L.R.C. The members of the Triumph team were frankly outclassed, and most of them abandoned the race, although Stan Saunders, the team captain, took second place on one of the early stages, and Dave Robinson (no relation to Brian or Des) finished less than an hour behind Thomas overall.

Whether Triumph would have come back for more in 1954 is an academic question, for by then the company had ceased to exist. The bike market was booming at this time, and the giant Raleigh company was eager for an ever-greater share of it. In the spring of 1954, Raleigh took over Triumph, and its entire operation was absorbed into the Nottingham factory. The Triumph brand-name survived for several years before it was phased out. The London agency on which Monty and Wally Conway had founded their business was abruptly ended. By this time however the Condor identity was sufficiently established for the business to survive, and at the same moment Monty was fortunate in finding a highly talented frame builder, Bill Hurlow, who shared his own sense of design and quality. The 1950s was a great era for hand-built frames: the pencil thin seat-stays, the chrome forks and rear ends, the scrolled or spear-pointed lugs. Each frame-builder tried to add distinctive touches of his own that were both imaginative and functional. Bill Hurlow had learned his frame-building in the1930s and worked for Freddie Grubb, and then after the war, in which he was an an armourer in the Royal Engineers, for Holdsworth. He became briefly involved with Paris Cycles, although he never built their frames. The Paris business foundered in 1953, and Hurlow made a short-lived attempt to rescue and re-launch it himself. When it became clear that this had no future, he moved to Condor early in 1954. Hurlow was a keen time-triallist who rode for the Galena C.C. and then for the Marlborough A.C., and he was capable of riding 4:32 for the 100 in 1951.

His first and most lasting achievement was to come up with a series of lug designs that were to become classics. The "Superbe" and the "Number 1" embodied motifs such as the fleur-de-lys, with much additional and perfectly symmetrical scrollwork. The "Number 2" and the "Number 3" were spear-points with slightly less elaborate scrolling. The "Italia" was a clean, open design. The head-tube and fork crown were the focus of the designs, but the patterns extended to the seat tube, bottom bracket and rear brake-bridge. It was a day's skilled work to cut a set of these lugs from the plain cast originals, and only around three frames were produced each week. When lined by hand, or better still, when chrome-plated, these lugs added a new level of artistry to the familiar bike frame, inspiring pride in their owners. These designs were universally admired, and fifty years later they are still being produced and sold, an extraordinary link, in the age of carbon-fibre frames, with the craft metal-working of yesterday. The brazed joints were meticulously finished, and when the lustrous metallic colours were added, the early Condor frames became works of art, and quickly established their reputation for quality and design which they have held ever since. After only six years in existence Condor were able to advertise with the slogan "Our claim to fame is in the name". Bill Hurlow's name and reputation were strong enough to be featured in their adverts and their early catalogues; no other bike manufacturers of this time named their builders in this way. But Hurlow did not remain with Condor: a hugely talented craftsman, he was also a rather difficult man, fastidious and uncompromising, and he had frequent conflicts with colleagues and customers alike. In 1958 he opened his own workshop near his home in Kent, and supplied Condor on a contract basis for a further ten years. Their relationship was finally dis-

Bill Hurlow, outstanding designer and frame-builder.

W.B.H. No. 1

W.B.H. SUPERBE

W.B.H. No. 3

FLEUR DE LIS

ITALIA

The Hurlow frame designs, illustrated in a 1959 Condor catalogue.

solved in 1968, but Hurlow left an invaluable legacy behind him.

These were exciting days in the Condor shop, developing a range of top-class lightweight frames and seeing them raced at weekends. But by modern standards the business was very small and personal: the frames were priced at from £15 to £20, and if there was £50 in the till at closing time it was reckoned a good day. Of course they sold other bikes besides their own - lightweights from Hobbs of Barbican and Holdsworth, and roadsters from Hercules or Coventry Eagle. As well as the frames themselves, it was Condor wheels which rapidly became famous for their build-quality. With an eye for publicity, Monty persuaded the Council for Industrial Design to examine and test his wheels in the late 1950s. The Council published an impressive report that a hand-built Condor wheel weighing less than two pounds had sustained an axle load of 1200 lbs before distorting; a tyre inflated to 120 pounds per square inch having been squashed flat long before this point. An interesting spin-off from this test was Monty's conclusion that tandems can be fitted with perfectly standard lightweight wheels, provided they are built correctly - a principal that has been proved to be correct.

Monty was always conscious that he was doing more than running a shop: he was building a specialist business in a very crowded field, and this demanded ideas and commitment that would spread the Condor name among serious cyclists. He saw it as essential to become directly involved in racing, and from the mid fifties onwards he was out most weekends with the Condor van helping at road races around London. Many of the riders at these races were his customers, from clubs such as Ealing Manor, Barnet, Highgate, Finsbury Park, Castille or Acme, and it was from this pool of riders that the Condor racing team would be formed in 1959. With the Barnet C.C. he sponsored an early-season road event which ran for several years, the Condor Grand Prix, a sixty-mile race through the Hertfordshire lanes which attracted some well-known names such as Ron Jowers, Vic Stark, Les Gill and Alan Shorter. It was in the 1955 Condor G.P. that Billy Holmes rode his first road race, but the first edition in 1954 was won by a man who later worked for Condor before opening his own shop. Ted Gerrard had become a top road-man while serving in the RAF, and in 1953 he won the N.C.U. massed-start championship. Gerrard later enjoyed - to put it mildly - a colourful career in England and abroad, making and losing several fortunes, and, rather like an Evelyn Waugh character, he disappeared from time to time to the Outer Hebrides, Mexico or the Cape Verde Islands. It was Gerrard's shop that became the focus of the powerful Barnet C.C. racing team, including riders such as Engers, Woodburn, Bennett, Rochford and Munford, a tradition that continued when Alan Shorter took over the business.

The original Condor head-tube badge from the early 50s.

The years 1952 to 1954 which saw Condor's move into road racing were highly significant ones in British cycling history because of the truce between the N.C.U. and the B.L.R.C. In 1952 the N.C.U. had reversed its earlier policy and had begun to promote massed-start races on open roads. This move was greeted with amazement and dismay by the traditionalists, who argued that the N.C.U. had betrayed its principles and was simply aping the B.L.R.C., although still avoiding any reconciliation with its rival. In June 1952, in the first N.C.U. open-road race, a 90-mile event in Staffordshire, Dick Bowes, winner of the 1951 Manx International, out-sprinted Bill King to take his niche in cycling history. A dozen further open-road N.C.U. events followed throughout that summer, alongside the restricted-road races in parks and airfields. So now two organisations were promoting road-racing along identical lines, but refusing to cooperate with each other for the good of the sport. How long could this bizarre situation continue? The B.L.R.C. considered that it had won a moral victory, and had established its chosen form of competition after years of poisonous official opposition. But the N.C.U. would still not permit riders from the two camps to compete against each other. The professional-amateur split was also a feature of the conflict as many (but not all) of the B.L.R.C. riders had backing from trade sponsors. The sums of money involved were tiny by modern standards, yet they were clearly professionals, backed by relatively big names such as Viking or Dayton Cycles, or by smaller trade sponsors such as Pennine Accessories or Jack Taylor.

Several factors helped to break this log-jam. Firstly a number of larger manufacturers decided in 1952 to form professional teams to compete in B.L.R.C. events, among them Ellis-Briggs, Sun and B.S.A, while Hercules would follow in 1953. They did this because the publicity surrounding the B.L.R.C. Tour of Britain stage race, now sponsored by the Daily Express, was a major attraction to cycle manufacturers,

*Bob Maitland
(left), leading roadman
of the period, with the
B.S.A team in the 1953
Tour of Britain, Alf
Newman (centre) and
Stan Jones (right).*

compared with the hidden world of time-trialling. The sensation of July 1952 was the decision by Bob Maitland, probably the leading N.C.U. road rider as well as a respected time-triallist, to sign a contract with B.S.A. and enter the professional ranks. Maitland had been incensed at being omitted from the 1952 Olympic team, despite being the top British finisher in the Isle of Man road race, and he made his big decision within days of being told that he was not going to Helsinki. Maitland was to be the lynch-pin of the new B.S.A. team, and two months later he was riding alongside the professionals in the Tour of Britain, finishing third behind Ken Russell and Les Scales. Among Maitland's team-mates were three other former N.C.U. champions, Peter Procter, Alf Newman and Gordon Thomas. This 1952 Tour saw a famous finish, when Russell, a lone Independent riding for Ellis-Briggs, suffered a mechanical failure just twenty-five miles from the end on the final day, after 1,445 miles of trouble-free racing. Summoning all his limited French, he asked his breakaway companion, Marcel Michaux, for help, and Michaux selflessly gave Russell his bike, thus saving his race for him. Russell wept on Michaux's shoulder at the finish, and the press acknowledged that sportsmanship was not dead in the professional ranks.

In March 1953 the U.C.I. at last gave temporary recognition to the B.L.R.C. as a representative body within British cycling. From the British point of view, this was both sensational and illogical, since the U.C.I.'s own rules specified that only one authority be recognised for each member nation. The N.C.U. was stunned, and was put under further pressure to compromise: the truce of April 1953 was the result. The truce was very far from being a merger of the two warring bodies, but its great step was to allow the riders from both camps to compete against each other in events promoted by either body. The Independent and Aspirant categories - apprentice professionals - were adopted to permit riders to move between the amateur and professional groups, although the exact definition of these terms would be a lasting cause of confusion and friction. The B.L.R.C. was to promote up to 750 events per year, the N.C.U. up to 250. The N.C.U. would continue to control track racing, while the R.T.T.C. remained aloof from the dispute, keeping its control of time-trialling, but recognising the Independent and Aspirant categories, and permitting time-triallists to take part in massed-start events promoted by either governing body. The two bodies would cooperate to select teams for international amateur events, while the B.L.R.C. alone would field international professional teams. The political in-fighting and the complex regulations are hard to grasp today; for example in the 1950s there were three road race championships in Britain - for N.C.U. amateurs, for B.L.R.C. amateurs and for B.L.R.C. professionals.

Behind all this conflict and confusion there was clearly a cultural change in progress: British cycling was being guided, or forced, out of its insularity and into a form of competition based on the international model. The agreement was certainly not the go-ahead for open racing, for only a minority of events were open to all categories, and the understanding of the different classes and licenses was sometimes confused. In October 1953, Fred Krebs of the RAF C.A. won a fine victory in the Tour of the Chilterns, at 160 miles the longest amateur road race in the country. Krebs outsprinted Brian Robinson, now riding as an Independent for Ellis-Briggs, and the amateur Ron Jowers of the Ealing C.C., but Krebs's reward was to lose his amateur status. It seems that Krebs had neglected to provide himself with an Aspirant's license, and his offence was riding alongside Robinson rather than winning the victor's prize. Evidently the officers of the governing bodies were studying the names on the start-sheets and checking them against their records of licences issued.

Despite the truce, it seems that riders from N.C.U. or B.L.R.C. backgrounds tended to stick with the group they knew, and not enter each other's events, while other major established N.C.U. races such as the Isle of Man road race remained closed to profession-

Club road-racing in the 1950s: Monty (in T-shirt) was out most weekends with the Condor van, servicing events in north London; no-one seems to be taking much notice of the riders here.

als. This made it difficult to settle the hotly-debated question as to which class was the strongest, the traditional N.C.U. riders bred up on time-trialling, or the rebel B.L.R.C. men. However several races in 1953 did provide the answer, namely that the B.L.R.C. professionals were the stronger at this form of competition, and were almost certain to win any race they entered. One of the first was the Bournemouth two-day race in April, which was dominated by Maitland, Ken Jowett, Frank Seel and Bill Bellamy, all in trade teams. This pattern was repeated in the other mixed-category races of that season, the Dover-London, the Peaks Road Race, and the Tour of the Wrekin, before the professionals departed to campaign in Europe, in the Peace Race, the eight-day Six Provinces of France stage race, and the Tour of Calvados, races in which Maitland, Bedwell and Steel competed with some success. The newly-established Route de France - promoted as the amateur Tour de France - was opened to British Independents and Brian Robinson, Tom Fenwick and John Pottier gained valuable experience there. But in the strictly amateur races, it seemed that the B.L.R.C. amateurs were no match for the leading N.C.U. roadmen like Arthur Ilsley, the two King brothers, Bernard and Bill, Les Willmott, Brian Haskell, Dick Bowes, John Perks and Bernard Pusey. By the summer of 1953 each weekend saw half a dozen races on the open roads in all parts of the country, contested by a growing band of amateur rid-

ers who had made the transition from time-trialling and who evidently liked what they found. At the same time a number of B.L.R.C. men rejoined their former clubs, and were now able to mix time-trialling with their massed-start racing.

Ted Gerrard, Condor employee and champion rider, bike-shop owner and racing team manager. His business was continued by Alan Shorter.

The 1953 truce was short-lived. In March of the following year the U.C.I. withdrew its recognition of the B.L.R.C., and the N.C.U. took advantage of its strengthened position, reminding all British riders that they must have a N.C.U. licence to race abroad. The B.L.R.C., which had of course pioneered overseas racing, was furious, and matters came to a head in May 1954 when the Hercules team, including Bedwell, Steel, Parker and Greenfield, were refused permission to start in the Flemish classics the Fleche Wallonne and Liege-Bastogne-Liege. This problem of overseas licences drove the two bodies still further apart. The reputation of cycling as a sport was suffering, and in the winter of that year the Daily Express decided to end its sponsorship of the Tour of Britain, tired of dealing with two quarrelling sets of officials who both claimed to represent the sport. This news came in spite of the highly-successful 1954 Tour of Britain, in which Eugene Tamburlini of France was the victor, ahead of Brian Robinson and Dave Bedwell. Worse was to come in 1955 and 1956. The major trade sponsors, BSA, Viking, Hercules and Wearwell, all disbanded their teams, disillusioned with the progress that road sport was making in Britain, and this signalled the end of the first brief experiment with professional racing in this country. Hercules had made a calculated attempt over the past two years to break into the European racing scene, and the 1955 Tour de France was virtually the Hercules team in all but name. The gamble cost a great deal of money and Hercules decided to pull out - although this did not prevent the company from rather cynically market-

*Stan Saunders,
captain of the Triumph
team in the 1953 Tour
of Britain, which rode
Condors branded as
Triumphs. Stan later
ran his own bike-shop
in south London.*

ing a new model in 1956 called the "Tour de France Equipe", said to be identical to the machines ridden in the great race.

When all these ex-professionals found themselves without sponsors, it seemed that dozens of good riders would be lost to the sport, for there was no way back for them into N.C.U. racing or into time-trialling. The situation was largely saved by Dave Orford in Derbyshire, who formed the B.P.I.C.A., the British Professional and Independents' Cycling Association, and organised an energetic programme of road-racing over the next few years, in which Ron Coe built his reputation for invincibility. At the same time it emerged that the N.C.U. and the B.L.R.C. could not even agree their definitions of permitted competition between professional, amateur and independent. The B.L.R.C. was ready to let former professionals revert to independent or amateur status, but the N.C.U. was not. In the Condor Grand Prix of April 1956, the situation erupted, and several dozen amateurs who competed in that race were suspended for competing with Graham Vines, a former top B.L.R.C. professional. Category chaos ensued, and the uncertainty and frustration would not be removed until the following year, when mixed-category racing - that is, amateur and independent or professionals and independents, but not amateurs and professionals - was clearly approved by the N.C.U. and the R.T.T.C. Road-racing in Britain had become an accepted fact, but the hatred that existed between the two governing bodies prevented the obvious solution, which was amalgamation. In part it was the struggle between the old amateur ideal and the new forces of professionalism, but it was also a personal power struggle between two sets of determined and embittered men. A similar split in the sport in Scotland had been healed relatively easily in 1952.

In the winter of 1956-57 the U.C.I. lost patience, and threatened to expel Britain unless the two authorities could settle their differences and create one official body with whom the U.C.I. could deal. This forced both sides to accept amalgamation as inevitable, and by the autumn of 1958 an agreement was ready to dissolve the N.C.U. and the B.L.R.C. and replace them with a new body – the B.C.F. The sponsorship deal by the Milk Marketing Board for the Tour of Britain was instrumental in preparing the ground, for the MMB wanted the race to feature all the best British riders, regardless of category, and the two bodies hammered out a common set of rules, and opened the race to trade team riders, although it reverted to all-amateur from 1960 onwards. The years of conflict were finally ended in February 1959, when both the N.C.U. and the B.L.R.C. voted themselves out of existence, and transferred all their powers and functions to the newborn B.C.F.

A significant group of riders had stayed loyal to the N.C.U. including Stan Brittain, the two King brothers Bill and Bernard, Eric Thompson and Bill Bradley, who would later prove himself probably the strongest amateur roadman in Britain. One reason why these men kept faith with the N.C.U. was their wish to ride in R.T.T.C. time-trials, but a far more important one was the desire to gain selection for international races, above all for the World's Championships and the Olympics. Among these N.C.U. amateurs were many riders who moved easily between road-racing and time-trialling, and were clearly among the best in the country in both fields: Ray Booty, Ron Jowers, Billy Holmes, Owen Blower and Brian Wiltcher. Each week the N.C.U. men and League men would fight their own battles, or occasionally mix with each other if permitted, depending on who was promoting the race and which other groups had entered.

Leaving aside the politics for a while, is it possible to highlight some outstanding rides and riders of these years, achieved both at home and in international competition ? Historically the most important figure was undoubtedly Brian Robinson, who served his apprenticeship riding in the Tour of Britain in the early fifties, and after various trips abroad, came to the big decision that this was where the future lay. He based himself permanently in France, and with quiet determination set about making the transition to the European professional standard. His success made him the natural choice to lead the first British team in the Tour de France in 1955, in which he and Tony Hoar finished with credit, although Bedwell, Steel, Maitland and all the rest of the team had to abdandon. In 1956, riding in a composite international team, he became the first Briton to win a stage, and finished 14th overall. Slight in build, displaying no special magic or fireworks, Robinson possessed the immense stamina, recovery-power and cool judgement essential to a good stage-race rider. His example prepared the way for Tom Simpson, indeed his achievement inspired a whole generation of British riders to follow his path to France, often living on a shoestring in caravans - or a converted ambulance as Tony Hewson and Vic Sutton did - or seeking the backing of a local club or a trade team, with a place in the Tour de France as their great burning ambition. Reg Harris had already succeeded brilliantly in Europe, but that was in the specialist world of professional sprinting, where none could follow him. Robinson changed forever the horizons of British cyclists, completing what the B.L.R.C. had begun – the internationalisation of British cycling. Robinson's success, and the stream of riders who followed him across the channel to race, created a sense that we

were on the verge of a real breakthrough into top-level European competition. But British riders would find again and again in the following decades just how difficult it was to make that transition. Ian Steel had won two historic victories – in the 1951 Tour of Britain and the 1952 Peace Race – which in the climate of the time were barely reported in the cycling press. A few years later road-racing was bigger news, and Steel's start in the 1955 Tour of Spain and Tour de France was well-reported, but he was unable to finish in either. Other casualties in that first British Tour were Maitland, Bedwell, Pusey, Jones and Krebs, all big winners at home, but who all retired in the early stages.

Similarly, there was Ron Coe, the tall strongly-built Yorkshireman who set

Alf Howling, later to ride for the Condor racing team, after victory in the 1956 Martini G.P.

up a fine record between 1952 and 1954, then turned his back on the sport, during which time he admitted that he smoked and drank heavily. After a two-year layoff however, he came back in 1957 to such good effect that he had four wins in four rides in March, became an independent for Wilson Cycles, and wrapped up the B.L.R.C. pro-independent championship in a 90-mile race through the toughest roads in the Peaks, beating among others Bob Maitland, Arthur Ilsley, Dave Bedwell and Brian Haskell. One week later he was the victor in the two-day Tour of the Lakes, and he confirmed his superiority in July

by taking the first N.C.U. professional-independent championship. Signing for the new Elswick-Hopper team, he started 1958 in the same tremendous form, taking all three stages of the Buxton Spring Road Race, and continued winning so regularly that he was selected for the composite international team in the Tour de France, alongside Robinson, Elliott and Stan Brittain. Before going off to France he stormed through the first Milk Race, taking four stage wins and finishing seventh. The difference in the level of racing in the Tour de France however was too great, and Coe retired on stage six, ostensibly with a knee injury. There was little sign of this however when, just days after his return home, he flew over 146 miles of the Kentish hills in less than six hours, to win the B.L.R.C professional championship by the huge margin of nearly eight minutes. In the two seasons since his come-back he had won 65 races, and in 1959 the pattern continued with victories in the Archer G.P. in March, the Huddersfield Road Race in April and the Tour of the Cotswolds in May. The scene was set for what should have been the highlight of the year – the second Milk Race in June, but this race ended for Coe in controversy. True to form, after the first week Coe had won two stages, was leading the points classification and was lying second to Bill Bradley. Bradley was Coe's team-mate in the England team, as was Harry Reynolds, but, outside of this race, Coe and Reynolds were both members of the same Elswick-Hopper team, and were in turn rivals of some of the other

Brian Robinson, the man who opened the door to the continent for other British riders to follow, although few could emulate his achievements.

England men who rode for the Viking team. On stage nine tensions between these "ghost teams" came out into the open, and Reynolds attacked, wiping out all but one minute of Bradley's big lead, while Coe sat in with Bradley and did nothing to help him. The furious manager of the England team, Gordon Thomas, demanded from the race organisers the expulsion of both Reynolds and Coe for "bad sportsmanship and conduct prejudicial to the good running of the race". It was a humiliating exit for Coe, who picked up the pieces later in the summer and won a number of good races, but he did not come back in 1960. His contract with Elswick-Hopper expired, and he went to race in France, where he was briefly sponsored by the Bertin-Milremo team, but the results did not come. He returned to Britain to compete in the Isle of Man professional road race, but failed to finish, and after that a serious accident disrupted his progress. In 1961 his obvious class gave him a second chance in the British Tour de France team of that year, but he retired early, along with most of the team. Coe could not make the transition to the higher continental standard, but his experiences there seemed to undermine his home-based racing, and he never regained his top form; the huge natural talent of this prolific winner was lost to the sport for reasons which will never be fully explained.

Ron Coe, prolific winner at home, but victim of Tour de France ambitions.

For the British road-racer, to be selected for the Tour de France was the ultimate dream, and to finish it made them seem like a god. But Stan Brittain was one of these early heroes who made no secret of the suffering involved at this level of the sport, and the disillusion afterwards if it appeared to lead nowhere. He described his 1958 Tour as three weeks of agony, not knowing what town he was in or what day it was, just eating, sleeping and keeping the legs turning round, clinging on behind the leaders. Beginning as a time-triallist (he was second to Booty in the historic sub four-hour 100 of 1956) Brittain became one of the toughest British roadmen of the fifties, having won stages and twice claimed a podium place in the notorious Peace Race, in 1955 and 1957, and taken overall victory in the Tour of Sweden in 1957. In the 1958 Tour, Robinson was forced out by injury, and Brittain's reward for his three-week ordeal was a half-share with Shay Elliott of about £700. There was no team place for him in 1959, and although he started in the 1960 Tour he failed to finish, and returned to England to ride for the Viking team. Brittain's greatest achievements were in overseas races, and after 1959 the Milk Race was closed to him, so that he is perhaps less of a memory than some of the riders who raced at home. More than Brittain's, the name of Dave Bedwell seems to evoke the whole British road-racing scene throughout the 1950s. He won the B.L.R.C. championship in 1951, the same year that he took the King of the Mountains prize in the first Tour of Britain, and exactly ten years later he won the B.C.F. professional road title. In between the pocket Hercules from Romford had scored dozens of victories and still more near-misses. Tiny in stature - he rode an 18-inch frame - he could race all day and still pack a devastating sprint. In the 1956 Pro World Championship race, Bedwell battled for 178 miles to finish just six minutes behind van Steenbergen, van Looy, Bobet and Coppi. He made many ventures into continental racing, but always returned to the British scene, riding for a succession of sponsors – Dayton, Wearwell, Hercules, Rory O'Brien and Viking. Always explosive in temperament, when his strength to pedal had gone he could still shout his defiance: in September 1959 he was trying for his third successive win in the Criterium des Vainquers in Essex. Hurtling towards the line with Ron Coe on his wheel, Bedwell suddenly died and freewheeled over the line, screaming that the 200-yards-to-go marker was too far out. "I went from there", he pointed,

Stan Brittain, Tour de France pioneer in 1958.

Dave Bedwell (above) iron-man sprinter of the 1950s and twice pro road champion. Ray Booty the roadman (below) winning the 1958 Commonwealth Games race in Cardiff.

" I had it in the bag. I couldn't help but blow up". The chief judge reminded him that since he'd won the race twice before, he should know the finish better than anyone else. Bedwell's strength came from a training regime of huge mileages, 300 miles on a winter weekend being normal; when leaving to take part in the 1954 Paris-Nice, he and his fellow Hercules professionals, Parker, Talbot and Buttle, pedalled from London to Paris two days before the race.

If Bedwell was one icon of the fifties, an even greater one was Ray Booty, who must have towered a foot above Bedwell when they occasionally raced together. But Booty was the pure amateur, and his historic time-trialling achievements have tended to overshadow his many great road-racing exploits. Booty was a relatively unknown 21-year-old in 1954 when he won one of the hardest Manx Internationals ever run, on a wet, gale-torn day, taking the King of the Mountains prize on the way. It was on an almost identical day four years later, a day of cold, swirling, wind-blown rain, that Booty took his other great international title, the Empire Games road race in Cardiff, where he finished alone, minutes ahead of, among others, Bill Bradley. In the years between these two legendary victories Booty rode many fine races, winning some and losing many, but he took them all philosophically. In the world championship race in Solingen in 1954, the year of his Manx triumph, he crashed heavily in the first mile, gashing his leg and bruising himself all over, but he rode on alone over the entire course, to finish almost half an hour down. In the 1955 World's in Rome he finished ninth, two minutes down on Ranucci, the Italian winner. In the 1956 World's in Denmark, history repeated itself, when another disastrous crash took him out in the first mile. He was severely criticised after the 1956 Manx International, in which he finished third, because the three Britons could not prevent an unknown Italian from taking the victory when they were all together for the final half-lap. The unknown Italian was named Baldini, and he would later win the Olympic road race, break the world hour record while still an amateur, and then win the world professional road race title. Booty accepted all these experiences without drama or despair: like his victories and the adulation he received for them, these were not steps up or down a great career ladder, but mere incidents in this most challenging of sports. Slightly unpredictable, and certainly not known as a sprinter,

Booty could occasionally exert his immense strength, especially when conditions were hard, and take off and time-trial to victory alone, as he did in the 1958 Birmingham to Barmouth race, when he covered 115 hilly miles in 4-38-47, leaving top sponsored riders like Maitland and Bedwell literally miles behind on the road.

Physically somewhere between the Bedwell and Booty extremes was Bill Bradley: slight in build, of average height, modest, casual, polite, apparently unremarkable, he became a giant of British cycling. Between 1957 and 1961 he won stages in the Peace Race, and the Tours of Sweden and Austria - in the latter his climb of the Grossglockner pass has become legendary for his beating of Charly Gaul's record for the ride. Second three times in the Manx International, his real dominance at home came in the Milk Race, with a very close second place in 1958 behind the Austrian Richard Durlacher, and then two out-standing wins in 1959 and 1960, during which he spent only one day out of the yellow jersey. No one in England had seen the Grossglockner climb, they had only read about it, but the second act of the Bradley legend occurred here on stage four of the 1959 race, a battle without mercy across 123 miles of Pennine roads, from Whitley Bay to Morecombe. Bradley, already race leader by just 25 seconds, attacked with team-mate Brian Haskell and spread-eagled the field over an end-less succession of mountains, where professional riders walked the unclimbable gradients, until Bradley left Haskell to win alone nearly seven minutes clear of his nearest rival, having increased his lead to over 9 minutes; a third of the field fin-ished more than three-quarters of an hour behind Bradley that day. Among those unable to get near Bradley in the whole race were Stan Brittain and Vin Denson, the former a Tour de France finish-er in 1958, the latter preparing to ride his first Tour.

Bill Bradley, legendary climber who uniquely won two successive Milk Races.

In 1960 Bradley won the National Road Race Championship and his dominance in the Milk Race was equally impressive, with Billy Holmes second almost five minutes down, and the third man almost twenty minutes back. Once again the trans-Pennine stage had been the key to Bradley's victory, a mirror-image of the 1959 race, this time from Morecombe to Whitley Bay, which splintered the field so dramatically that all time-limits had to be abandoned, because riders were coming in an hour and more after Bradley. The same year he went on to finish twelfth in the Rome Olympic Road Race. In 1961 Bradley retained his National Championship, but his other results were less brilliant (11th in the Milk Race behind Holmes) and he was passed over for international selection, despite finishing 19th in the Tour de l'Avenir, the 14-stage amateur Tour de France. Bradley, who had never before felt drawn to professionalism, resented having his career determined by a selection committee, and he turned Independent first for Harry Quinn and then for Falcon, win-ning events such as the Tour of the Peaks, the Chequers Grand Prix and the Tour of the

South-West, before bowing out in 1965. Unselfish, relaxed, philosophical about his riding, it was always said of Bradley that he enjoyed winning, but didn't mind losing; perhaps he was always the amateur at heart. Like his contemporaries, Bradley trained little during the winter months. His spring training consisted of the traditional long run at the weekends, and a couple of shorter faster rides mid-week. This was exactly the same training as all his rivals, and one is left wondering what was the source of Bradley's special strength.

These men have all left enduring reputations behind them, but there were so many others who were close behind, and indeed could occasionally beat the star names. There were the two King brothers, Bernard and Bill, who rode very much as a team, and made a speciality of dominating the big road race at the Isle of Wight Easter festival, winning every year from 1954 to 1958, when Brian Wiltcher finally ended their reign; Bernard also became the N.C.U. road-race champion in 1955. Another famous pair of brothers were the Batys, Bill and Norman: in 1958 they finished first and second in the B.L.R.C. national amateur championship, and for good measure Bill inflicted a rare defeat on Ron Coe in the Harrogate International Road Race in the same year, a race in which all three national champions competed, Coe being the pro champion and the third being Bill Seggar, the N.C.U, champion. There was Eric Thompson who preceded Booty as Empire Games champion, winning the 1954 road-race at Vancouver. There was the Austrian-born Fred Krebs, who was forced into the pro ranks at the age of 21 when he rode against, and beat Brian Robinson in the Tour of the Chilterns in 1953. Winner of numerous events at home, Krebs performed well for the Hercules team and seemed to be on the edge of an exciting career, but he was one of the British casualties of the 1955 Tour de France, and little was heard of him afterwards. There was Jim Hinds, so often overshadowed by Bradley, but his conqueror in the Manx International of 1959. There was Alan Jackson who has a place in history as Britain's first national cyclo-cross champion in 1955, but who was also a great roadman, taking the bronze medal at the 1956 Olympics in Melbourne. That same year Jackson had won the N.C.U. national road-race championship, but under bizarre circumstances: first across the line was Peter Ward, but Ward was disqualified for receiving from his wife two aspirins for a headache during the race, infringing a technical rule that riders must take no food from unofficial helpers; few people would have blamed Ward if he had turned his back on cycling. There was Bernard Pusey, who won an unbelievable Tour of Ireland in May 1954, one of only 16 survivors from a field of 74 that was decimated by a blizzard on the penultimate stage through the mountains. There was Brian Haskell, Graham Vines, Arthur Ilsley, Clive Parker, Tony Hewson, Gil Taylor, Viv Bailes, Dick McNeill, and so many other names from that era, all with their own battles, achievements and victories, star riders and lesser men, who all helped to build the momentum of road-racing in these few years, as it became evident that beyond all the political squabbling, there was now an unquenchable thirst in Britain for this form of competition.

Time-Trialling: the Traditional Heartland

The history of time-trialling in the 1950s is easier to document than that of road-racing, first because the R.T.T.C. remained aloof from the political conflicts and confusions, but secondly because in time-trialling there is a clear sequence of championships and a clear line of progress in speed over all the distances. The 25-mile test has always been the most popular event in British cycling, contested week after week by several thousand riders, most of them taking the hour barrier as their target. Logically, the 25 must be the strongest of all the records because it is attacked so incessantly. When the 1950s opened, and the number of sub-hour men on the scene was still less than a dozen, the king of the 25 milers was George Fell, national champion and holder of the record at 58 minutes dead. It was fitting that 1951 should see a new star name, that of Bob Inman who took the championship with a sensational new record of 57:17, and on that day no less than fifteen riders were inside the hour, an unprecedented number for one event, and a sign that a new era of speed was beginning. Inman was never destined to reach such heights again, for the following year saw the beginning of the three-year domination of the event by the Higginson brothers. The twins Stanley and Bernard, who looked even younger than their twenty years, had taken turns to win races for years, but now in 1952 Stan began his habit of coming out on top in the big events. Missing Inman's record by just 18 seconds, he was the victor over Dave Keeler, with Bernard in third place. Stan would take the championship for three successive years, from 1952 to 1954, and also lower the competition record three times, leaving it at 56:29 in 1953. Dave Keeler was a tall powerful stylist who had a remarkable career, ranging from track pursuiting to all the time-trialling distances and finally the End-to-End record, and he twice shaved the 25-mile competition record by seconds in 1951, but he was never to win a national championship. The two

The Higginson twins, Bernard on the front and Stanley behind - or is it the other way around? When the brothers rode solos, time-keepers had problems.

Higginsons, Keeler and Ken Craven were among the small elite capable of beating the hour on a 72-inch gear. Another of the top 25-milers who would not win the championship but who would break the record twice was Billy Holmes, later known as a top roadman. Two years later he was to clip the 50-mile record set by the great Ron Jowers.

The 1950s saw a continuous refining of the record, by a few seconds at a time, so that no less than a dozen new marks were set between 1951 and 1959. 1955 was the year in which Holmes shaved the record twice, and in between his two rides came yet another new record, this time from Norman Sheil, as he was building up to his sensational world pursuit victory. Sheil came back in 1957 to take the championship, but on the whole the record-breakers and the national champions seem to have played musical chairs in this period, for Holmes, Dave Evans, Alan Shackleton and Alf Engers all brought down the record, but never took the champion's gold medal, while the champions Gordon Ian, Mike Gambrill and Mick Ward never broke the record. Evans, of Acme Wheelers, Rhonda, was the first Welshman ever to break a national competition record, although the ride took place in Dorset.

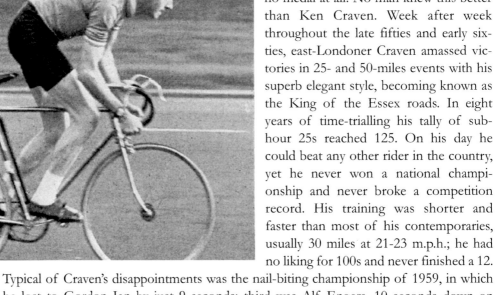

The 25 is the most intense and the most uncertain of time-trials, in which a handful of seconds can make the difference between the gold medal and no medal at all. No man knew this better than Ken Craven. Week after week throughout the late fifties and early sixties, east-Londoner Craven amassed victories in 25- and 50-miles events with his superb elegant style, becoming known as the King of the Essex roads. In eight years of time-trialling his tally of sub-hour 25s reached 125. On his day he could beat any other rider in the country, yet he never won a national championship and never broke a competition record. His training was shorter and faster than most of his contemporaries, usually 30 miles at 21-23 m.p.h.; he had no liking for 100s and never finished a 12.

Ken Craven, "King of the Essex Roads", prolific time-trial winner who so often missed out championship honours.

Typical of Craven's disappointments was the nail-biting championship of 1959, in which he lost to Gordon Ian by just 9 seconds; third was Alf Engers, 10 seconds down on Craven. The first six men all had 56-minute rides, from Ian with his 56:3. to Holmes on 56:55. Despite his near-misses on so many big occasions like this, Craven's name remained almost legendary among London cyclists twenty years and more after he had stopped racing. All these riders, without exception, raced on a fixed wheel, usually around 84 inches. As the decade ended, the nineteen-year old Engers, had cut the record to 55:11, where it stayed for two whole years, although Gordon Ian remained the man to beat, taking the championship again in 1960. Surely Engers can never have guessed how far in the future his greatest days would be, or that he would have to wait another ten years before taking the championship.

In the 50-mile competition, the great question was who would be the second man to beat two hours? Fleming had done it twice in 1947, but four years went by without a repeat performance, until Walter Fowler rode a 1:59:34 in June 1951. Fowler was always the most likely to succeed, having ridden a 2:0:16 in 1950 and then a 2:0:11 just weeks before breaking the barrier. His new time however was not a new record, Fleming having ridden 20 seconds faster back in 1947. Fowler went into the National Championship one week later as the hot favourite, but in a shock result he was beaten into second place by Keith Bentley who took the record down to 1:58:29. Both Fowler and the third man, Dave Keeler, were under two hours. Bentley lowered his own record again in the 1952 championship, to 1:57:46, then later in the same year he set the mark at 1:56:44, where it remained for the next three years. Bentley, a tall London-domiciled Yorkshireman whose glasses often appeared to be slipping off the end of his nose, was revered as the master 50-miler of his day, superior to Fowler, Gibbons, Keeler and even to Ken Joy. For the next eight years the 50 record, like the 25, was nibbled away by 10 seconds here and 20 seconds there, by great names like Vic Gibbons, Gordon Ian and Ron Jowers. Jowers was one of sever-

al big, powerful riders who pedalled furiously to produce 1:55 rides on their 84-inch fixed wheels. One has to ask what a man like a Jowers would have achieved on a set of gears reaching up to 110 or 115. Billy Holmes broke the 50 record but never won the National Championship, just as he did with the 25, while Mick Ward took the title no less than three times without breaking the record. The decade was brought to a close by another six-foot wonder-man, Bryan Wiltcher, from the club appropriately named after the king of the gods, the Zeus R.C. Like Jowers and Holmes, Wiltcher had already proved himself to be an outstanding roadman, and he was foremost in leading the new trend towards time-trialling on gears. To win the 1960 National Championship in 1:55:36, he pushed a

Ron Jowers, powerhouse 50- miler of the mid fifties.

top gear of 112, while Ken Craven was still whirling his 84-inch fixed, to post a time just 70 seconds slower. In 1959 Wiltcher had lowered the 50 record to 1:53:56, the biggest improvement in the post-war era, and in the following year he took more seconds off to leave it at 1:53:40. Bear in mind that 50-mile events at this time almost invariably included dead turns in the road, and sometimes two or three.

There is something central and classical about the 100-mile time trial, forming a perfect balance between speed and endurance. To beat the four-hour barrier was seen for decades as the ultimate time-trial challenge, while the symmetry of the four sub-hour 25s provided an obvious parallel to the symmetry of four sub-one-minute laps in the four-minute mile; both these great sporting feats were of course first achieved in the mid 1950s. The top 100-milers have always been the supreme time-triallists of their era, and the distance has formed the key to victory in the B.A.R. competition. The undisputed time-tri-

*Gordon Ian,
three times champion
at 25 miles and twice
record-breaker at 50.*

alling giant of the 1950s was Ray Booty, but he was preceded by a rider only marginally less phenomenal as a setter of new standards: Ken Joy, winner of four B.A.R. titles from 1949-52, which he achieved by taking a multitude of National Championships and competition records on the way. Yet Joy was no prodigy, in fact he got into his stride rather slowly, finishing third in the 1948 B.A.R. at the age of 26, behind Peter Beardsmore and Derbyshire, although significantly Joy's 50 and 100 times that year were both better than Beardsmore's: only his 12-hour time was inferior. In 1949 Joy topped the B.A.R. list with a 50 and a 100 that were both faster than the second man, Ken Whitmarsh and the third man Beardsmore, yet once again Joy's 12 was noticeably inferior to theirs. Joy won no championship and broke no competition record that year. In the winter he built up his regime of long, hard, solitary training rides, and he began the 1950 season with a clear proof of his growing strength: on the 1st of June he set a new 100-mile mark of 4:14:30, a three-minute improvement on the old competition record, and an eight-minute margin over second man Alf Hill. Almost two months later, on a wet and windy day, Joy took the National Championship event in 4:18:22, but his margin of victory over Ken Whitmarsh was just three minutes. On that same very difficult day, Alf Hill had triumphed in the South Western 12-hour to set a new competition record of 259.25 miles, and take the lead in the B.A.R.

The classic Bath Road 100 in August - an event which Joy never won throughout his career - was eagerly awaited, and it brought the biggest time-trial sensation of the year: the 19-year-old Les Willmott., a promising massed-start racer riding only his second 100-mile event, smashed Joy's record by two minutes to win with 4:12:22. Vic Gibbons was just 25 seconds behind Willmott, while the only consolation for Joy, third in 4:13:34, was that he too had got inside his old record. On the 17th of August, no less than five different riders topped 250 miles in 12-hour events around the country, while Joy's figure was 249.75. To make the competition even keener, Walter Fowler improved his 100 time to jump ahead in the B.A.R. In those days all serious time-triallists rode two or three 12s in a season, and Joy's answer came in the 12-hour championship in mid-September, in which he improved his figures to 258.5 miles, the second fastest 12 ever ridden, beating Hill the record-holder by two miles. Joy had sealed his second B.A.R. victory; he had won two championships and broken a competition record, yet he ended the season with the second fastest 50, the second fastest 12, and the third fastest 100 of the year. It had been an impressive year of middle-distance record-breaking, and voices in the cycling press ventured to suggest that records were "approaching finality", that speed and physical strength could not go on improving endlessly.

The 1951 B.A.R. campaign followed a similar pattern, with Joy posting the second fastest 100 in history in June, not contesting the 100 championship, which Willmot won, and finishing fifth in the Bath Road event, in which Gibbons triumphed for the second time. In mid August Alan Hill took the 12-hour competition record from his namesake Alf Hill with 260.5 miles, while Joy rode 252 in a another event. This gave Joy third position in the B.A.R., so just one week later he rode a second 12, this time achieving 259.9 to take the lead. Strangely however, both Hill's and Joy's 12-hour figures were subject to revision: Hill's was reduced to 258, depriving him of the record, while Joy's was increased fractionally giving him a new record of 260 miles. This had been a tense and difficult competition, but Joy had emerged with his stature greatly enhanced, and in 1952 his domination was unchallenged. He set a new 100-mile record, again in June, smashing Willmott's figures by a massive six minutes with 4:6:52, and in August he raised his own 12-hour mark to 264.8. Gibbons had risen to second in the B.A.R. by virtue of outstanding performances in both the 100 and the 12, but fittingly Joy defeated him in the final 50 of the year, to end the season the undisputed master. To appreciate the impact that Joy's four wins created, we must remember that the legendary Frank Southall had won the first four B.A.R. titles in the early 1930s, following which there had been a succession of single-year winners, until Derbyshire took his two full-distance victories after the war. Joy's string of four titles therefore inevitably made him seem to be the new Southall – a virtual superman, far ahead of all his contemporaries.

The Ken Joy story did not end here however, for in January 1953 he turned professional for the Hercules team. His main purpose was to attack R.R.A. time-trialling records, but in the following two years he performed astonishingly well in road races too, riding alongside men of the calibre of Steel, Maitland, Parker, Bedwell and Ilsley, in single-day events and in the 1954 Tour of Britain, in which he finished 17th, nineteen minutes behind the winner Tamburlini, an outstanding feat for someone who had been a pure

Ken Joy, supreme time-triallist of the pre-Booty years.

time-triallist for ten years, and who now found himself plunged into massed-start at the top level. Nevertheless Joy's years with Hercules are best remembered for his record-breaking campaign, in which he targeted many of the classic records which Bob Maitland, who turned professional for BSA in 1952, had set up. Over a period of eighteen months a dozen records fell to Joy: all the out-and-home records from London; Brighton and back, Portsmouth and back, and Bath and back; then the to-London records: Pembroke-London, Land's End-London and Liverpool-London. The last was perhaps one of Joy's greatest ever rides, as, admittedly with the help of a strong following wind, he flew down the old A5 to beat the old record by more than an hour, and average over 25 m.p.h. for the 201 miles. Joy was defeated in his attempt on the End-to-End record, retiring after 590 miles, but he did take the 24-hour record, and he put up a sterling straight-out 100 miles of 3:45:12. Maitland retaliated by taking back the Land's End to London record, with a tremendous

ride of 23 m.p.h. for the 287 hilly miles, which even Joy failed to recapture, and which was to stand for forty years. Joy was something of an enigma: always immaculate on and off the bike, tall, formal, reserved, he looked like a company director or a diplomat. He married and soon turned his back completely on the sport in which he had been a dominating presence for six years. His wife, Janet Gregory, was herself a star rider, having held competition records at 50 and 100 miles, and finished second to Eileen Sheridan in the 1950 women's B.A.R.. Had Booty's record not been so outstanding, Ken Joy would probably be looked on as the giant of time-trialling for the entire period from 1945 to 1975.

A great deal has been made of one of Joy's rare failures, one which occurred in the full glare of publicity: in October 1953 he and Maitland were invited to take part in the Grand Prix des Nations, the classic French time-trial for professionals. Run over 87 miles, this should have given Britain's undisputed time-trial champion the chance to shine in international company. In the event, Joy finished a full twenty minutes down on the winner, the young Jacques Anquetil, while Maitland was little better at nineteen minutes down. A similar fate overtook two other great time-triallists, Ray Booty and Owen Blower, in 1958 when they conceded more than 7 minutes in a 50-mile time trial in Switzerland. In both cases there were inquests and soul-searching about what was wrong with British time-trialling when its greatest stars could lose by such margins. But were these defeats really so surprising ? These riders were sent to foreign countries where the roads were different, the food was different, the course was unknown, the whole atmosphere and task before them were different from their normal racing. Any rider, even on a cycling holiday in a foreign country, knows how these things affect you, but after a few days acclimatisation you start riding much more confidently. A week's settling-in and practice on the course would surely have given very different results. At the same time another question was being asked: what would the top continental riders do in a English time-trial ? They might probably win - for no one imagined that an amateur club-rider could really defeat the hardened professionals - but by how much ? Experts in the late 1950s guessed that Anquetil might ride a 100 in 3:45, but was it possible that a supreme rider like Booty could really be left trailing by almost 15 minutes over his specialist distance ? The question has still never been answered. Joy's successor as the B.A.R. was a very different figure: Vic Gibbons was stocky, round-faced, bespectacled, a punchy rider, not one who glided impassively through the miles, but a man who showed the effort as he battled with the

Vic Gibbons, twice B.A.R. and later super-veteran, with his trademark black socks.

wind, with his rivals and with himself. Strangely, he was the only rider who always raced in black ankle-socks. Before Joy left the scene, Gibbons was already pressing hard on his heels, indeed he had the beating of Joy several times. He won three Bath Road 100s, took the 50 competition record, which Joy never did, as well as the 100, and he won three National Championships. He never pretended to be enthusiastic about the 12-hour, but in 1954 he achieved a ride of 264.3 miles, only half a mile outside Joy's record, and a figure which Booty himself would exceed by less than a mile in his great year of 1956. Gibbons was always the pure amateur clubman, and unlike Joy he retained his enthusiasm and his speed for decades after his glory days were over, putting up tremendous times as a veteran in his 60s. Gibbons was tough and talented champion in his own right, although it has been his fate to be remembered as the man who came between the Joy and Booty eras.

The simplest way to gauge Ray Booty's dominance of the sport in the mid-fifties is to set out his record. He was three times winner of the B.A.R.. competition in three years; he was the national 100-mile champion five times in succession; he was the national 12-hour champion five times in succession; he broke competition record for the 100 three times, and competition record for the 12-hour twice; on the right day he was the strongest amateur roadman in Britain. If there is one slight weakness in his record it was over 50 miles, where he was not unbeatable, never taking the championship or breaking competition record. But over the classic distance, the 100, he was supreme for several years, regularly winning events by ten minutes or more, and Booty's name was raised from greatness to immortality by one classic ride at the distance, on 6 August 1956, when he smashed through the four-hour barrier for the first time, with 3:58:28. This target had bewitched the imagination of the time-trialling world for years, just as the four-minute mile had been a dream of the athletics world, and as long ago as 1952 *Cycling* magazine had struck a unique gold medal which was to be awarded to the first rider to achieve this feat. The four-minute mile had come in May 1954 (curiously, from an athlete whose initials were R.B.) but the four-hour 100 was apparently an even tougher challenge. When Booty arrived on the scene in 1954, competition record stood to Gibbons at 4:6:31. Booty himself reduced it to 4:4:30 in 1955, but it was his 4:1:52 ride in July 1956 which made the four hours seems a real pos-

Ray Booty, unique and unmistakable.

sibility; few people however expected it to come just two weeks later, in the August Bank Holiday Bath Road Club event.

Booty's own recollections of the ride were typically undramatic. He had cycled down from Nottingham two days before the race, and spent the evening before at the cinema, watching *Reach for the Sky,* a typical fifties war film about the famous crippled pilot, Douglas Bader. Next morning it was cool and damp at the start, and he set off with no special hopes on his usual 84-inch fixed. He went a little faster than he had expected to the 50-mile mark, drawn out by tussles with his friend Jim Ogden and with Vin Denson. Only at the final turn, three-quarters of the way through the race, did he begin to realise that he was still averaging 25 m.p.h. and that this might be "the" morning: then he really poured on the power to the finish. Stan Brittain, who would be riding the Tour de France two years later, was second, twelve minutes down. Yet Booty was far from exhausted, and he certainly did not share Roger Bannister's dramatic "collapse-at-the-tape" style, for where Bannister sank into a lethargic reaction for weeks, Booty was back on his bike six days later winning the national 12-hour championship and setting a new competition record for that distance too. He added a final touch of brilliance at the end of September when he set a new R.R.A. straight-out 100 record with an incredible time of 3:28:40, smashing Joy's old record by 16 minutes. Booty's feats made him a legend in British cycling, nothing less than a superman: for the ordinary club rider whose greatest ambition was to beat the hour for a 25, it seemed utterly impossible to conceive of doing it four times in succession, while the idea of maintaining almost 29 m.p.h. for 100 miles, even wind-assisted, appeared quite miraculous. Yet Booty was known to be an unpretentious, likeable clubman, who enjoyed his cycle-touring holidays, including trips to the Alpine passes, and his social life. He was in fact a member of one of the smallest clubs in the country, the Ericsson Wheelers, formed by the twenty or so cyclists who worked for the Midlands electronic company. He was endearingly modest, and always slightly bemused by

Owen Blower, road-man and B.A.R. in 1958 with a 12-hour record that lasted for 9 years.

his fame and by the adulation showered on him by the cycling world. He never claimed to be a superman, and pictures of him collapsed in the road after the 12-hour championship of 1957, when he had been pushed to his limit by John Finch, showed plainly that he was human after all.

The comparisons with Bannister can be extended, not least because they both shared the same old-fashioned amateur ideal of sport. Neither of them ever earned a penny from their sport, but where Bannister became a world celebrity overnight, and has remained so ever since, nobody outside the cycling world ever knew Ray Booty's name. In one respect we can say with certainty that Booty's ride was an even greater achievement than Bannister's: within weeks of the four-minute mile at Oxford, other runners had equalled it, and indeed had run even faster than Bannister did. Within a couple of years, dozens of athletes were running four-minute miles regularly, and the world mile record had been taken down dramatically, to a level that Bannister could never have dreamed of in 1954. Yet Booty's record remained untouchable for a full six years. Booty himself never repeated his achievement, and champions of the calibre of Blower, Wiltcher, Wilkings, Kirby and Baylis could never break the four-hour barrier. We have to conclude that Booty's ride was an inspired one, a feat that was genuinely ahead of its time, and beyond the range of all his contemporaries: his place in cycling history is deservedly a unique one. In the many interviews and talks which he gave, Booty never revealed any unusual training methods: it was all long steady miles on winter weekends, and short fast evening dashes home from work. As with Bill Bradley, we are left wondering what was the source of his overwhelming superiority.

Booty's reign in the B.A.R. was ended in 1958, when Owen Blower pushed the great man down into second place. Slower than Booty at 50 and 100 miles, Blower smashed the 12-hour competition record with his 271.8 mile ride, achieved on the same day that Booty was winning his last 12-hour National Championship with 263.4 miles; this 12-hour record would survive for a full nine years. Blower was better known as a road-man, one of the best in the country, and immediately after the end of the 1958 season he turned professional for Elswick-Hopper. Like Joy, Blower continued his time-trialling with a number of R.R.A. record attempts in the autumn of 1959, but Blower found to his cost just how tough were those records which Joy and others had set in earlier years. Attempts on Portsmouth-London, Cardiff-London and London-York were all defeated by unfavourable winds, the last being lost by a handful of seconds after battling for 197 miles. But at last in late October, with a westerly behind him, he covered the 162 miles from Cardiff to London in 6.27, an average of 25 m.p.h. However his satisfaction at getting into the R.R.A. record lists was short-lived, for the ride was disallowed, on the grounds that he had received assistance from an unauthorised car. Blower was a tenacious rider, who made a remarkable come-back a full twenty years later, at the age of almost fifty, to finish ninth in the B.A.R. of 1979.

One sometimes has the feeling that so many of the time-trial stars of the fifties were larger than life – almost literally giants: Joy, Keeler, Bentley, Jowers, Booty and Craven, while Blower's successor at the head of the B.A.R. table in 1959 was another six-foot powerhouse, Londoner Bryan Wiltcher. Only 22 years old, Wiltcher was already established as a top roadman, and had brought the roadman's use of gears into time-trialling. In contrast to Booty, Wiltcher was unbeatable at 50 miles, setting a competition

Bryan Wiltcher, double B.A.R. winner; he was the primary influence in bringing the use of gears into time-trialling.

record of 1:53:56, so far ahead of everyone else that it undoubtedly won him the B.A.R. Second man Roger Wilkings was in fact substantially faster over both the 100 miles and the 12-hours, and many considered him unlucky to be stuck with a slow 50 time of 2.0.1., and then to become ill towards the end of the season and be unable to improve it. Wiltcher's final B.A.R. average speed was the slowest for some years, and his 100 time of 4:8:5. was actually bettered by seven of the other top eleven finishers. Booty slipped down to third place this year, but his 100 was still five minutes faster than Wiltcher's and his 12 was identical at 259.5. But if there was a slight question-mark over Wiltcher's title in 1959, he made no mistake in 1960. He trimmed his own 50 record to 1:53:40; he radically updated his 100 best to 4:1:17; and he pushed his 12 up to 267.8. His average speed of 24.5 m.p.h. was a record, surpassing even Booty's 1956 figure, and Wiltcher's right to victory was beyond dispute. Perhaps Wiltcher had something else to prove too, having suffered a good deal of criticism for his mysterious performance in the Milk Race, where he never got into the action, and pulled out on stage five. Second in the B.A.R. was John Baylis, virtually unknown before this season, with Wilkings third this time. One side-effect of the 1960 time-trial season was to bring into the spotlight the question of who would achieve the second four-hour 100. Wiltcher himself, Wilkins, and Vin Denson had all clocked rides of 4:1, while Baylis had a 4:3. As the years went by, Booty's historic ride of 1956 was increasingly seen to be ahead of its time, since to the rest of the cycling world the four-hour barrier was still as forbidding as ever. Any one of four or five riders might break it, with Wiltcher the obvious favourite, but in 1961 he decided to return to road-racing, signing as a professional for Condor. His later time-trialling was restricted to some R.R.A. record attempts, but like Blower, he found them impregnable, even to the power of a former B.A.R. winner. Wiltcher freely admitted that, despite his great physical gifts, he had problems with mood and motivation during his cycling career, and it is doubtful if he ever achieved his full potential.

Dennis White, the first 24 hour rider to top 480 miles - the magic evens.

In July 1956, two weeks before Ray Booty smashed the four-hour 100 barrier, another historic time-trialling milestone had been passed, but one that was destined to be always overshadowed by Booty's ride. Dennis White became the first man to beat evens for a 24-hour event, riding 484.6 miles in the Wessex R.C. event. The nearest anyone had come before to the magic figure had been Cardiff's Ken Price in July 1955, when he rode 478.5 to win the National Championship. White was an accomplished 12-hour man, but this was his first 24-hour ride, yet he maintained a miraculously even pace, whirling his 79-inch fixed, completing 246 in the first 12 hours, and scarcely slowing at all to 238 in the second. White's achievement was quite unexpected by himself or by anyone else, so that the event organisers had to hurriedly insert a twenty-mile detour for him, to keep the race together after he had gone right through the field. White had scheduled a ride of just 459 miles, aiming to set a new club record, but the race took on an entirely different aspect when he realised with six hours to go that he was well inside evens. After that point he was truly riding into the unknown, wondering if he would blow up, or if he could survive on a road which no rider had ever taken before. Two years later the National Championship came to the Wessex event, and White rode his second 24-event to produce a carbon-copy of his first ride, this time edging his own

record up by a matter of yards to 484.7. Once again White's 12-hour splits were 246 and 238, once again he was riding his familiar 79-inch fixed (all other 24-hour men had by now switched to gears) and once again he finished fresh and unruffled. No other 24-hour rider can claim that his only two rides at the distance have both been competition records. Good but not outstanding in the shorter time-trials, yet gifted with the mental and physical toughness to endure huge distances at a metronome pace, White was a modest clubman who rode for pleasure, yet he took 24-hour riding into a new realm, and set a record which lasted for six years.

The delights of time-trialling in the 1950s.

This form of long-distance competition was, perhaps more than any other, rooted in the club-life of the time. Its slower pace enabled those with grit and determination, including many older riders, to achieve a distinction which was beyond them at 25 or 50 miles, while the teams of helpers who came out for the weekend created an involvement in the race that, again, was not possible as spectators of a speed contest. These long-distance rides had an epic quality which stirred the imagination, and this explains the tremendous interest in 24-hour racing throughout the late forties and the fifties. Riders like Stan Butler had an appetite for endless miles that now seems incredible, competing in two or three 24s within two months. He, Ron Mynott, Gus Andrews, Eddy Munday and George Laws pushed the competition record up rapidly each year from the 454 miles with which Gordon Basham won the first national championship in 1948, to 467 miles by 1952.

In 1953 the championship went north to the Mersey Roads event, and it was a northern rider, Nick Carter, who won through on a wet and gusty day, to finish on 459.2 miles. But this victory was inevitably overshadowed by the sensational trike ride of John Arnold, who was only two miles behind with a record-breaking 457 miles, having led the field for much of the race. Even the new national champion himself generously agreed with the amazed gallery of spectators, that it had been Arnold's day. The competition record had survived in 1953, but in 1954 and 1955 it took a real battering, first from Stewart Thompson who won the championship event. Thompson was already an experienced long-distance man, and having added two miles to the competition record on a very punishing day, much was expected of him in the future. These hopes were fulfilled, for in the following year, again in the championship, he raised the record to 474 miles, but he did not become the champion: that honour went to Ken Price who, with 478.7 miles, pushed the record to within a mile and a quarter of the magic evens barrier. This was the gap which Dennis White was to close in 1956 with the first 20-m.p.h. ride in history.

More than any other event, 24-hour riding in the post-war era seems to have been a tradition fostered by certain clubs, the same clubs who set team competition records year after year. There was the south London club, the Addiscombe, who took the national team title and the team competition record for three years in succession from 1950-52. This feat was surpassed by the Rutland C.C., who lifted five championships between 1955 and 1959, including two team competition records, through the efforts of Thompson, John Liversedge and Ron Coukham. It is hard to imagine a rider more alone than the 24-hour man, more reliant on his own courage and strength; and yet there is no doubt that that courage and strength are both upheld by the sense of being the spearhead of a team, supplying food, drink and moral support throughout the ordeal. Of all the dozens of stories that made up the 24-hour history in the 1950s perhaps two deserve special mention. There was Fred Burrell who won the 1956 championship with a distance of 477.7 miles, and who did not ride another 24 for four years: when he did, in the 1960 championship, he once again took the title with 477.7 miles. And there was Dave Keeler, former 25-mile speed-man who progressed steadily up the distances until, in June 1958 he successfully tackled the End-to-End record. Six weeks later he was battling with Dennis White in the 24-hour championship, finishing fourth with 466.3 miles. Then four weeks later still he was, incredibly, on the start-line for the North Road 24, which he won to become the second man to beat evens, with 481.5 miles. Yet this splendid result disguised a near-tragic misfortune, for Keeler had gone off-course for 36 minutes, without which he would surely have amassed a further 10 miles, to take White's record and place it over 490 miles, and out of reach for some years to come. Conditions for the race were perfect, and the incident occurred in the hours of darkness when Keeler missed a turn, and had to be chased for several miles by

Albert Crimes (front) and John Arnold, whose tandem-trike records will probably never be broken.

one of the marshals who vainly tried to catch him before Keeler realised his mistake and turned back. Without this disaster, Keeler must surely have become the only man to break competition record at 25 miles and 24 hours.

The culture of long-distance record-riding, the solitary battle against time, exhaustion and the invisible riders of the past, was the sphere of the Road Records Association, and the early fifties was a golden era for the up-dating of their place-to-place and straight-out record lists. To the cyclists of the fifties, the improvements in roads and in bikes since the 1930s made the records that were set then look vulnerable, even though there does not seem to have been any great development in training methods. The most famous of these solo rides were those already referred to by Eileen Sheridan and Ken Joy. Together these two put most of the solo, two-wheeled records on the shelf for some years, but

Dave Duffield, who was inspired by Crimes and Arnold to set his own amazing trike records, including his End-to-End which stood for 20 years.

there was also enormous interest in the other categories, tandems, and three-wheeled racing, and a special magic has always been attached to the tandem-trike exploits of Albert Crimes and John Arnold. This pair broke eight records together, four of them on their one legendary End-to-End ride of July 1954, in the course of which they took the 12-hour record, the 24-hour record, and then went on to add the 1000-mile record, all of which still stand today. Their End-to-End figure of 2:4:26 and their 1,000 mile time of 2:13.59 were the fastest for any category, bettering the then solo bicycle and tandem records. They had prepared for their ride earlier in the year by touring the entire route over Easter. Then they really showed their form in June when they destroyed the old tandem-trike 50 and 100 records, with times of 1:49:55 and 3:46:30 respectively, achieved in the course of the same ride, up the A1 with a favourable south-west breeze behind them. Individually both Crimes and Arnold had both broken every R.T.T.C. record from 50 miles to 24-hours, and together they formed a unique team. Both from Manchester, Crimes a railway worker and Arnold a joiner, they shared a devotion to trike riding that spurred them to set records which will perhaps never be broken, which will remain as memorials to an all-but extinct form of cycling.

There has always been tremendous camaraderie among tricyclists, and when a third record aspirant, David Duffield, appeared, he received every possible help and encouragement from the two men who had inspired him. When Duffield set out on his historic reverse (north-south) End-to-End attempt in June 1957, he was amazed to find John Arnold waiting by the roadside north of Perth with breakfast for the tiring Duffield, who already had 300 miles in his legs, but who went on his way a new man, and took the record with 2:20:9. But, as often seems to happen with the End-to-End record, Duffield

Les Blackhurst and Alan Griffiths, two ordinary club riders who set some extraordinary tandem records in 1954 and 1955.

only kept it for a couple of months before Albert Crimes regained it by a huge margin, with 2:12:37, apparently disproving all Duffield's ideas about the advantages of a north-south run. It took Duffield some years to steel himself for a new attempt, but in 1960 he triumphed again, but south-north this time. In a nightmarish ride, battling against adverse weather and sickness, he brought the time down to 2:10:58, where it remained for twenty years. Earlier, in 1956, Duffield had tackled the ultra long-distance trike record of them all, the 1,000 miles, and had clocked 3:12:15, but in 1958 Albert Crimes pulverised those figures with 2:21:37, and Duffield decided to leave that one on the shelf, where it has remained ever since. Duffield rounded off his career by setting new trike records at 50 and 100 miles, with times of 1:57:4 and 4:22.50, and with a 239-mile 12-hour, all of which also stood the test of time well. Whatever the reason, Crimes and Arnold never joined forces again after their historic 1954 campaign, but both continued to race and set solo trike records, although they rarely raced against each other. As late as 1963, John Arnold came back into the fray to show what real quality record-breaking was about. His target was the York to Edinburgh ride, the record standing at 10:4:24: Arnold pulverised this with a new time of 8:48:28, which stood for over 30 years.

Since these records are not attacked every week, as the R.T.T.C. time-trial records are, it is hard to say how good they are, therefore this form of competition tends to go in waves, every few years witnessing a campaign to up-date the record times. From the fifties the great names of Joy, Sheridan, Crimes, Arnold and Duffield have tended to overshadow those who were riding at the same time. A second tandem-trike pair, Tweddell and Stott, set half a dozen endurance records between 1950 and 1953, and if their times were not better, they had some heroic rides: on their 1950 London-Edinburgh, they were stampeded by some runaway horses in the borders, and their machine damaged, forcing them to walk for miles, as they watched their margin of victory slip away. Edward Tweddell was a remarkable veteran, for many years Scotland's only racing tricyclist. He had set his first record in 1930, and as late as 1957, partnered by Chris Sandham, he broke the tandem record for the now almost forgotten Scots End-to-End, from Gretna Green to John O'Groats, a 393-mile marathon over Britains' wildest roads, which they completed in 20:53. On the tandem, Smith and Collins set a 24-hour mark of 467 miles in 1950, while Needle and Young tandemed the 197 miles from London to York in a fraction under 8 hours. The Lancashire R.C. tandem pair, Cowshill and Denton beat the 1938 End-to-End record by six hours in August 1952, with a time of 2:8:47, and after a full nine hours sleep they established the first tandem standard of 3:7:41 for the 1,000 miles. At the shorter distances tandem speeds were remarkable: in 1954 and 1955 Les Blackhurst and Alan Griffiths of the Mid-Shropshire Wheelers set new records for the 50 and the 100 of 1:35:45 and 3:33:49. Their 50 record was achieved in cool, wet and far from ideal day on a mid-Wales course, while the 100 record was significantly faster than Joy, and not far below what Booty would achieve solo in 1956; but Blackhurst and Griffiths were ordinary club riders, while Joy and Booty were the supreme champions of their day. Blackhurst and Griffiths also set a Liverpool to London record of 8:4, just eight minutes slower than Joy's 1954 time, and that particular ride of Joy was one of his greatest. This was the attraction of record-riding, that it offered good but not outstanding riders the chance to write their names in the history books alongside those of the immortals. A comparison of the tandem and the solo records seems to show that the tandem offers a pair of average riders a distinct speed advantage up to 100 miles, beyond which the advantage fades rapidly.

The early fifties saw a tremendous wave of record-riding which pushed the standards very much higher, and consequently in the latter years of the decade the vogue for this form of competition had rather exhausted itself. However 1958 brought a double epic from two outstanding riders on the End-to-End course. Dave Keeler, although still only 26, had graduated from being a 25-mile record-breaker to the point where he would tackle anything, and he felt strongly that the 1937 End-to-End mark of fellow-vegetarian, Sid Ferris, was ripe for up-dating. He scheduled for an extremely fast ride of 48 hours exactly, and secretly hoped to be the first to beat that formidable barrier. This proved optimistic, and he never got on terms with his own schedule, but had enough advantage to take the record by well over three hours at 2:3:9. He made no prolonged stops, and took no sleep at all, and it was this which prevented his adding the 1,000 miles record, for 50 mile after leaving John O'Groats he was falling asleep in the saddle. Keeler had suffered various physical problems (which observers said never marred his superb pedalling style), in particular a persistent story has grown up around this ride, that Keeler's back troubles were caused by his rather perverse use of the Campganolo Roubaix gear, which was operated by reaching back to turn a rod on the right-hand seat-stay; but Keeler always denied that this was the cause of his troubles. The tall, powerful, smooth-pedalling Keeler could never have imagined that, having up-dated this blue-ribbon record after eleven years, he would hold it for just two months, or that it would be taken by a man who was his complete physical opposite. At five foot two inches,

Dave Keeler's 1958 End-to-End record ride.

The team car 1950s style: Dave Keeler's following car on his End-to-End

Reg Randall of the Harlequins C.C. was a foot shorter than Keeler, and he had an unusual build for a long-distance cyclist: his nickname was Tubby. Where Keeler had good conditions, with favourable wind, and night-mist the only hazard, Randall suffered hours of cold, drenching rain, mechanical mishaps and more than one crash on the wet roads. Yet at the end he bettered Keeler's time by more than an hour, with 2:1:58, and with better conditions he could possibly have cracked the two day barrier. Perhaps the most praiseworthy aspect of Randall's ride was this: he had been preparing seriously for it since the preceding winter, with a certain target in mind, and then in June he learned of Keeler's new record, and had to adjust his sights completely to a new and much higher level, and yet he still persisted and he won through. Between them Keeler and Randall had brought the 2-day record within reach, but seven more years would pass before it was finally achieved. Keeler did make an attempt to recapture the record in 1959, but was unsuccessful. Another ordinary club cyclist who used his powers of endurance to achieve fame was Arthur Render, who in June 1956 took up the challenge of Sid Ferris's 19-year-old 1,000 miles record. Render had covered 24,000 miles in one year's training, and this mammoth preparation paid off with a six-hour beating of the old record, giving him new figures of 2:16:12. During the ride, Render suffered from sickness and double-vision, but this did not deter him from stopping en route to telephone for an entry-form for the Mersey 24, which he had forgotten to enter ! Like so many End-to-End riders, Reg Randall had been too exhausted to go on to capture the 1,000-mile record, but he added this achievement too in a separate ride four years after Render, with a 17-m.p.h. ride in 1960, giving him figures of 2:10:40.

At the opposite extreme from long-distance time-trialling and record-breaking were the competitions which bring the British racing season to an end, the hill-climbs. The long, steadily-rising roadman's type of climb lay still in the future, and the traditional climb was the short, fierce hill that reared up at a gradient of 1 in 6 for half a mile or so, requiring two or three minutes of gut-wrenching effort on a fixed gear in the mid-fifties. The hill-climb champions were a breed apart, rarely being top riders in other branches of the sport, appearing each October to take their moment of glory ahead of the star roadmen and time-triallists, before disappearing again for the next eleven months. In the south of the country, the classic event was the Catford C.C. climb, held since the 1880s on the hills of north Kent such as Westerham, Toys, Brasted and Yorks. Between 1953 and 1958, Arthur Pursey of the Medway R.C. made this race his own, winning it five times in succession, yet Pursey was never able to crown his efforts with a national title. The Catford event, like many in the south, was run on deep, wooded lanes, often wet and littered with fallen leaves on which the wheels would spin. They were at least sheltered from the winds, but were so narrow that the crowds left only a couple of feet for the riders to pass, and to remount after a slip or a jumped chain was often impossible. By contrast the classic Pennine climbs such as Winnats and Holme Moss had a moorland character, exposed and treeless, so that on many occasions the wind became an even greater enemy than the gradient. The championship would move between north and south, and take in famous climbs such as the Cotswold edge at Saintbury Hill, Barbers Hill at Llangollen, Ambergate in Derbyshire, or one of the steep pulls on the slopes outside Bath. The first post-war star climber was Vic Clark of Coventry, who took three titles from 1946 to 1948. Bob Maitland was one of the few big names to become hill-climb champion, winning twice on Pennine hills in 1945 and 1949. He was followed in 1950 by the 21-year-old Ron Stringwell, who claimed his only victory of the season in the championship event. The 1951 title battle was a classic race on Saintbury Hill near Broadway. A week before, Stringwell had been beaten on Holme Moss in a snowstorm by Brian Robinson, but this time Stringwell rose to the occasion magnificently, pushing Robinson into second place by just 4 seconds, with two more roadmen, Peter Procter and Ted Gerrard third and fourth. Stan Higginson was fifth, Brian Haskell sixth and Maitland eighth. This event showed clearly that the longer, less intense climbs - Saintbury is a mile and a quarter at 1 in 10 - would attract wider fields, including top riders who did not regard themselves as specialist climbers. The following year Robinson took his revenge with his championship win on Mow Cop in a very close race in which five seconds separated the first five riders. Stringwell was fifth, but came back in 1953 to finish second on Winnats to Roy Keighlel.. For the rest of the decade the hill-climb championship continued to be decided among a handful of specialists, and the event was often presented as a north-south battle. Les Ingman of the Norwood Paragon won twice in 1954 and 1956; Eric Wilson of Rossendale R.C. became a triple champion in 1960, following his wins in 1955 and 1957; Peter Graham of the West Pennine R.C. won in 1958, and again twice more in the 1960s. On a wild day on Winnats in 1959, Huddersfield's Gordon Rhodes won by less than a second from Russell Foster of the Birdwell Wheelers, in an icy wind that blew so hard down the gully that several riders could not finish the course, and hardened roadmen like Bill Bradley and Billy Holmes struggled and died. Different as it was from from long-distance cycling, the hill-climb also offered the virtually unknown club rider the chance to show his strength, and sometimes to triumph over much bigger names.

Hill-climbing in the south of England: deep wooded lanes, fallen leaves, wheels spinning on the wet road. The rider is Alan Shorter, famous North London bike dealer and racing coach.

Women's Racing Takes Off

By the summer of 1951 Eileen Sheridan was considering the offer of a professional career as a road record-breaker for Hercules, under the management of Frank Southall. Although still the biggest name in women's cycling, she missed much of that season with an injury, and the way was open for other girls to fill the top places. At this period, and for many years afterwards, there was no mixed time-trialling: women had their own events, and there were not many of them - perhaps four or five each weekend scattered around the country, and their season started later than the men's. As in men's racing, there were a dozen riders who dominated the scene, and who repeatedly clipped the competition records by seconds, reducing the 25 from 1:5 at the beginning of the decade to 1:1 at its end, while the 50 came down from 2:15 to 2:5; both these rates of improvement were greater than the men's in absolute terms. Stella Farrell was still claiming many victories, but championships and records now eluded her. Elsie Horton, a Coventry C.C. club-mate of Eileen Sheridan, took the 1951 women's B.A.R., although Daisy Stockwell won both the 50 and the 100 championships, the latter in the course of her first ride over that distance. The 25 championship was something of a sensation when all the established names were beaten by the virtually unknown Christina Bellet, riding only her fourth race over 25 miles. As Christina Brown she retained her title in 1952, and added the B.A.R., although she was beaten in the 50 and 100 championships by Joyce Dean, who was now making a great comeback as Joyce Harris, and who went on to take B.A.R. honours in 1953.

By 1954 new names were appearing at the top: in June the 25 championship was won by Daphne Hackney - but was her name really Daphne ? Apparently not, for when she came back to win the 50 title in July, the press had discovered that she was Doreen. That same year saw a remarkable string of record rides in Scotland by Janet Sutherland of the Musselburgh R.C. She came south on several occasions to challenge for top honours, and missed the 25 title by 44 seconds. In the 100 championship however she triumphed, taking the title by two minutes from Mary Dawson, although Dawson was desperately

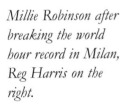

Millie Robinson after breaking the world hour record in Milan, Reg Harris on the right.

unlucky to puncture in the closing stages, having led for much of the race. Sutherland finished second in the B.A.R. to Dawson, becoming the first Scot to figure in the British women's honours. Mary Dawson was the strongest at the longer distances, taking the 100 championship, breaking competition record and winning the B.A.R. twice, in 1954 and 1955. In 1955 Daisy Stockwell, now Daisy Franks was second, while Millie Robinson was third. Robinson was probably the strongest woman rider of the pre-Burton era, and she won the 25 championship for three years in succession from 1955 to 1957, but at the longer distances she was more than matched by the outstanding multi-champion Iris Miles. In the 50 championship of 1956, Miles beat her own competition record with 2:10:39, and beat Robinson by 4 minutes, on a course that included three dead turns. She had trained for the event during the preceding week by riding 400 miles in the Yorkshire Dales. A month later she won the 100 championship, this time finishing 9 minutes ahead of Mary Dawson. Miles took the B.A.R. in 1956 and 1957, with Robinson in second place on both occasions. In the Rosslyn Ladies 12 of 1954, Chris Watts had beaten Eileen Sheridan's 12-hour time-trial record by a narrow margin, achieving 237.9 miles, and she repeated her victory in this unique event the following year. Eileen's road records had the appearance of being on the shelf as far as ordinary mortals were concerned, but one wonders what Iris Miles or Millie Robinson might have achieved in this field, even before the advent of Beryl Burton.

Millie Robinson was important too as one of the most successful early women road-racers. The Women's Track Racing Association had been formed in 1949 by a group of pioneers led by Eileen Gray, but road-racing was not part of its original programme. The introduction of road-racing seems to have come about in a curious way, through an invitation for a British team to be sent to France to compete in a women's race there. The selection event for this race was run on a closed circuit, and it was also designated as the first women's road-race championship for the Association - now renamed the Women's Cycle Racing Association. Beryl French won the race, but Joy Bell was the first W.C.R.A. finisher, so she became its first champion. The French event was an enormous success for Britain, with Millie Robinson and June Thackray taking first and second places. In the following year, Millie was leading the race again on the final day when she suffered mechanical failure, leaving Beryl French to take the victory. As a result of this experience, the N.C.U. was persuaded to accept women's road-racing, its first national championship being held in 1956, which Millie duly won, as she did an international women's race held at the Harrogate festival in that year, and the W.C.R.A.'s own championship. The B.L.R.C. was now also staging its own women's races including a national title-race, won in 1956 by Jacqueline Hewson, so duplication and confusion reigned, as it did in the men's road-racing scene. By the end of the 1956 season, the W.C.R.A. was threatening to organise its own women's world championships if the U.C.I. refused to respond to requests for it to do so. The W.C.R.A. was to remain the guiding influence in British women's racing, but only N.C.U. licences could be recognised abroad, so international matters had to be controlled by the N.C.U. Not surprsingly relations between the two bodies, and later with the B.C.F. were often strained and bitter, the one group representing the grass-roots, the riders themselves, the other being the head office, remote and dictatorial. The two bodies both continued to run their separate national championship races for many years.

In the history of women's cycling, 1958 marked the year of the first women's world championships (won largely through the advocacy of the British), while in British time-trialling it will always be remembered for the tremendous season-long battle between

A young Beryl Burton at the outset of her extraordinary racing career.

Millie Robinson, the established champion, and Beryl Burton the sensational young challenger. The competition between these two produced a string of new records at all three distances, pushing both riders to new heights. Beryl's name had first begun to appear in the press in 1956 when at the age of seventeen she beat 40 minutes for the 15-mile race, and later in the year she beat Iris Miles in a 25 by just a handful of seconds. In 1957 she had progressed to riding all the B.A.R. distances, finishing fifth in the competition, and in one 25 late in the season, she beat all the stars – Robinson, Miles and Dawson, and was being spoken of as a future champion. The 1958 dual really began with the 25 championship, with Beryl taking the title ahead of Millie by 27 seconds, but within a few weeks Millie responded by lowering the 25 competition record to 1:1:49. But Beryl also gave proof of her increasing strength when she clipped the 100 record to 4:33:26. The next round of the battle came at the 50-mile distance, in which Beryl took the championship by two minutes on a very hard, windy day. In a revenge match exactly one week later, both women broke the competition record in the same event, with Beryl finishing ahead on 2:9:17, one second ahead of the time Millie had posted ten minutes earlier. Three weeks before the 100 championship, Millie broke competition record at the distance and took the lead in the B.A.R., but in the championship itself, Beryl's gave the final proof of her superiority when she took the title and in doing so reclaimed the record, taking it below 4:30 for the first time at 4:29:21. Beryl and Millie were a full fifteen minutes clear of the third finisher that day. Beryl had won all three championship encounters, but Millie was still on top of the B.A.R. table, on the strength of her faster 25 time.

While Beryl spent the last few weeks of the season vainly chasing that elusive fast 25, Millie departed for Italy to attack the women's world hour record on the track at Milan. In this she succeeded, setting a new mark of 24 miles and 1197 yards. She returned satisfied, as British B.A.R. and world record holder, but perhaps apprehensive about what she could do in the following season to counter Beryl's dominance. Her mood cannot have been improved when, in November, Elsy Jacobs of Luxembourg destroyed her new world hour record by a big margin, riding 25 miles and 220 yards also on the Milan track. Jacobs had earlier become the first women's road-race champion at Rheims, an event for which, inexplicably, neither Millie nor Beryl had been selected. Jacobs finished alone almost three minutes clear of a group which included six British girls, of whom Joan Poole finished the best in fifth place. On the track a few days later, Jean Dunn was third in the sprint behind Ermolaeva of Russia, while Stella Ball and Kay Ray were second and third in the pursuit behind another Russian, Kotchetova. On a personal level, it had been an amazing year for Kay Ray, a striking beauty who had won a national competition to find Britain's most glamorous cyclist, and thereafter had acted as a hostess for *Cycling* magazine at numerous events. For women's cycling as a whole it had also been an unforgettable season of time-trialling, while new horizons were opening in the international and road-racing fields. Great things were expected from Beryl Burton, but no one could have imagined that the 21-year-old was on the threshold of a unique domination of both aspects of women's cycling that would last for a generation.

On the Track

Alone among all the forms of cycling, track-racing is first and last a spectator sport. Before the television age the watcher by the roadside could hope for only the briefest glimpse of the riders, but at the trackside he came face to face with the great champions of the day. The skilled trackman could, in an afternoon of varied racing, build up a real rapport with the crowd, not only through his athletic strengths, but through his appearance, his sportsmanship, his humour, and his body language. The sprinters were the real stars, with their gamesmanship, their explosive bursts of speed, and their terrifying crashes. But the sprint was over almost too quickly, while the crescendo of the pursuiters' final laps in a close-fought race would keep the crowd on its feet for minutes. Track racing is an exception to the rule that cycling is purely a participation sport without great spectator appeal, for in track racing, the intensity of effort, of victory and defeat, all become visible and shareable. Following every World Championship there would be a series of revenge matches, officially billed as "Meetings of Champions", where the crowds could see the new title-holders, and perhaps see them dethroned by their own special heroes. The sprinters have always been the track's own stars, but part of the track's appeal has also been to bring the great roadmen before a personal audience. On the continent the great names of the Tour de France and World Championships would regularly race in the winter velodromes, while in Britain the "Invitation Pursuit" or a special paced event would bring top time triallists and roadmen to the big meetings at Herne Hill or Fallowfield; Joy, Bedwell, Booty, the Higginsons, Stan Brittain and Brian Robinson all competed in this way. In the early fifties however it was slightly unusual for top road riders to be serious track competitors too. Among the exceptions were Cyril Cartwright who switched from time-trialling to become national pursuit champion, as did Keith Bentley, the great 50-miler, while Dave Keeler won the pursuit title in 1951, the same year that he broke the 25-mile record. Cartwright took the pursuit silver medal in the World Championship in 1949, and the gold at the Empire Games of 1950. The link between pursuiting and short-dis-

What the British crowds wanted to see: Harris beating Derksen by inches at Fallowfield.

tance time-trialling would become even clearer a few years later, when Norman Sheil and Mike Gambrill were supreme in Britain in both fields. Track racing was a form of urban entertainment, and there were a dozen major track venues in cities like London, Manchester, Coventry, Birmingham, Cardiff, Brighton and Portsmouth. In the smaller towns grass-track racing also flourished, for which no special facilities were needed except a good sports ground, and national grass-track sprint and five-mile championships were keenly contested. Throughout the 1940s and 1950s there was no national championship track gathering; instead the individual titles were decided at different meetings scattered around the country. At most of the tracks there was strong local interest in certain trophies, some of which had been established in the Victorian era, which were competed for each year; among the best-known was the Muratti Gold Cup at Fallowfield, awarded to the winner of a 10-mile bunch race.

Unlike time-trialling, which was a purely British affair, track racing had always had an international dimension. The successful track rider would soon be faced with the question of how far he wanted to go, for a national championship would almost certainly mean selection for the World Championships or the Olympic Games, and at the same time stardom on the track depended on international success. With the exception of the hour record, track racing has never been primarily concerned with times or records: it was always winning that mattered. For these reasons the history of track racing inevitably focuses on the riders who have won international honours. From 1947 to 1960 Britain produced half a dozen cyclists who reached the finals in world championships, the highest

level at which any track-rider can aim. International success also opened up the possibility of a professional career. There was no professional structure in Britain, but almost all the major track meetings invited pros from the continent to come and race here, and in this the personality of Reg Harris was paramount, for the British fans all wanted to see him compete against men like Scherens, van Vliet, Derksen, Plattner, and Maspes, and above all to win. Crowds of ten thousand or more would fill Fallowfield or Herne Hill to see these great names. In 1951 and 1952 the six-day event at Wembley, established in 1936, was revived after a twelve-year break, and this provided another forum for invitation sprinting. But the costs of erecting the temporary track, with its hardwood frame and thousands of feet of birch boarding, proved prohibitive, and the Wembley Six lapsed for many years.

Harris at home: look at that calf muscle.

The presence of Harris on the British track scene, from 1947 to his retirement in 1957, was enormous. He was Britain's first world cycling champion for 25 years, and his was no one-off victory, as he proved by taking four professional titles in addition to his amateur one, and in between, he won every major sprint honour in every velodrome in Europe. Probably the only reason he did not win still more world titles was the shift in 1952 from straightforward two-up matches to three- and four-up sprinting, for in terms of sheer speed Harris was well-nigh unbeatable, but in three-up races, tactics and alliances played a much greater part. The idea that a British cyclist could live with, and repeatedly out-ride, the giants of the European track was exhilarating. In 1950s Britain, Harris's name became a household word, like those of Roger Bannister, Dennis Compton, Stirling Moss or Geoff Duke. Supremely powerful, clever, articulate, his achievement in breaking into the tough, enclosed world of continental racing was no less outstanding than that of Brian Robinson. Like Robinson he inspired a number of followers, but they found it not merely difficult but impossible to equal what he had done. Harris's contract with Raleigh increased the sense that his victories were the patriotic triumphs of a British team against foreign opposition. From his humble background in the Lancashire cotton towns, Harris acquired considerable wealth and sophistication, and was always the immaculate professional on and off the bike. His come-back in 1974 at the age of 54 to win the British sprint championship seemed utterly incredible to those not familiar with the extraordinary qualities, physical and mental, of this outstanding athlete.

Immediately after the war, the top amateur sprinter was still Alan Bannister, a former Manchester Wheelers colleague of Harris, with whom he won the silver medal for the tandem sprint in the London Olympics in 1948, the same year in which he reached the last four in the world's amateur sprint. He won three British titles between 1948 and 1950, the first when he actually beat Harris, although the competition was then decided by a points system and not by a straight match. Wiry and slightly built for a sprinter, he was an ideal tandem stoker, who would take no less than six British tandem sprint titles, with three different partners. Bannister's position at the top would be threatened and then ended by the two Cyrils, Bardsley and Peacock, who took the national sprint championship in 1951 and 1952 respectively. Bardsley, another Manchester Wheeler, was fourth in the world's amateur sprint, then turned professional for Raleigh, perhaps prematurely, for he never gained any outstanding successes. Peacock, a south Londoner, was a higher achiever than Bardsley, who became a Raleigh professional after winning the world amateur sprint championship in 1954, the year when Harris took his last world title. Peacock seemed to typify the indefinable problems of the British cyclist trying to make the transition to the European professional level, for after that high-point he failed to gain a single significant victory, and after just two active seasons, he retired. His pro career began on an ominous note when he was responsible for a tragic car crash in France, in which he was badly injured and which claimed two other lives, including that of the Australian Olympic gold medallist, Lionel Cox. Peacock's worst moment on the track came in the 1957 World's series, when he had beaten the Frenchman Gaignard twice, but, in an incomprehensible judge's decision, was ordered to re-run; he refused on principle and was eliminated. No British rider since Peacock has won the sprinter's rainbow jersey, yet ironically he is remembered as a failure, rather than as a world champion. The departure of Peacock into the pro ranks left the way open for Lloyd Binch's ascendancy, becoming master of the British track scene for the rest of the decade, winning every national sprint title from 1955 to 1960, yet never quite being able to gain international victories or medals. Throughout these years Binch resisted the challenges of Dave Handley, yet it was Handley who scored a great personal triumph in the 1960 World's by taking the bronze medal after Binch had been eliminated. The programme of track events which we now know was still emerging then, for example the kilo sprint did not feature as a British championship event, although it was an international one, and Neville Tong won the gold for England at the 1958 Commonwealth Games in Cardiff.

The line of top-class pursuiters that began with Tommy Godwin, Cyril Cartwright and Charlie Marriner continued through the time time-triallists Keeler and Bentley, but nothing quite prepared the British track fans for the brilliance of the next wave of pursuiters – Sheil, Brotherton, Holmes, Gambrill, Simpson and Geddes. From 1954 to 1959 these riders took the time necessary to win a top-class 4-kilometre pursuit down from around 5:30 to the 4:50s, they won international honours and formed formidable team pursuit squads, and in Sheil Britain found a world champion able to defeat the Italian and French masters on their own tracks. The story began in 1954 when the tall lean Sheil, who bore a striking resemblance to Coppi, went to the Empire Games in Vancouver as national champion and took the gold medal, with Pete Brotherton second. At the World Championships a month later, Brotherton and Sheil took the silver and the bronze behind the winner, Leandro Faggin of Italy. That winter Sheil trained like a demon under the guidance of Liverpool coach Eddie Soens, and showed his early form in 1955 by breaking the 25-mile record in June. In September history was made at the famous Vigorelli track in Milan when the world pursuit championship was decided between two

Englishmen, Shiel and Brotherton, after Sheil had beaten Faggin and Brotherton had dismissed Hansen of Denmark. The semi-final with the reigning champion was perhaps the real final, in which Sheil produced the blistering finish which became his trademark to finish with a 4:57 ride. After this great victory, Sheil, then aged 22, might have turned professional and become a top European rider, but he was driven by no such ambitions. He returned to England, married, fell out with Eddie Soens, and seemed to lose his way. In 1956 his results were less than convincing, and meanwhile a strong challenge to his supremacy had appeared in Mike Gambrill, the sensationally fast Londoner. First Gambrill beat Sheil for the 25-mile title, and then took his national pursuit championship - indirectly, for Sheil was actually knocked out by another great Liverpool talent, John Geddes. The result was that Sheil, the reigning world champion, was not even picked for the World's or Olympic teams in 1956. (There was no individual pursuit in the Olympic Games until 1960; Sheil missed being part of the team pursuit squad). Brotherton was also eclipsed in the championships by another rising star, Tom Simpson, who was being coached by Cyril Cartwright. In the World's pursuit, Geddes was third and Gambrill fourth, and in the Melbourne Olympics late in the year, these two were joined by Simpson and Don Burgess to take the bronze medal.

In 1957 Sheil rebuilt his relationship with Soens, and plunged back into racing to such effect that in June he at last broke Charlie Marriner's 10-year old hour record, with a ride of 26 miles 1392 yards at

Norman Sheil at the moment of his triumph in Milan, 1955

Fallowfield, but still he could not master Gambrill in the national championship. In the World's in Belgium, Sheil finished fourth, losing to the ultimate winner, Simonigh of Italy, while Gambrill went out in the quarter-finals, unable even to equal the times he had achieved in Britain. Sheil had underestimated just how difficult would be the climb back to the top, but in 1958 he made few mistakes. He scored a great psychological blow when he beat his two rivals, Geddes and Gambrill, at the season-opening meeting at Herne Hill. He lost narrowly to Simpson at the national championships, but turned the tables at the Commonwealth Games in Cardiff, where he took the gold medal from Simpson by just 0.3 seconds.

Then in Paris in September he at last reclaimed his world crown, in a tense, desperate final with the Frenchman Guadrillet, who led for much of the race, but cracked dramatically in the final two laps to leave Sheil a clear winner. After three years of doubts, disappointment and intense effort, the elation of regaining the supreme title was greater even than his first victory had been. Yet Sheil's career once again veered into uncertainty: in 1959 he was again national pursuit champion, this time beating top time-triallist Gordon Ian, in a series which saw a great challenge from a young Barry Hoban. But at the World's in Amsterdam, he and Gambrill both failed to qualify for the final rounds, and would in any case have stood little chance against the new champion, Rudi Altig, who set a phenomenal standard with his 4:53 ride. That winter Sheil turned professional in France and embarked on a brief road career, which saw him start quite unexpectedly in the 1960 Tour de France: he was asked at very short notice to replace Shay Elliott, and in view of his lack of special training, Sheil performed very creditably for almost two weeks, but was eliminated in the Pyrenees. By his own choice his pursuiting days were over, but at the age of 27 he had delayed too long his move into top-level road racing; he had never longed for a pro career, and had never really sought to capitalise on his world championship status.

Mike Gambrill: when Sheil's motivation lapsed, Gambrill took both his national pursuit crown and his 25 mile title.

He remained an English club rider at heart, but one whose burning ambition was to ride supremely fast. In this he was the complete opposite to Simpson, for whom track success was merely a stepping stone to his pro road career, which took off as Sheil's dissolved.

In continental Europe the great crowd-pleaser at the track was the motor-paced event, but the pacing motorbikes were only rarely seen in England, where the traditional pacer was the tandem, for which teams of tandemists were recruited from the local clubs. In the early fifties, the veteran Reg Waters was still winning the national paced 50-mile championship with times between 1:35 and 1:40. But a few years later Vespa scooters were introduced to pace an experimental 100-mile event at Herne Hill, in which roadman Stan Brittain won by a big margin in a time of 3: 31:22. In that event, even Waters was defeated and retired, like most of the other competitors, and the spectators lost interest in the buzzing scooters over such a distance. The tandem pacing obviously had more charm for the real enthusiasts, and for some years there were even 12-hour events, and we have to wonder how these events were managed, and who the tandemists were who

The Olympic track team of 1956: Dawson, Thompson, Gambrill, Burgess, Brotherton, Geddes, Simpson.

circled the track with them all day, hour after hour at 25 m.p.h. The big motor-pacing machines were usually brought in only for invitation and professional events, and there was considerable interest in a little-known Englishman living and racing on the continent who had made a name in this specialist field and took the bronze medal at the 1954 World's: some of Joe Bunker's celebrity must have come from his having a name that once heard was never forgotten. The track was an arena where novelties and experimental events could be staged, and none was more sensational than the "Sputnik", the streamlined bike that the French rider Francois Lahaye unveiled at Fallowfield in July 1958. Lahaye, a good but not outstanding rider, competed in a special pursuit against a crack four-man team that included Sheil, Gambrill and Geddes, and such was the effect of his aerodynamic shell that he beat them by 8 seconds. During further outings with other riders, the results were the same, but the aerodynamic lessons appeared at first to have little practical relevance.

In addition to Britain's own sprinters and pursuiters, the press and public in this country "adopted" a series of top Australian riders as if they too were British. There was Sid Patterson, who after winning the world amateur sprint title in 1949, lost it in 1950 but switched immediately to pursuiting and won that world championship instead; he went on to win two professional world pursuit titles. Russell Mockridge was a double gold-medalist at the 1952 Olympics who later turned pro roadman and rode the 1955 Tour de France. Like Patterson, Mockridge was a favourite performer on British tracks in the early fifties; he was killed during a race in Australia in 1958. Dick Ploog - another unforgettable name - defeated England's Karl Barton to win the Empire Games sprint in Cardiff in 1958, the same games which saw the arrival in this country of New Zealand's Warwick Dalton, who became a popular trackman and road-racer. Dalton started as favourite for the pursuit title, and rode fractionally faster than Sheil and Simpson, but not in the vital rounds. In cycling terms the early Empire Games in 1950, 1954 and 1958 were virtually Britain versus Australia affairs, but in European competitions there seemed to be a feeling that if a Briton could not beat the continentals, an Australian was the next best thing.

Womens' track racing was pioneered by the W.C.R.A., and was officially sanctioned by the N.C.U. in 1947. In that year Dorothy Hobbs, won the first women's national sprint championship at Herne Hill, beating Joyce Dean into second place. Joyce Dean, as Joyce Harris, later set a new hour record of 23 miles 1096 yards at Herne Hill. The record that she broke belonged to top time-triallist Stella Farrell, who in 1951 convincingly won the first women's metre pursuit title from Winnie Shepherd in a time of 6:13 for the 4,000 metres; the women's pursuit distance would soon be brought down to 3,000 metres. The story of women's track racing in the 1950s, like the story of time-trialling and road-racing, inevitably culminates in the figure of Beryl Burton. Totally inexperienced in track-racing, she was not considered for selection in the 1958 inaugural world championships, but in 1959 she showed that could pursuit better than anyone else, and she was sweeping all before her in the time-trialling world; she was therefore a natural choice for the pursuit event in Belgium. Millie Robinson went out in the quarter finals, while Beryl disposed of Yvonne Reynders, the Dutch girl who would win the road race title that year, and who would become her great international rival during the 1960s. Years later Reynders was implicated in drug-taking, and Beryl wondered with some bitterness how many world titles she had been unfairly deprived of. In her final, Beryl then defeated Elsy Jacobs, winner of the world's road race in 1958 and holder of the world hour record. This was the first of Beryl's five rainbow jerseys, and it was achieved with no special preparation, but through natural speed and strength. With hindsight, there was nothing especially surprising in her triumph: in Britain she was head and shoulders above all her rivals at every facet of the sport, so why should her superiority not carry over into the international sphere ? At the time however it was a cause for tremendous celebration, a vindication of all the efforts of Britains' women riders and administrators to put women's cycling on an equal footing with men's.

Jim Hinds en route to his famous victory over Bill Bradley on the Isle of Man in 1959.

Retrospect

In retrospect, the pattern of cycling history in Britain from the war's end to 1960 is clear. The period began in the enclosed world of club-runs, time-trials, and fixed wheels, but when it ended, very different international horizons were opening up. An island nation with its own cycling traditions was being exposed to new ideas, new ambitions and new challenges. Harris was the early symbol of this process, but Harris's achievement was in the highly specialised world of professional sprinting, where few if any could attempt to follow him. The real focus of change lay in the road-racing revolution, where riders trained in both the B.L.R.C. and the N.C.U. traditions now set out to emulate continental-style racing, and many dreamed of a professional career as their ultimate objective. This change was encouraged by the dramatically increased press coverage of the Tour de France, which in 1947 or 1948 received only one paragraph in *Cycling,* but which, ten years later, dominated the magazine. The change was seen too in the cycling trade, where "continental" styles and components suited to road-racing came to replace British ones. Brian Robinson's move to the continent and his success there inspired scores of British riders to try to emulate him. The British suspicion of professionalism in sport was to some extent modified by admiration for him, while stars like Coppi and Anquetil were spoken of with adulation. Yet there was still a feeling that professionalism, while it was alright for

The historic first issue of J.B. Wadley's magazine "Coureur", winter 1955, featuring Bobet, Sheil, Millie Robinson, and the British Tour de France team. This magazine helped to foster the passion for all things continental.

top European riders, just did not belong in British cycling, that it was out of place here. In some senses perhaps this was correct, for the lure of road-racing on the continent produced heartache and disappointment for many riders who could not make the crucial transition, and returned disillusioned with the sport. In the many interviews which Robinson gave, the professional scene sounded hard, calculated and mercenary, a form of cycling from which joy and spontaneity seemed to have been removed.

Were all these changes inevitable, or was isolation still a feasible option? Throughout these years the time-trialling scene glided on, serene and immune from the historic changes at work around it. The fifties produced some brilliant champions, with whom the ordinary club rider could easily identify, while marvelling at the new heights to which they were taking cycling records. Of course time-trialling was intensely competitive, but the competition was contained within an ethos of amateur sportsmanship, it was part of a wider cycling culture. The new standards of road-racing, professionalism, and the drive towards international success seemed to belong to a very different and more ruthless world. Cycling had been a way of life, and it was now becoming a sport, in a different and more modern sense.

So the new forces within cycling brought losses as well as gains. Commentators frequently asked if we

had become obsessed by racing, and if the health of British cycling was to be measured only by international success. Year after year the headlines following World or Olympic Championships would read "British riders fail", inducing a crisis of confidence throughout British cycling, a feeling that other nations possessed the keys to success and excellence which we just didn't have, and that perhaps we had been doing things wrong all these years. As it happens, this questioning, this sense of doubt and failure, this uncertainty about our relationship with continental Europe, was entirely typical of Britain's history during the 1950s and still more during the 60s. The Empire was dissolving fast, our social traditions were being questioned and challenged, our industries were being squeezed by foreign competition, and our news was dominated by international events quite beyond our control. We were waking up to a more difficult and complicated world, and we had to decide if we wanted to be fully part of it or not. Thus in a strange way cycling was a microcosm of the forces of change that were facing British society as a whole.

Road-racing became news by the end of the decade, in a way that time-trialling never had been, and Condor quickly gained a reputation for supplying bikes to the press and media, partly because Fleet Street was just around the corner. They lent a fleet of bikes to Hammer Films for the 1960 comedy "A Weekend With Lulu", starring Shirley Eaton, about a group of innocent Brits abroad who get mixed up with the Tour de France.

Chapter Two

The Sixties: Years of Transition

In February 1960 Harold Macmillan made his famous "winds of change" speech in Cape Town. He was speaking specifically about the post-colonial era in Africa, but the phrase soon came to be seen as prophesying the revolutionary era that was beginning, and by 1960 the winds of change were certainly blowing through most aspects of British life including the cycling world. Bicycle ownership, and with it the basis of cycle sport and of the cycle industry, was shrinking. The two great enemies were the car and television. The spread of car ownership through all the social classes meant that for thousands if not millions of people, the bicycle was no longer the primary means of transport. In fact in a consciously affluent society, even to be seen on a bicycle would soon become a confession of social failure. The freedom offered by the bicycle seemed childish compared with that offered by the car. Health consciousness and environmental awareness lay far in the future, and in 1960 there seemed no reason not to foresee an endless growth in motor traffic. For the young, a motor bike or scooter rather than a car was the preferred style symbol. This in turn was just one aspect of the rise of youth culture - the music, the films, and the fashions - which competed for their attention, and which made pastimes like cycling seem dull and old-fashioned. Then there was television - the hypnotic time-killer which had simply not existed in 1950, but which by 1960 had arrived in ten million British homes. Television engendered a culture of inactivity, a reason not to go out and explore the world, but to sit at home and be told about it. Behind the cars and motor bikes, the televisions and hi-fis, lay the extension of credit through all the social classes, creating the consumer society which now surrounds us.

These signs of a new lifestyle were not merely things which sociologists - another invention of the 1960s - could enjoy studying; instead they had a very real impact on the world of cycling. First, they diminished the social base of the sport, the pool from which serious cyclists would come. Cycling became something that children did, but for adults there were easier and faster ways of getting about, and more exciting ways of spending one's time. So cycling's position as a minority sport lacking in glamour was confirmed. Second, they had a severe impact on the cycle trade, shrinking the market for all types of bike. As early as June 1957 readers of *Cycling* had been staggered to find the historic journal of their sport transformed overnight into *Cycling and Mopeds*, a move which the editor claimed reflected "the new age of personal transport". In spite of being given this exciting new identity, the magazine shrank steadily in size, from the sixty pages of the mid-fifties to less than thirty pages a decade later. In 1960 the contraction of the market forced the merger of the two great bicycle manufacturers, Raleigh and the Tube Investments group, bringing into the hands of one giant company marques such as Hercules, Phillips, Sun, Norman, Sunbeam, BSA, Triumph and Rudge, as well as component makers such as Sturmey-Archer, Brooks and Reynolds; Carlton would soon be added to the empire. Part of the industry's trouble was that their bikes looked dull, old-fashioned and distinctly unsporty. But if there was a design or marketing way out of the malaise Raleigh could not see it, for in 1958 they rejected a design for a revolutionary new bicycle offered to them by a man named Alex Moulton; "an overgrown fairy cycle" was Raleigh's verdict. When he heard this, Moulton promptly went away to develop the new concept himself. For the specialist lightweight builder too, the sixties were difficult years which saw the demise of many small London builders - such as Ephgrave, Gillott, Maclean, Hobbs and Carpenter - while those that remained had to struggle for their survival.

These social changes cast a shadow over the future of cycling as a whole. Yet the sixties in Britain witnessed some superb cycling from both roadmen and time-triallists: Colden, Engers, Beryl Burton, Roach, Watson, Cromack, Chisman, West, Metcalfe, Hitchen, Lewis, Porter and many more. The decade had its disappointments, quarrels and tragedies, but these names still evoke an era of great records and great victories. A curious historical milestone was passed in March 1960, when bike-racing on Britain's roads came within the scope of the law for the first time. The new rules, which had been hammered out through several years' negotiations with the cycling bodies, made a clear distinction between time-trialling and massed-start races. In the case of time-trialling, the police now had to be informed about the race twenty-eight days in advance, and details given as to the route, the size of the field, marshalling arrangements and so on; so long as this was done, the race was legally authorised and the police had no powers to stop it. Road-racing had more restrictions, principally that the maximum field was forty, and that the race must take place entirely in daylight hours; but in addition, the police were given additional and very wide powers to "impose such conditions on a race as they might think fit", especially in respect of the route, the timing, the marshalling and so on. Nobody quite knew if this meant that the police could actually prohibit a race if they wished, but in practice this never seems to have happened. In a sense the introduction of these regulations was the final act in the drama of the cycling conflicts of the 1950s. The efforts of the B.L.R.C. had been vindicated, and road-racing was established as a legal but controlled activity, but time-trialling's special position as a race that was not really a race, over which the police had no powers, had also been recognised.

Colin Lewis and Dave Nie in a fierce sprint in 1968. When the sixties opened, no one at Condor imagined that they would soon be part of a high-profile professional racing scene.

The Condor Road Team

In the road-racing scene from 1959 onwards, there was reason for optimism. The healing in that year of the long-running massed-start war and the creation of the B.C.F. seemed to promise a new era in which commercial sponsorship could benefit both the riders and the bike trade. The publicity offered by road-racing tempted many manufacturers, some large some small, to set up teams to showcase their bikes, and Condor was among the first south-of-England bike businesses to take the plunge into the world of trade-team sponsorship. After the collapse of the professional sport in the mid fifties, an independent class had existed, mainly in the north, where many of the former B.L.R.C. professionals had built up a weekly racing circuit, but independent racing had not flourished to the same extent in the south of the country, and few new sponsors were entering the sport. Yet the 1950s had established beyond any doubt that there was a tremendous appetite in Britain for this form of competition, a type of racing whose psychology was quite different from the traditional time-trialling culture. Road-racing was a direct, hands-on battle between man and man, requiring a tactical brain, and a deep self-knowledge and belief. Experienced road-racers would coach newcomers by telling them bluntly "stop thinking like a cyclist": stop plodding away at steady club-runs and long lonely time-trials, and start thinking how to win, how to defeat your opponents. They drew surprising parallels with other sports, such as boxing. A boxer does not hammer away non-stop round after round; instead he cruises with two aims in mind, how to save himself from getting hurt, and how to strike at the strategic moment. So the cyclist should save his strength and watch his rivals until the crucial point when he can exert his power to win. Speed was the key: to reach that crucial point in the race when a fierce attack would break up the field or win the final sprint, but one had to learn how to reach that moment with one's strength intact. Good coaching for this

Terry Jeoffroy, Edmonton R.C., and Condor independent, the team's first big winner during 1959 and 1960.

Albert Roberts riding alongside former world champion Andre Darrigade in the Isle of Man Premier race of 1961.

type of racing did not involve scientific measurement and physiological build-up, but getting inside the rider's head, training his instincts, building his confidence, setting him targets and analysing his defeats and victories. This type of competition was more aggressive and personal than time-trialling, but it was far less lonely, and bred a camaraderie between rivals in opposing clubs and teams. It was a different culture from time-trialling, and it suited a different type of rider, although a few could successfully cross over from one discipline to the other. But many time-triallists retained the suspicion that the roadmen were all lazy and crafty, sitting in and sprinting for the line, and that this was not a race of truth.

Condor's participation in this type of racing was to last eleven years, involving some of the best riders in the country, and placing the Condor name at the heart of British cycle sport. Yet it all began quietly enough in July 1959 with the signing of four riders: Terry Jeoffroy, Laurie Cook, Peter Barrett and Graham Vines. Actually "signing" is too grandiose a word, because it was all quite informal, since there were no big fees and no written contracts. All the riders were Londoners, known to Monty Young as customers or from his weekend race-going. No one would claim that they were star riders, with the possible exception of Vines who had been national road race champion twice, once as an N.C.U. amateur in 1952, and again as a B.L.R.C. professional in 1955 when he rode for the Wearwell team; but Vines was now probably past his best, and took several placings but no victories for Condor. The rewards for this new team were pretty modest too: they were each given a bike, which of course would be serviced for them, plus a few spare tubs; they got racing jerseys in the purple and white team colours; and they sometimes got a lift to the race at the weekend. They were not paid a salary, although of course they could win any prizes that were on offer, and they received small bonuses for any top-three places. They were not professionals in the full sense, but independents, the class which had been dreamed up in the mid-fifties as a half-way house to professionalism, permitted to race against both pros and amateurs. But since that time there had been a significant change in the status of independents. The original two-year limit after which the independent was supposed to move up to become a full professional, had been quietly discarded, and a rider could remain independent as long as he wished. This suited the smaller trade sponsors, especially in the bleak economic climate of the early sixties, who could run a racing team at minimal cost. The team strength at Condor was usually three or four, and riders came and went periodically: about twenty-five men wore the Condor colours between 1959 and 1970, some of them famous names, some of them now forgotten. There was a certain degree of glamour in the independent scene, but not a great deal of money; however most of them felt it was one step up from time-trialling. The prize for a typical race might be £10 or £20, although a few top races, such as London-Holyhead carried a first prize of £100 - a month's salary in 1959 - while a similar sum awaited stage winners in the Milk Race, the richest amateur race in the country. Over the years the precise relationship of the independent rider with his sponsor would vary a great deal, and a small salary or retainer would often be paid; Condor were able to do this when they set up their co-sponsorship deal with Mackeson. The cash prizes for amateur races were actually paid via the tortuous voucher system, where a winner was given a voucher for £5 or £10 which he must present to his local lightweight shop, theoretically to exchange for equipment. In practice the dealer simply wrote a bogus receipt for the equipment, which the rider then sent to the race organiser, finally receiving back his postal order for £5 or £10. This form of "shamateurism" was criticised pretty widely, but it went on for years.

From the outset the original four Condor riders worked well together, and began winning team prizes regularly, especially in London area road races. Terry Jeoffroy, of the Edmonton R.C., was clearly the strongest in the team, winning three events in the late summer of 1959, taking second spot behind Ron Coe and Dave Bedwell, and finishing ahead of riders of the calibre of Jim Hinds and Owen Blower. For the first few races the team name was simply Condor Cycles, but before the season ended Monty found a co-sponsor in Britanica Tubulars, who were near-neighbours of Condor just off Gray's Inn Road. Britanica was run by Nick D'Alessandro, a member of the famous Italian tubular manufacturing family, who had decided to set up a separate UK operation, and for the rest of 1959 and through 1960, Condor-Britanica was the name on the jerseys. The bikes they rode were the "Number 1" models, built by Bill Hurlow and soon they were being equipped with Zeus components, an alloy range imported from Spain; not so classy as Campag, but still excellent quality. These first months were highly successful: the team showed that they could compete at a high level and get results, and the Condor name was appearing alongside those of the country's top lightweight manufacturers like Viking and Elswick-Hopper. In order to strengthen the team still further for 1960, two new riders were signed up, while Laurie Cook and Graham Vines dropped out. The new men were Alf Howling of the London club Castille, and Albert Roberts of the Highgate. The

Alf Howling's racing career in France started with a bang, and his former sponsor celebrated with this press notice.

CONDOR

Congratulations to Alf Howling (Condor Britanica) on his many successes in France

Some of his latest wins :—
The Ploemeur, R. R.
„ Hennebont, R. R.
„ Sante-Helene, R. R.
„ Brennilis, R. R.
„ Gran Prix de Kervignac
Plus many track events

Date of the Condor Frame Show in next issue

Send for Condor Frame Catalogue. Stamp Please
211 BALLS POND ROAD, N.1 - CAN 2192
90 GRAYS INN ROAD, W.C.1 - CHA 7896

21 year-old Howling - a self-trained commercial artist by profession - was a very promising rider, out of the army the previous year, with several good wins to his credit, including the classic early-season time-trial, the North Road Hardriders. He had finished 30th in the 1959 Tour of Britain, and he still has vivid memories of the murderous trans-Pennine stage which Bradley won.

Competition from the other teams in 1960 would be stiffer, for Viking had signed Dave Bedwell and Stan Brittain, while Falcon had now decided to field a team composed of John Perks, Harry Reynolds and Frank Clements, and which would soon become much stronger. The dominant team in 1959 had undoubtedly been Elswick-Hopper, with the all-conquering Ron Coe, backed up by Owen Blower and John Geddes, but 1960 saw the arrival of Albert Hitchen riding for Ellis-Briggs, beginning a brilliant career which would take him to countless victories over the next ten years. The independent class was growing, for Condor's example spurred several other small lightweight firms - Sid Mottram, Rory O'Brien and Ken Ryall - to set up heir own teams. Ryall's rider was inter-

Post-race publicity for Mackeson from George Drewell.

esting choice - Ron Jowers, the former time-trial giant, now coming back as a roadman. Condor's Pete Barrett won the first big race of the year, the Chiltern G.P. in March, and Condor took the team prize. A week later however all the independents were soundly beaten by Billy Holmes in the classic Archer GP. It was still an open question who was the best roadman in Britain for there were still a few top amateurs capable of beating the big-name independents: Holmes was one, Bradley obviously another, and young Alan Ramsbottom and Jim Hinds were two more. The two classes still had separate championships, and after the 1959 experiment, the 1960 Tour of Britain was not open to independents, so a final showdown never seemed to arrive.

Alf Howling took over from Terry Jeoffroy as the star of the Condor team, winning three races in the early summer, but then in June he packed his bags and went off to live and race in France, where he was so successful that by the end of the year he had won a dozen races and secured a pro contract with the Rapha-Gitane squad, alongside Robinson and Simpson. In 1961 he would perform so well that he was selected to ride for Britain in the Tour de France, which was then organised in national teams, but he became ill just before the start and could not race. Later in the year he married and set up his own business in France, so his serious racing days were over. But more than a decade later Howling would once again play a significant part in the Condor story, for he was commissioned to re-design the Condor badge along more modern lines, and the linear, stylised bird with the outspread wings which has appeared on their frames and clothing ever since, was his creation.

The winter of 1960-61 brought a major change in the fortunes of the team: the

Whitbread Brewing company, sponsors of many sporting events, was signed up as co-sponsor of the team, and they chose to promote just one of their many products - Mackeson stout - so that the team was subsequently to be known as Condor-Mackeson. This was the first time that a major sponsor from outside the industry had put money into cycle sport in this way, and their financial resources would provide far better support for the riders than Condor alone could offer. In addition to financing the team, Mackeson would also sponsor a number of road races each year, and a season-long points competition. They were willing to commit themselves for several years ahead, and the building of a stronger team now became possible. The contact with Whitbread came about in a quite informal way: one of Condor's many customers worked at the Whitbread offices in Britannia Street just off Gray's Inn Road, and he provided Monty Young with the all-important introduction to the Whitbread management. They were impressed with the approach which Monty and Wally Conway made to them, with the photographs of the races, and they were particularly keen to partner a neighbouring business. Each year thereafter there would be a formal team launch at the brewery's head office in Chiswell Street, and one of the attractive spin-offs of the sponsorship was a generous monthly allowance of Mackeson stout; the riders used to mix it with lemonade and refresh themselves with it during races, purely for publicity purposes of course.

The new era for the team coincided with several changes of personnel. Jeoffroy moved to Fred Dean Cycles, to ride alongside Dave Bedwell. With Howling and Peter Barrett gone, there were three vacancies for the new season, filled by three notable riders, all Londoners. First there was Doug Collins, a very experienced rider who had finished a fine fourth in the first Milk Race in 1958, less than three minutes behind the winner, Durlacher of Austria. He had also succeeded in finishing in the 1960 Peace Race, and had taken third place in the Manx International. Collins was a rather fragile-looking rider, who glided along unobtrusively in the bunch, concealing his strength and earning himself the nickname "the Ghost". Next there was Alan Jacob, a Milk Race stage winner who had beaten all the favourites in one of the 1960 Olympic trial races, but who had not made the Olympic team, and had decided to turn independent. And thirdly there was no less a rider

The Ted Gerrard road-racing team of 1962: time-triallists Harvey, Engers and Woodburn. Woodburn won his first race, and Harvey later won the national championship.

than Bryan Wiltcher, time-trial champion for the previous two years, and now returning to his first love, road racing.

But Wiltcher did not settle well in the team, staying only one year and scoring only one win, although he narrowly missed breaking the R.R.A. 50-mile record after a super-fast ride that was ruined by punctures. He was also the best Condor finisher in the London-Holyhead event in May, in which he was seventh, two minutes down on the winner Albert Hitchen. Roberts performed very creditably in the Manx Premier professional road race, finishing 17th, just two minutes behind the winners De Roo and Darrigade. Mainly on the strength of this ride he was selected for the World Championship road race in Bern in September, alongside Robinson, Simpson and Ron Jowers. Roberts and Jowers were clearly out of their depth at this level, but they stayed well through almost five hours of racing, until the killing 177-mile distance forced them out. The 1961 season had been satisfactory if not brilliant for Condor: Wiltcher, Collins, Roberts and Jacob had all scored individual victories, and there had been half a dozen team wins. Wiltcher, Jacob and Roberts were also selected to ride the Meeting of Champions at Herne Hill, riding a professional omnium in two teams captained by Robinson and Simpson. Condor-Mackeson was recognised as the strongest independent team in the south of the country, although they probably could not rival the Wolverhampton-based Viking team. But the next six or seven years would see a steady development, until the Condors were acknowledged as the strongest force in British road-racing. Nothing was static in the world of the independents: Falcon had head-hunted Albert Hitchen for the following season, while one of the most intriguing new team announcements was that of Ted Gerrard Cycles, who signed up three star time-triallists from the Barnet C.C. - Alf Engers, John Woodburn and John Harvey, who would make their debut as roadmen in 1962. Woodburn had a dream start to his new career, notching a clear win in his first race, and recording several more victories. Engers soon left the team for personal reasons - he started his own business - but the team was short-lived in any case, falling a victim to Ted Gerrard's business problems.

There is no doubt that there was a degree of north-south needle in the road racing scene. Road-racing's heartland was in the north of

Dennis Tarr's greatest victory, outsprinting Albert Hitchen at the finish of the London-Holyhead, 1962.

You didn't find road-racing company much classier than this in the sixties: Dennis Tarr riding beside Jacques Anquetil in the Isle of Man in 1962. Unfortunately, Dennis couldn't stay with him to the finish.

England, firstly in Liverpool and Manchester, but even more in the Sheffield-Leeds axis. Over the years an apparently endless stream of top riders emerged from this area to hammer the softer southerners. Whether it was the Yorkshire character, the moorland air, or the dour life of the steel-and-coal towns no one knew, but something seemed to breed exactly the right blend of grit and aggression that road-racing demanded. London and the south could produce fast, talented riders by the score, but the champions, the Milk Race winners and those who went on to dominate the independent and pro class were usually northerners. In time-trialling, the post-war B.A.R's had all been southerners, but here too the pendulum had now swung decidedly to the northerners. The Condor riders were very much the London representatives on the road-racing battleground, and the two years 1962-63 saw them restore the balance, and become a team to be feared.

A disillusioned Wiltcher parted from the team during the winter, and his replacement was the diminutive but immensely strong Dennis Tarr, a former national junior champion and a stage winner in the previous year's Milk Race. In fact the Condors began to be teased around this time as being a team of midgets, for several of their riders were distinctly small-scale. Tarr, who was also a weightlifter and boxer like Dave Bedwell, was an interesting rider who possessed the roadman's two classic assets: an extremely shrewd tactical brain and a sprint that was feared by everyone who ever rode against him. His partnership with Alan Jacob during 1962 and 63 was one of the two highlights in the team's story - the other being the Bonner-Lewis-Porter years of 1967 and 68. Tarr started scoring victories for Condor immediately in March of that year, and his greatest triumph was to take the London-Holyhead classic in May, getting the better of the sprint king himself, Albert Hitchen. Tarr had improved his victory chances by riding Ron Coe off his wheel just a few miles before the finish. Doug Collins was third, and Condor-Mackeson took the team prize. Tarr had known Hitchen as a friend and rival for many years, and he was confident that he could out-jump him, in fact it was part of his self-belief that if he got to the last mile of a race in the front group, however long and hard that race had been, he could unleash a sprint as fast as a standing quarter-mile, and he would not be beaten. On the basis of this ride, Tarr was selected for the Tour de l'Avenir in July, riding alongside Bradley, Metcalfe, and Chisman, but he retired after four stages. Alan Jacob had better fortune in the Peace Race in May, where he was the best British finisher, although down in 42nd place, returning absolutely shattered. Condor confirmed their strength in depth by taking the team prize in the road race championship in July, with Jacob, Collins and Roberts all finishing in the first ten. The surprise winner was the twenty year-old John Harvey, riding in the Ted Gerrard team in his first year as an independent. He outsprinted none other than the defending champion Dave Bedwell, fourteen years his senior.

Alan Jacob, the big winner for Condor in 1963.

In 1963 it was the turn of Albert Roberts and Doug Collins to quit the team, to be replaced by Brian Willoughby and Harry Willison, but this was to be Alan Jacob's year. Strong, fiercely motivated, able to climb and sprint, Jacob (who was incidentally Billy Holmes's brother-in-law) had matured into a roadman of outstanding class who worked brilliantly with Tarr, and only narrowly missed top honours. As it was he took a dozen victories that year, the highlight being his triumph in London-Holyhead, beating men like Bradley, Holmes, Hitchen and Brittain, and out-jumping the master sprinter Bedwell on the line, just as Tarr had done to Hitchen the year before. It was a great double for the Condor team, and Jacob underlined his class by taking third place that year in the national championship behind Hitchen, who had replaced Ron Coe as the big winner among the independents.

1963 had been a splendid year for Condor and their new co-sponsor, with a dozen individual and team wins, but it ended on a deeply sad note with the sudden death from a heart attack of Wally Conway. Wally had been Monty Young's trusted partner since the founding of the business; he had managed the shop in Ball's Pond Road, and had shared in all the risks, difficulties and successes of those years, and had been instrumental in winning the sponsorship deal with Whitbread. Aged only in his mid-forties, his death was a tremendous blow, but it was at this point that Frank Westell emerged as an important figure in the business, becoming manager of the Gray's Inn Road shop, and taking a bigger

Dennis Tarr and Alan Jacob, a hugely succesful combination in 1962 and 1963. On their wheel is sprint expert Johnny Clarey.

role in the running of the team, seeing to their equipment, transport and service during races. This role was to be his first step into the field of coaching and sports physiotherapy, in which he later acquired a strong reputation.

Because the win-bonuses were so important at this time, the independents were always sizing up their rivals, and calculating whether they might do better by moving to another team: this explains the constant transfers among the independents, although the new team formations did not always work out as planned. At the beginning of 1964, the annual round of transfers saw Alan Jacob leave Condor to join Ken Ryall's squad, and Dennis Tarr go to Witcomb, but neither of them subsequently enjoyed the level of success which they had achieved together with Condor, and the demands of family and business soon took them out of the sport. Their replacements at Condor-Mackeson were first, but very briefly, John Harvey, whose successes since winning the national championship in 1962 had been very few; in mid-season he vanished from the scene anyway when he emigrated to Australia. Second there was Ged Coles from Suffolk, the first non-Londoner ever to ride for Condor. Coles was a wiry, endurance rider and a brilliant climber who had finished second in the 1961 Manx International and won the King of the Mountains title in the 1962 Milk Race; Coles had already ridden as an independent for Falcon for a year. Third was George Drewell, a young Smithfield meat-porter who had emerged as one of the top riders in London-area races; a little short on staying-power, he was a clever rider with an excellent sprint. Another intriguing candidate for a place in the team was Dave Bonner, superfast youngster and reigning 25-mile champion, but Bonner was hanging on for possible Olympic selection later in the year, and the discussions between him and Condor were put on ice. Coles's climbing strength gave him the King of the Mountains title in the six-day Tour of the South-West, in which Alan Jacob finished a close second overall to Billy Holmes. Holmes was now racing as an independent for the Falcon team,

Dave Bonner, spearhead of the Condor team from 1964 until 1970. Fast, clever, flamboyant, he made the difficult transition from 25-mile champion to leading pro roadman.

to which Hitchen had returned yet again. Another top amateur rider, Wes Mason, would also join the independent ranks in the late summer, becoming a team-mate of Bill Bradley in the Harry Quinn colours; Mason's move was prompted by his failure to be selected for the Olympic road race. During the year Coles won two races and was third in the independent road-race championship. The surprise winner of the championship race was Keith Butler, an experienced time-triallist and roadman who was based on the continent and riding for the Rapha-Gitane team, and who relegated Hitchen to second place. Drewell was placed several times, but would have to wait another year before gaining some excellent victories. The most significant event for the Condor team's long-

term future came in August, when Dave Bonner finally signed up. Bonner had had his season ruined by a series of crashes on the road and on the track, and even by accidents in his own home. Like Mason, he had been chosen only as a reserve for the Tokyo Olympics, and decided that the scramble for international selection did not justify remaining an amateur.

Bonner was a south-London lad, a printer by trade, not yet twenty-one years old but already in his seventh year of racing. Confident, extrovert, cocky perhaps, but his talent was a brilliant one and his determination was fierce and competitive. He rode a 57-minute 25 at the age of sixteen, and 1:57 for the 50 at eighteen. He had firm views on gearing and fast-pedalling, and although he soon forsook fixed wheel riding like most other people, he did not join the growing move towards big-gear pushing. In 1962 at the age of nineteen he smashed the 25 competition record in a mid-October ride, the latest the record had ever been beaten, with Ken Craven once again taking second in a big race. The national 25 title became his in the following year, in a championship record time, with a narrow victory over Hugh Porter. Bonner's speed made him an excellent track pursuiter, although not yet a championship winner, and his real ambitions lay in road racing. His extrovert character may have led him to take too many risks, for he certainly appeared to be accident-prone, suffering numerous crashes that interrupted his racing career. Yet he had that touch of flamboyance that was just right for an independent career, and he was to remain with the Condor-Mackeson team for a full seven years, longer than any other rider, scoring several good wins each year and becoming central to the team's identity. His first win as an independent came in early October in a Sheffield criterium, and two weeks later in the final race of the year's pro-gramme, he won again in Kent, outsprinting the aggressive south Londoner with the cannonball

finish, Johnny Clarey. Like quite a few other riders at this time, Bonner honed his speed by regular training behind a moped, a technique he learned from the Continental pros - in fact this was probably the single great benefit that the moped age brought to cycling.

1965 started well for the Condors, with wins for Bonner, Drewell and Coles in early season events in the south, including the Dover-London race. A few weeks later however in the Tour of the South-West, now extended to eight days, Bonner's jinx struck again after a good start, and he crashed, badly injuring his back, while Drewell retired. For a time it was feared Bonner might never race again, but he did recover. The race was won by Bill Bradley, now a member of the immensely-strong Falcon team, alongside Hitchen, Holmes and former amateur road champion, Bob Addy. Wes Mason had now gone to the Viking team, and Raleigh had appeared in the independent race scene, riding Carlton bikes in a team co-sponsored by the engineering firm BMB, led by Peter Chisman. For the London-Holyhead marathon Bonner was out injured, and in any case that year's race was clearly going to be a very different one, in which neither Drewell nor Coles fancied their chances, for all the continental-based British professionals - Simpson, Elliott, Denson and Hoban - decided to return en masse to compete. Simpson won from his friend Elliott in a sprint that has long troubled cycling historians, for photographs show the Irishman clearly pulling on both brakes a yard out from the finish. Hitchen was third by a yard, he and Bradley having stayed brilliantly through the all-day race, run at a record 25 m.p.h., leaving the bunch almost twenty minutes down. Bonner had piled in 2,000 miles of train-ing while recovering from his crash, and started in the of Isle of Man Premier race in July, but he trailed in fourteen minutes down on the victorious Anquetil, who outsprinted a young first-year pro named Eddy Merckx. Soon after the race, in an attempt to give new impetus to his disappointing season, Bonner announced that he intended to attack the British hour record, held since 1957 by Norman Sheil. This attempt never materialised, but it was just two weeks later that the record was broken anyway - by Les West. In August Hitchen underlined his superiority by winning the independents' championship, a race in

Albert Hitchen, probably the most success-ful Independent of the early sixties. A prolif-ic winner, including two national champi-onships and two London-Holyheads.

*The new professionals:
Porter leads Billy
Holmes, Heaton Park,
1967.*

which Bonner was fifth and Drewell ninth. Coles and Drewell both had excellent victories in the following weeks, and then in the last event of the season, the Brighton-London, Drewell and Bonner were out on their own for half the race and heading for a one-two, but were swept up just before the finish by the winner, Hugh Porter.

The 1965 season ended with the announcement from the B.C.F. that, following U.C.I. decisions, the independent class was to be abolished: in future all non-amateur licences would be out-and-out professional ones. This was a change in name more than anything else, for it did not revolutionise overnight the contracts between sponsors and riders: it did not force sponsors to pay good salaries so that riders could live purely from cycling, although they could do so if they wished. Nor did it create a programme of professional events for them to ride, for former independent events were simply re-classified as professional. There was no big injection of new money into the sport, and the expectations of the new pros were little changed. What it finally did however was to draw a clear line between amateur and professional racing, and to declare an end to the independent experiment which had begun more than a decade before.

So what had the independent era really achieved ? In career terms the independent was very little different from an amateur, for they all had jobs outside cycling, but they had agreements with their sponsor and received prizes, win-bonuses and some expenses. This was the concept of the independent accepted by the B.L.R.C. and the N.C.U., and taken over by the B.C.F. The independent class became so firmly established that neither the B.C.F. nor the trade sponsors saw any need to go to full professionalism. So although the independent class was supposed to be a first step towards professionalism, in practice it never worked that way in Britain, and voices were periodically raised to ask how professional cycling could ever develop here while the independent system prevailed. The career length of the average independent was fairly short. He was racing each week against the same twenty or thirty riders, and a small handful of winners picked up virtually all the prizes. If he was not one of these, he must ask himself again and again where his career was going - was he going to make money from the sport, and if not what was the point of it all? Then there was the curious situation where some amateur races, notably the Milk Race, carried cash prizes bigger than any independent race, further confusing the picture about the structure of the sport. Frustration could easily set in, since even for those who won, the rewards were not huge, and many riders in their late twenties, with career and family to think of, dropped out sooner than they should have.

The other great headache for the independent was his exit route if things did not work out for him. Already by signing as an independent he was barred from representing his country at international level - ever, at any time in the future - while the question of reinstatement as an amateur was one that had been left deeply obscure when the B.C.F. was founded. A joint committee of the B.C.F. and the R.T.T.C. was given the task of hearing requests for reinstatement, but they were not compelled to give reasons for their decisions, and their standpoint was generally very negative. Riders were strongly discouraged from "chopping and changing" in and out of the amateur ranks, and would only be reinstated under exceptional circumstances. Exceptional circumstances meant something like having ridden only a handful of races as an independent, having won no prize-money, and having quit two full years before. A big-name, successful independent like Coe or Hitchen, or later the Condor trio of Bonner, Porter or Lewis, would have no chance of being reinstated for years to come. Many ex- independents and ex-pros were barred from returning to the sport in this way. Reg Harris himself was denied reinstatement in 1963 when he wanted to come back to coach younger riders: what can one make of offcials who thought that his presence would corrupt young amateurs?

This sense that the amateur-professional dichotomy was absolute and immutable was something that was deeply rooted in many British sports. It is difficult for us to understand in today's culture of open sport, where star performers are paid large fees simply to

Ged Coles, a top climber and a winner for Condor-Mackeson from 1964 to 1966.

appear at events. The avowed motive was to defend the amateur from unfair competition, to ensure that the man who raced purely for enjoyment, and who worked forty or fifty hours a week, as a bank clerk or a coal miner or anything else, was not deprived of victory by rivals who were free to devote their entire lives to training. This sounds fine in theory, but in practice it meant that officials had the right to inquire how you earned your living and what rewards you received from your sport, not merely now, but going back years into your past. An amateur cyclist who even competed against a professional would find himself banned, as if professionalism were some kind of taint or disease which had to be fought by isolating the diseased subject. Today we no

Bonner's electrifying series against Simpson at Herne Hill in 1966. Simpson came out the winner, but only after some sharp practice by the rainbow jersey.

longer care: the only thing that matters is how a man rides. What he does with his life, how he earns his living, is his affair. We don't call him an amateur or a professional: he is simply a cyclist. The point about these structural problems in the sport in the 1950s and 1960s was their potential to confuse the riders and misdirect their careers. The rider had to navigate his career along one of several pathways: amateur, independent, or continental-professional, and if he made the wrong choice and pursued the wrong goals, failure and disillusionment awaited him, and his talents might be lost to the sport. The role of the sport's governing body should be to create a clear but flexible structure, that would bring the talents of any individual to their fulfilment, and in this they so often failed.

Some of these doubts and ambiguities were settled by the decision at the end of 1965 to draw a line under the independent era. The terminology and the thinking at last became a little clearer, but the simple fact remained that bike-racing in Britain was not big enough in economic terms or in popular appeal to offer any great support to a professional class, and this fact could not be altered by a change of language. The importance of the Condor-Mackeson team, and the other teams of that era, was that they were attempting to develop the sport: they were offering to young riders the possibility of making cycling a career, and they were bringing in finance from outside the bike trade. On the other hand the great criticism of the independent system was that, instead of leading on to other things, it had become a caste in itself. Its members were barred from representing Britain as amateurs, but none of them had gone on to make an impact against the European professionals either. The original aim of making it a stepping-stone to a full professional career had simply not happened. The idea at the outset of 1966 was therefore to wipe the slate clean and move to a straightforward amateur-professional set-up, and see which teams and which event organisers embraced the new system.

The change of title altered very little on the ground: the leading teams were still Condor, Viking, Falcon and Raleigh, and now they all paid their riders a small retaining salary and gave them written contracts, so that they were genuine professionals. The 1966 season opened in great style for Dave Bonner when he was invited to race against Simpson at the Easter meeting at Herne Hill. In a series of three Derny-paced events, Simpson, showing off his rainbow jersey as world road-race champion, was pushed to the limit, with Bonner taking one of the three races to Simpson's two. Behind this result there is a controversial story, because Simpson took a longish time out with chain trouble in the deciding fifteen-mile race, and Bonner was fairly convinced that the trouble was self-inflicted. This was noticed by the crowd, who felt strongly that Bonner should have won and actually booed Britain's world champion. The next month Bonner won the pursuit title that had eluded him as an amateur, beating Billy Holmes in the final. There could be no doubt that running the team for the past six years had achieved its object: it had placed the

Colin Lewis, Condor's complete professional: tough, dedicated and reliable, he was twice national champion.

Condor name and identity at the forefront of British bike racing. Bonner and his team-mates always figured in the top listings of the race results, and Bonner's grinning face looked out of the pages of *Cycling* so often that some of his rivals derided him for being cycling's pin-up boy, a role which delighted him immensely. Still, there was a feeling that the team still lacked a really big hitter, a man capable of winning championships or stage races, and before the 1967 season they set about finding one, and found two instead.

Condor's first choice to strengthen their team as the 1967 season opened was one who might well have made it on the continent. Colin Lewis - Lulu to his friends and rivals - was born in South Wales but moved to Devon with his family as a child and was always regarded as a West country rider - probably the best ever. He joined the Mid-Devon R.C., discovered racing at the age of nineteen, and immediately revealed an outstanding talent for road-racing - he was never too interested in time-trialling. Long training runs over the Devon hills gave him his special climbing edge, and he was soon matching and beating the top roadmen in the region – Brian Sandy, Roy Hopkins, Chris Barretto and Dave Andrews. A string of local victories led to selection for the

Hugh Porter, top roadman when he wasn't winning international pursuits.

1963 Milk Race as part of a Commonwealth team, and he finished very strongly in ninth place. In the following year he was in the England team, and his race started with a bang when he won the first road stage with a lone break through the Peak District, but thereafter he worked for Metcalfe's victory, finishing seventh overall. He was the best British finisher in the World Championships at Sallanches behind Eddy Merckx, and he and Mike Cowley were with Merckx again in the Olympic road race in Tokyo, in a last-lap break which came close to success, the trio being swept up close to the finish. In the spring of 1965 he seized the chance to go to one of the sponsored clubs in Brittany, V.C. Vannes, where he was well looked after, and he spent the next two years winning many local events and riding for Britain in the Tour de l'Avenir and the world championships – he was behind West at the Nurburgring in 1966.

Decision time for Lewis came at Christmas 1966, when he had to choose between moving on to the famous ACBB club in Paris, and remaining an amateur, or accepting the offer which Condor-Mackeson had made to come and join Dave Bonner in what was undoubtedly an expanding pro scene in the UK. He chose the latter, and one of the factors in his choice was the announcement that had been made that summer that the Tour de France would now switch to national teams. Lewis reasoned that good results in the home pro scene would give him the best chance of selection in a team that would be built around Simpson, and would certainly include Hoban and Denson. While Lewis was preparing for the 1967 season, the news came in March that the team would be further strengthened by the signing of Hugh Porter and the Bristol rider Derek Green from the Falcon squad. Porter was already one of the country's top roadmen, who had also begun to carve out his career as world-class pursuiter, having won a World Championship bronze medal in 1963 and the Commonwealth Games gold in Jamaica in 1966. There was no doubt that the combination of Bonner, Lewis and Porter made the Condor Mackeson team a formidable force in the home pro scene, while Green would come into his own in the following year. Their constant rivals would be Albert Hitchen and Falcons, the Carlton team of Metcalfe and Chisman, supported by Bernard Burns and John Aslin, and the Trumann-Steel group of Wes Mason, Dick Goodman, Peter Gordon and George Halls. For Lewis in particular, selected to ride the Tour de France, 1967 would be probably the most eventful year of his cycling life.

Although the Condor trio were highly placed from the start, the victories were slow to come: Porter's first win came in June in Gravesend, while in the now professional Vaux International, Lewis was third behind Anglo-Belgian star Michael Wight and Arthur Metcalfe. Bonner won the historic Llangollen to Wolverhampton race in July, the event that commemorates the birth of massed-start racing in 1942. Porter and Bonner took first and second in the national professional pursuit championship at Leicester, Bonner joking that as team captain of Condor-Mackeson, he should have won by right.

A historic postcard from France, sent to the Condor shop by the 1967 Tour de France team, and signed by Colin Lewis, Tom Simpson, Barry Hoban, Arthur Metcalfe, Michael Wright, Vin Denson and Albert Hitchen.

Two weeks later Porter went in optimistic mood to the World Championships in Amsterdam, where he took the pursuit silver medal behind Timoen Groen. At the beginning of August Lewis had crowned his first year as a pro by winning the national professional road-race championship, finishing alone almost three minutes clear of the field after a hot, punishing 146 miles. The Condor riders were now proving their class at the highest level, and the bikes themselves were being raced in the Tour de France and the World's. But in amongst these victories had come the most traumatic event to hit British cycling in the post-war years: the death of Tom Simpson in the Tour de France.

A disturbing portrait of Tom Simpson shortly before his death; his face seems to be haunted by ...what?

This event was like the spectre at a feast, destroying much of the glamour that surrounded continental racing and the euphoria of Simpson's previous victories. It brought out into the open all the doubts, the rumours and the secrets that had surrounded professional cycling for years. Colin Lewis was riding in the Tour alongside Simpson, with Hoban, Denson, Metcalfe and Wright; Chisman and Hitchen and Peter Hill had already retired before the fatal Ventoux stage. Lewis had suffered like never before, but he had ridden through it well, and, along with the other Tour first-timer Metcalfe, was steadily making his way towards the honour of finishing in Paris. Lewis, like many others who knew Simpson, had no illusions about him, in two senses: they saw that he was a great rider, but that he was also a self-destructive rider, who would launch reckless attacks, who would crash too often, who would drive himself beyond normal limits, and who undoubtedly used drugs. This was the picture that only slowly emerged in the months and years after his death, but the Simpson episode shook British cyclists to the core. Simpson had been built up as a demi-god because he had gone out and stormed the heights: he had achieved what no other British cyclist had ever achieved before, and proved that Englishmen could rival the European stars like Anquetil, Van Looy, Altig and the rest. But now we knew that to achieve all this he had thrown away his

integrity: he had tried to buy success, and had brought about his own death.

Or had he? Had the drugs caused his death, or merely contributed to it? Had he taken them habitually or not? Did they make any difference anyway, and weren't his rivals all using them too? Almost forty years later, the facts of what actually happened, and still more the implications of what happened, still divide cyclists in this country more than any other event of the past fifty years, and still raise bitter arguments. There are those who maintain that he was both a cheat and a fool, while others argue that he was a heroic rider whose death was nothing more than a tragic accident. Perhaps there will never be a final verdict because they are both right. He was probably the most determined and talented rider ever to cross the channel in search of the great prize, but he also became a cynical professional, prepared to do whatever was necessary to get to the top. Simpson's death obviously did not mark the end of drugs in cycling, but it did mark an end to the secrecy and rumour that had surrounded the subject. The death of a rider was a stark, uncompromising fact, which could not be excused or explained away as some kind of mistake. In the long history of the Tour, with all the intense demands that it makes on mind and body, no rider had ever collapsed and died in this way: there must have been an extraneous cause. Drug-testing became universal, but so too did the search for more scientific drugs that would genuinely enhance performance, without the risks of the crude stimulants implicated in the Simpson case. It was also as a result of the Simpson tragedy that Tour riders were allowed to take drinks from their team cars, for people realised that something as simple as a pint of cold water on that last climb might have saved his life.

Bonner riding the 1967 London Six partnered by the Dutch rider Seeuws. This was the first of modern London sixes, at Earl's Court, before the move to Wembley.

But, as after any tragedy, life went on, and bike-racing went on. Lewis and Porter won their championships and their medals, then returned to the business of preparing for the next home season, each with a clear aim in mind: Lewis was determined to ride again in the Tour de France and to make an impact this time, not merely to hang on and suffer, while Porter knew how close he had come to a world championship, and felt sure that the top prize was within his grasp. Lewis, always a stamina man who believed in long, steady state training, pushed up his mileage to 2,000 a month in preparation. Derek Green, less experienced but a similar kind of rider to Lewis, felt that maybe he could match his team-mate if he made that final extra effort. Bonner had no illusions about defeating Porter on the track, but his character was not one to be overshadowed, and he too stepped up his training. These four would be a formidable force when the 1968 season opened, but for Porter the immediate aftermath of his world's silver medal was a big let-down: he crashed midway through the Skol six-day event at Earls Court in September, breaking his collarbone, and losing the chance to cash in on his star status. Porter admitted that he had been petrified during the high-speed Madisons on the tiny track, a totally different experience from pursuiting on an open-air circuit. This was the first London six-day since those at Wembley in 1951 and 1952, and Bonner was also riding, partnered by the Dutch rider Seeuws. They finished well down on the winners, the Danes Lykke and Eugen, but still these were heady days for the Condor-Mackeson team, riding in such company and showing off the Condor name yet again on the international stage: it was a far cry from the modest team that had contested north London road races in 1959, and more was to come.

Derek Green, over-shadowed by Porter and Lewis, but a top rider in his own right.

The 1968 season was enlivened by the arrival of several new pro teams. The most talked-about was the Clive Stuart squad, financed by two brothers who were wealthy Hatton Garden diamond-merchants, and who opened a string of bike shops in London and elsewhere. The riders signed were George Drewell, Johnny Clarey and Reg Smith, and the team was certainly the most stylish on the home scene, with big contract money and flashy cars; every day was Christmas day said one of them later, but it was not to last. Another new face in the pro ranks was Peter Hill, the former B.A.R. who had been racing in Europe for four years, but who now returned to ride in the Bob Jackson colours, while another great time-trial star, Dave Dungworth, signed for the Sun team, together with Chisman, Aslin and Trevor Bull. It was a huge transition for 25-mile champion Dungworth, but he was not outclassed, and notched up several excellent performances, including victory in the classic Llangollen-Wolverhampton commemoration race.

1968 was a vintage year for the four Condor riders, who won more than a dozen individual victories and half a dozen team prizes, including several occasions when they took first and second, and even first, second and third. The honours were evenly divided between them, Derek Green now proving his class alongside his more famous team-mates. Probably the best team win was in the Vaux International in June, where individual victory went to Vin Denson, home from Europe for the occasion. In the same month the team was invited to Germany, where Lewis won a city-centre race in Linz-am-Rhein, becoming possibly the first English-based rider to win a professional race on the continent. Porter won two stages of the Tour of the West, perfecting his technique of riding away from the bunch in the closing miles, using his unmatchable pursuiting speed. In that race, Lewis won a memorable 150-mile stage after a long, long break which saw Metcalfe take the overall victory. So successful was the team that no less than three of them - Lewis,

Porter and Green - were selected for the Tour de France, but the experience was not a happy one for any of them. Porter was the first to go on stage two, with a foot injury which chaffed unmercifully on his toe-strap. Green found himself out of his depth, and was eliminated on stage six, admitting defeat after two days of torment. The bitterest disappointment of all was Lewis's, who felt that he was stronger than at any time in his life, but who was forced out on the third stage over the dreadful northern pave near Roubaix, when he suffered mechanical problems and found himself without service, and finished outside the time limit. There would be no Condors finishing at Paris that year. Metcalfe also retired after trying a lone break on stage ten, which came close to succeeding. Our finishers that year were Hoban, Wright, Denson and Johnny Clarey. After the race it was announced that the national team experiment of recent years was over, and that 1969 would see the Tour return to the trade team structure. This was especially significant for the home-based British riders, because it meant the end to their chances of riding in the great race. Only those like Hoban and Denson with contracts in continental teams could look forward to a Tour future. It had been the experience of a lifetime for British pros like Lewis, Metcalfe and Clarey to ride and finish the Tour, but it could be argued that it had not led anywhere for them in career terms.

Lewis returned with just one burning ambition - to retain his national road-race title, and in this he succeeded, albeit in a hotly-disputed sprint with John Aslin. Porter, having won the British pro pursuit title for the second year, had his sights on an even bigger prize, and headed off to the World Championships in Rome, where he dominated the pursuit series, beating Ole Ritter out of sight in the final. One month later Ritter would break the world hour record in Mexico City, a record which could surely have been Porter's. It had been a long road for Porter, known as a very good roadman until 1963 when he discovered his pursuiting talent almost by accident, taking the national title from the reigning champion Harry Jackson, then going on to a bronze medal in the World Championships in Liege. He always looked superb on the track - tall, powerful, perfectly positioned, rock-solid in the saddle and very smooth-pedalling. He won the British pursuit title three times running, yet his was no easy progress to international success, for after 1963 he won no more medals until the 1966 Commonwealth Games in Jamaica, where he took gold. His hallmark was a comparatively slow start, but a storming finish, and on some smaller tracks this could be a disadvantage, allowing him to be threatened or even caught by a fast-starting opponent. For this reason the pro distance of 5,000 metres suited him much better than amateur 4,000 metres. The 1968 World's victory belonged to Porter himself: his was the talent and the strength built up over six years of endeavour in this most demanding event. But it was an extraordinary moment in the history of Condor Cycles too, founded exactly twenty years earlier as a small shop in the austerity of post-war London, and now building bikes that were being ridden to World Championship gold medals. Back home, in one of the last races of the road season, the Wills Weekend at Weston-super-Mare, the Condor team's dominance was complete, with stage wins for Green and Porter, overall victory for Lewis, the team prize and the mountains prize too.

In 1969 the Condor-Mackeson team increased its strength to five with the signing of Dick Goodman, the pro champion of three years before. Once again there were team prizes and individual wins for Lewis, Porter and Green, but there were big disap-

Porter at the opening of his world pursuit series in Rome, 1968. He looks unbeatable, and he was.

Post-race post-mortem: Porter tells Bonner what he did wrong, Bonner takes a philosophical drink, Lewis looks downcast.

pointments too. Lewis, not surprisingly, was unable to hold onto his pro road-race title for a third successive year, and on a roasting July day, the punishing 164-mile race was won by Bill Lawrie, the Australian who rode for the Falcon team. After the finish there were a lot of puzzled spectators and embarassed offcials when it was revealed that Lawrie did not even hold a B.C.F. license, and he spent an uneasy couple of hours while officials debated the matter. They soon realised that they could not possibly allow him to ride then disallow his victory, and no other rider wanted to object. Goodman was the best Condor finisher, in fourth place. This was to be his best result of the season, and it seemed that perhaps his best days were behind him. The same appeared to be true of Bonner, who was still only twenty-six, but who had been racing at a very high level now for ten years; had he done too much too soon? At the World Championships in Antwerp, Porter was devastatingly beaten in the pursuit final, when Ferdi Bracke caught him before the halfway mark, after deliberately risking everything on a superfast start. It was a great comeback by Bracke, who had won the title a full five years before, and who at thirty was a year older than Porter. But Porter was left reeling, despite having beaten six minutes, eleminated Peter Post and won the silver medal. Colin Lewis was the best British finisher in the road race over a flat Belgian circuit that was not to his liking: he was 27th alongside Van Looy, after Hoban, West and Wright had all been forced out by the heat and the distance.

At the beginning of the '69 season, Porter had naturally felt that his World Champion's status was worth a big rise in salary from his sponsors, but he had not got what he wanted, and he was now ready to switch teams. Lewis too had decided that three years in one team was long enough, and he was preparing to join West and Addy at Holdsworth. Porter joined Bantel, alongside the young Sid Barras, in a combination which would score so many wins in the next decade. All at once the Condor-Mackeson team was beginnig to unravel, for reasons which no one can now explain precisely. There was a delay in finding new riders to replace Porter and Lewis, and in April 1970 Derek Green suddenly announced that he was retiring. Graeme Gillmore, a talented Australian road and trackman, was quickly recruited, and he won an extended series of track events in the early summer. But then in June Goodman also decided that his career had gone as far as he could take it, and he too stopped racing. For the last couple of months of the season, Bonner and Gilmore were alone, and Bonner chose this moment to come back to form and win a couple of excellent victories on road and track, including the national pro pursuit title in Porter's absence. Bonner

The glory and misery of top-level racing: in the 1967 London six, Bonner races by while Porter lies in the centre with a broken collarbone.

also finished the London-Holyhead, well down on the leaders, but alongside Shay Elliott, Wes Mason and Bob Addy. Intriguingly there was now talk of bringing Martyn Roach, the top time-triallist and long-standing Condor rider, into the team, but it came to nothing. In November the expected announcement came that Whitbread would not renew its sponsorship in the following year. It was sad, but behind any team there has to be drive, vision and objectives, and these had now faded away. Some vital energy seemed to have deserted the team. The endless hours spent training, preparing the bikes, travelling and racing had taken their toll in the end; this is a feeling that all cyclists experience at some stage. There was no conflict or bitterness, but the personnel on both sides - Condor and Mackeson - felt that they had gone as far as they could, and it was time to pull out. Bonner too, after seven years as team leader, recognised that he had done all he could, that his life had reached a turning-point, and he did not attempt to find a new sponsor.

The Condor team had been part of the landscape of British cycling throughout the 1960s. They had supported some outstanding riders and won many top events. They had seen their bikes ridden in the Tour de France and in World Championships. They had brought money into the sport from outside the bike industry. For a small frame-builder it was a great record, and it placed their name at the centre of cycle sport in this country. This was apparent in the shop itself, where the walls now proudly displayed large photographs of the team riders: Dennis Tarr winning London-Holyhead, Bonner racing alongside Simpson, and Porter in his World Champion's jersey. The customer knew at a glance that he was in one of the country's elite bike shops, a real centre of racing expertise.

The Amateur Scene

While the trade teams had been developing along their own lines, moving towards full professionalism, what had been happening in the world of amateur road-racing? Who was coming through to replace Booty, Bradley, Haskell, Hinds, Seggar, Jackson, the Batys and the others who were either turning independent, or scaling down their racing? What had been happening in the Milk Race and the Manx International? How had the acceptance of open-road racing under one governing body, the B.C.F. worked out? It is clear that by the mid sixties there were two big issues that dominated discussion of the road racing scene: firstly the perceived failure of our roadmen at international level, and secondly drugs.

The overwhelming fact about British international road-racing in the seven years following 1959, the year the B.C.F. was born, was that no British rider had won a medal of any kind in a world or Olympic road race - with the outstanding exception of Beryl Burton. These were the years of Hinds, Bradley, Holmes, Chisman, Metcalfe and Lewis, so no one could possibly point to a lack of strength or quality in our riders. These riders had an excellent record in the Milk Race, delivering a string of home wins, and in the Manx International, after three foreign winners in 1960-62, British riders dominated the top ten placings for years. But when they went abroad for the big championships, the results simply refused to come. The exception was the Commonwealth Games, with Wes Mason's win in 1962, but in cycling terms these games were virtually a two-way contest between Britain and Australia. The track picture was the same: medals in Commonwealth Games, but in the Worlds and the Olympics, there were just two bronze medals - Dave Handley's sprint in 1960 and Hugh Porter's pursuit in 1963 - to provide relief in a medal-drought that was unbroken throughout the early 1960s. In any year, the mid-season would be marked by press reports hailing British victories on the Isle of Man and in the Milk Race, but would inevitably close with gloomy post-mortems on our performances in the world championships. Of course there was a certain lack of consistency in analysing these results. In the 1956 Olympic road race at Melbourne, Alan Jackson won the bronze medal after finishing two minutes down on the winner, Baldini, while Stan Brittain and Billy Homes were almost a further minute behind Jackson, yet together these three riders brought home the team silver medal. Yet in Rome four years later, Bradley, Hinds and Holmes finished in the bunch just twenty seconds down on the gold-medal Russian, Kapitanov, and won nothing. The margin between success and failure in road racing is often agonisingly close, a matter of seconds after 100 miles or more, and on the track it could be hundredths of a second. Yet the inescapable fact remains that, year after year for one reason or another, no medals except Beryl Burton's came home to England.

Everyone suffering except Bradley: he leads Baty, Taylor and Holmes through the Welsh hills in the 1960 Milk Race.

So the question became inescapable, and was asked more and more urgently in the press: What's wrong with British cycling? One obvious scapegoat was available: time-trialling. Time-trialling was a peculiarly British competition, practiced devotedly week after week by thousands of cyclists, which, its critics claimed, drained the pool of riding talent, but which had no relevance at all to real competition at international level. The continentals, it was pointed out, had never bothered with time-trials as we knew them; they had never become bewitched by the quest for speed against the clock for its own sake. This view was held by many roadmen, who argued that time-trialling was an unreal form of racing - some said bluntly that it was a pure waste of time. This view was loudly expressed too by the new editor of *Cycling*, Alan Gayfer, appointed in March 1964, who was far more pro-road-racing and anti-time-trialling than any of his predecessors had ever been (incidentally it was Gayfer who swiftly removed the "*...and Mopeds*", and gave cyclists back their own magazine again). This theory may have had some general validity: the culture of time-trialling may indeed have diverted some good potential roadmen into the "backwater" of 25s against the clock every Sunday morning. But it clearly failed to account for the fact that dedicated roadmen like Bradley, Metcalfe or West could tear fields to pieces at home, but were just part of the bunch abroad. It also left unsolved the mystery of one of Britain's most persistent failures at international level: the team time trial. This event was pioneered at the Rome Olympics and made the transition to the World's in 1962. It may have seemed tailor-made for Britain, but the results year after year were disastrous. Sometimes time-triallists were selected to ride, including national champions and B.A.R winners, sometimes roadmen including Milk Race and Manx winners, but it made no difference. No British team ever managed to finish bet-

Team time-trial blues, Mexico 1968. Watson, Smith and Cromack sit shattered and demoralised, having finished in 11th place, 9 minutes behind the winning Dutch team. Billy Bilsland was the fourth man, out of sight here.

ter than tenth, and they were invariably left trailing by margins of between ten and twenty minutes over a distance of 100 kilometres. The British were regularly beaten not only by top teams like Italy, France and Holland, but also by nations with no known cycling tradition, such as Turkey, Uruguay, Yugoslavia and Rumania. With hindsight, the real reason for these failures was nothing more mysterious than a lack of practice in this specialist discipline, but the perception at the time was that the British devotion to time-trialling did not even produce world class time-triallists, and this was baffling.

But if time-trialling in itself was not the culprit, what was? Given that British cyclists were not genetically different from European ones and were not simply incapable of riding as fast as the others did, was there a scientific answer? Was our training and coaching all wrong? Did we simply not know how to prepare ourselves for top-level competitive cycling? The difficulty in answering this question is that we did not really know how the top Europeans themselves trained. For the pros, training was a kind of trade secret, whose details they were never willing to reveal. In fact in the many interviews given by the Anquetil generation, they scarcely admitted to training at all, other than steady 60-

*Scientific training ideas
met some resistance in
the late 1960s.*

80 mile runs at 15 m.p.h. But this concealed the fact that the pros raced themselves fit: these 60-80 mile runs might take place during January and February, but then these men went into a regime where they were racing 200 days a year or more, a relentless programme forced on them by the relatively low financial rewards in the sport at that time. Therefore the training information which they gave was offered from the plateau on which they now stood: it gave no hint as to how they had reached that level. Many of their techniques were handed down from their mentors, and were purely empirical, based on what had worked before, and by modern standards they had no scientific basis. An obvious example of this was the dietary regime which they followed, with the huge breakfast of steak and rice, and the avoidance of drink, even during a long, hot race.

When the first British pros established themselves on the continent in the late fifties, they were eagerly asked for the inside story on continental training, but their answers were pretty cagey. Brian Robinson repeated the "steady ten-week build-up" advice, in terms that were vague and generalised, and which gave no explanation as to how this could possibly transform a man from a good club rider into a winner of big races. Brian and other top riders were periodically invited by the B.C.F. to give coaching courses, many of them at the National Recreation Centre at Lilleshall in Shropshire, but their advice was again the commonsense build-up, together with tactical tips on gearing, clothing, diet, and road-race tactics. All these things had their place, but the core issue of achieving physical condition tended to get lost in such details. If there were any fundamental secrets, Brian was not giving them away.

The simple fact is that at this period there was almost no formal coaching or body of scientific training-knowledge in British cycling. This is strange because it had existed in other sports, such as running, for many years. The core of the scientific method - interval training - had been pioneered by Zatopek in the late 1940s, and was known and practised by all runners, including in this country Bannister, Chattaway, Ibbotson, Pirie and that entire generation; in fact it was so prevalent, that by the late fifties a reaction against it had begun, and the great Australian and New Zealand runners, Herb Elliott and Peter Snell, practised a freer form of training based on even-paced endurance runs, rather than

A distinguished group during the 1962 Tour de l'Avenir: Holmes, Crinnion, Hill, Bradley, Metcalfe and Tarr.

the soul-destroying repetitions of the interval method. But whatever the reason may be, the concept of interval training did not consciously emerge in cycling until the late sixties, although many riders did discover it by accident, without giving it that name, and the traditional chain-gang training, with short, hard turns at the front of the group, did simulate it. The basis of all training in Britain was the long steady-state ride at the weekends, and the shorter, faster ride through the week. This was a correct basis as far as it went, to build stamina and add speed, but it was vague and unscientific: how long is long and how fast is fast? Without the precise language of aerobic and anaerobic, effort and recovery, pulse rate and training level, it was all subjective and unstructured. However it was a form of training which could be integrated into a social, club setting and enjoyed with friends, who would draw each other out, and this explains its prevalence. In the mid 1960s, probably the only countries in possession of scientific training secrets were Russia and the Iron Curtain countries, who were now emerging onto the world stage and beginning their domination of the endurance sports. We now know that their runners, swimmers, weight-lifters and cyclists were experimenting with many methods, legitimate and illegitimate, to secure their winning edge, and that they applied science ruthlessly to this end. It was only towards the end of the decade that studies in exercise physiology published by Loughborough College were widely read by British cycling coaches. The lesson which they taught was that of progressive overload - raising the workload of the heart and lungs in intense, measured steps to achieve racing fitness - in place of the traditional long, steady-state training rides.

So training was one problem area, but critics also argued that there were structural or organisational weaknesses in British cycling. The obvious difference between cycling here and cycling in countries like Italy, France and Belgium - who brought home regular hauls of gold medals - was the existence of a strong professional class. Cycling in those countries meant racing: it was part of their culture and it was a recognised career. Men like Coppi, Anquetil and Van Looy were national figures, and the ambition to become like them was what drew young talent into the sport year after and year, and it was what drove them on to aim for, and to achieve, the highest level. There was nothing equivalent in Britain, where cycling as a pastime had a much broader but a much more diffuse social basis. This situation could not be changed overnight by any organisation. The B.C.F. did indeed create a full professional class in 1966, but they could not at the same time magically conjure into existence the network of sponsors and events which had developed in Europe over the previous half-century or more. The B.C.F. produced its new initiatives, its five-year plans, but they had little money to back them up, and the B.C.F. management was not monolithic: its staff had policy disagreements, and it underwent its crises and resignations, such as that of Tommy Godwin after the dismal results at the Tokyo Olympics. The former track star had been appointed as the first national, but part-time, coach the previous year, and he would in turn be replaced by Norman Sheil as the first full-time salaried national coach. But what could these men do, working virtually alone, with no budget and no job description, except to improve the standards of British bike-racing, short-term and long-term? What more could they achieve than someone like Eddie Soens, the Merseyside coach who had inspired Sheil himself and so many others? The BC.F. was severely hindered too by its own financial problems: running a large deficit for many years in the sixties made it unable to address the future confidently, or evolve any plans which did not depend on low budgets. If they could not manage their own finances, how could they produce visionary plans to develop the sport?

Behind all these questions and answers there lay the whole problem of sport in society - how it is organised, how it is financed, and why people devote themselves to it. Sport is a voluntary activity, so nothing can be forced upon it in a free society. Any sport is the result of a slow evolutionary process involving small-scale and large-scale forces which are usually out of the control of any one individual: the sport changes as the society around it changes. When this book opened in the 1940s, cycling in Britain was a pastime which involved millions of people at various levels. For one large group of people - the club riders - it had a competitive dimension which took the form of time-trialling, a purely amateur form of racing, in which the top riders in the country competed alongside the unpretentious plodder. These top riders might occasionally be chosen to go to an international event, or even a world championship, to represent Britain, but the focus of their cycling, their heartland, was still the Sunday morning race with the other enthusiasts. This was an enclosed world, and if anyone had wanted to judge the health of British cycling, they would have asked how many people belonged to the clubs, how many went on

Bonner at the start of a Gentleman's Grand Prix in France with legendary cycling journalist Jock Wadley. Wadley's "Sporting Cyclist" ran from 1955 to 1968, and fostered the passion for all things continental among British readers.

touring holidays or how many took part in the Sunday-morning races.

By the 1960s this outlook had changed. With the advent of road-racing and with our exposure to the cycling culture of continental Europe, the goal-posts had been shifted, and the old amateur ideals no longer seemed to serve us. Whenever we sent riders abroad to world championships or the Olympics or the classic races of Europe, they were defeated, and these defeats seemed to demoralise us and raise doubts about the whole sport of cycling and what we were doing in it. At the top international level, winning is all that counts. At home you can race for recreation, you can take satisfaction from your own personal sense that you have done a good ride. But when you are chosen because you are the best in the country, and are sent abroad as its representative, the only reason you are there is to win; any other result, however creditable your ride, is judged a failure. The health of British cycling was now being seen in this very different light: if we could not win international medals, then we were failing, and the sport itself was in crisis. The very question What's wrong with British cycling, had pre-judged the issue: what was wrong was precisely this failure to win international medals.

And of course a second question naturally followed: What can we do about it? Could some form of planning, of central direction, improve the situation and bring home the medals? Could new talent be found and existing talent developed by planning? If so, where could that planning come from - from cycling's governing bodies, or from commercial sponsors or from the government? What would it cost, who would pay, and would it work anyway? Without realising it, cyclists in the sixties were being brought face to face with a world of changing values and hardening

Long hard miles in the depths of winter; but was this form of training mistaken?

choices, but this was something for which they were unprepared. It would take many years for the idea to crystallize that success at the international level could be achieved, but it had to be planned and paid for: aims had to be defined, strategies put in place and the money had to be found. People who knew the international scene pointed out that some countries - France and Sweden among them - already supported their amateur sportsmen through state aid, just as the Iron Curtain countries did, for reasons of pure national prestige. Other countries such as Italy and Belgium had a thriving professional class which acted as a spur to the amateurs. In both cases, there was a system in place, a pathway to sporting success: how far did British cyclists really want their sport to be organised and directed towards the single goal of international success, that was the question. These issues became especially relevant in the mid 1960s with the birth of the Sports Council, the body responsibile for formulating government policy towards sport and for subsidising sporting bodies like the B.C.F. Was national policy to be geared towards elite sportsmen who could win international glory for Britain, or towards encouraging sport as widely as possible - sport for all? Sports Council money became crucial to the running of the B.C.F., and there had to be some guiding principles, some philosophy about how it was to be spent. The equation of success with medals was easy to make, but was it necessarily the right one?

Not everyone was enthusiastic about the forces that seemed to be pushing cycling in this new direction - the direction of professionalism. People asked if the new approach meant that we had lost sight of the virtues of cycling as a pastime, and the ideals of amateurism. They asked why international success should be the overriding aim, and even if it were, they doubted if it were really possible to produce international champions to order. They asked how our few world champions - Reg Harris, Norman Sheil, and Beryl Burton - had achieved what they did. Had it come through science, coaching, financial sponsorship and outside support of that kind, or had it come from within, from their own personality and drive to excel? The dichotomy between the amateur and professional approach was becoming clearer and clearer, but these were issues that British cycling was not yet ready to confront. As a result of the conflicts and revolutionary changes within cycle sport during the 1950s, Britain had now entered fully into the international scene, but this awakening, this broadening of our horizons, had brought precious little joy, because of the perceived failure of our riders abroad, and the sense of discontent which it bred within British cycling. Before we had been insular and happy; now we were internationally-minded and discontented.

Drug stories became all too familiar in the cycling press in the sixties, and have never gone away.

The other issue that was casting its shadow over cycling - a shadow that spread its way from Europe to Britain - was drugs. It is hard to say exactly when this subject first came into the public domain. Those with inside knowledge of European cycling knew that professionals had been taking various substances for years which they believed to be stimulants, but before about 1960, public discussion of this subject, especially in Britain, was entirely on the level of rumour. Then in 1960 the Danish Olympic cyclist, Knud Jensen, collapsed and died during the team time trial, and reports immediately began to circulate that drugs were implicated. This was later officially denied after a post mortem, when heat exhaustion was given as the cause of death. Then a couple of years later, Roger Riviere, whose dreadful crash in the 1960 Tour de France had ended his career and almost his life, made the first public statement about the extent to which drugs permeated professional cycling. Riviere, world hour record holder and pro pursuit champion, was then as famous and as idolised as Anquetil, indeed he was just making the transition to Tour star when his tragedy occurred. After his statement there was no chance of putting the lid back on these stories. Drug testing began to be introduced in professional events, and one after another the great names were implicated: Altig, Anquetil, Aimar, Adorni, Gimondi, Jansen, van Steenbergen, van Springel - the list went on and on. Invariably the riders pleaded their innocence and blamed mistakes in the testing, but people asked if all these episodes could really be mistakes. And if these drugs were available to professional cyclists, surely it would be naïve to imagine that European amateurs knew nothing of them. British cyclists racing on the continent brought back stories of drugs, including Les West, who made no secret of the fact that he turned away from a pro career because he saw that it would be impossible to avoid being drawn into the drug habit. There were lurid stories of continental riders collapsing or crashing out of races because they were full of "dope", as it was then called. The most sensational case was that of Anquetil, who was first deprived of his victory in the 1966 Liege-Bastogne-Liege and then also of his 1967 world hour record, for failing to take drug tests on both occasions. By 1967 Anquetil had in any case decided to go public, and he not only admitted taking drugs, but claimed the right to do so, in order to help him endure the intense physical demands of professional cycling.

Winning in the rain: Porter demonstrates the reality of racing in England.

We now know that the drugs of that time were purely stimulants, such as amphetamines, which gave a rider a kick which was as much mental as physical; they were not performance enhancing in any great scientific sense, as later drugs would be. But to the average cyclist in Britain they were surrounded by an aura of mystery and potency. No one really knew the full medical implications of their use, or, on the political level, how to deal with them. In Britain they were spoken of as a poison, physical and moral, that threatened the whole sport; but the token fines and brief suspensions handed out to European professionals who were caught seemed to suggest that their use was regarded more as a peccadillo, and that the governing bodies were not yet prepared to take a serious stand on the issue. Anquetil was regarded as a god in England, partly because of his supreme time-trialling ability, and his statement dismayed his admirers here. No one was prepared to say that his whole career had been a fraud, for ability such as his could clearly not be bought; and if all his rivals were taking the same things, what advantage did he gain anyway? So the familiar arguments went on.

In the peletons in England, amateur and professional, there were whispers and rumours about certain riders, and anyone who was road-racing seriously at that time will now admit freely that these stimulants were around. By the mid-sixties there was sufficient concern for drug-testing to be introduced for the first time at the 1965 Milk Race, and it was then that the problem really exploded. The Spanish rider who was holding the yellow jersey, Santamarina, was disqualified on the last day of the race after testing positive for amphetamines, giving Les West his opportunity to take the race victory. At the same time the Liverpool rider, Ken Hill, became the first English cyclist to be caught and disqualified for the same offence. Hill was one of the country's top amateurs and had won the 1965 Manx International. He denied any wrongdoing and was supported by many who knew him, but the fact remains that he did fail the test, and he was suspended for a year. When the result of a test was not in dispute, the usual explanation was that someone had spiked a drink, perhaps maliciously, or perhaps trying to help the rider. Who knows what the truth was in any of these cases, when denial by the accused rider was the universal rule? Criticisms were voiced about the unsystematic testing that went on during that Milk

Billy Holmes, Milk Race winner after Bradley, then successful independent and one of the most respected of British riders; not much interest from these spectators though.

Race: West himself for example was not tested after that final winning stage, and the B.C.F. subsequently tightened up all its testing routines. Drug testing was introduced in British professional races at the 1967 national road-race championship, and later that year Albert Hitchen, for years the biggest name in British road-racing, was found positive and given a two-year suspension which threatened to end his career, although on appeal this was cancelled and he was fined instead. The whole issue made a deep impact on attitudes to top-level cycling and to the continental stars whom we had previously been prepared to worship. At the very least it made a continental career seem less attractive, and at the worst it cast a shadow over the whole of road racing. It was another argument in the armoury of those who opposed the culture of professional sport. In the amateur sphere such as time-trialling, it was claimed, there was no possible incentive to cheat. In fact there was a second major shadow over road-racing at the professional level, namely race fixing. There were endless rumours of races being bought and sold on the road, verbal auctions being held during a break, or riders being paid off before the race had even begun. These stories were well known to those on the inside, although again they were mostly covered by a conspiracy of silence, but when they did leak out, amateurs and ordinary fans of the sport were profoundly shocked. The twin issues of drugs and race fixing were seen as two of the evils that followed when a sport ceased to be a purely amateur pastime and became a profession, a career driven by money.

So amateur road-racing retained its appeal for many, and it remained extremely strong in the early sixties, with many riders, especially those with secure careers outside cycling, preferring the glory of Milk Race victories, followed by international selection for Britain, to the uncertain rewards of the independent system. The only man to make any impression on Bradley in the 1960 Milk Race had been Billy Holmes: in second place throughout, he steadily halved the eight-minute lead that Bradley had won on the savage Pennine stage, but of course he could launch no outright attack on his team-mate. Holmes's turn came in 1961 in a far more competitive and open race, in which he was free to ride his own race for his Northern regional team, while Bradley led the England team. The leader's jersey found a new wearer almost every day, and the expected hammer-blow from Bradley in the Welsh mountains never came. Holmes took the lead by a good margin on the long, hard eighth stage from Aberystwyth to Buxton, despite crashing, but then the struggle really began. The tall, powerful Spaniard, Juan Uribezubia, attacked remorselessly to erode Holmes's lead, continuing to do so into the final day, indeed into the final few miles into Blackpool, when Holmes had to battle alone to match his rival and save the race. In the 1962 Milk Race, the Pole, Eugen Pokorny, took a commanding lead by virtue of two fine stage wins. Holmes reduced this to just over one minute, but narrowly failed to bridge the final gap and finished second, otherwise he would certainly have emulated Bradley's double win. Holmes had a long career from his days as a time-trial record breaker in 1955, through the Olympic road races of 1956 and 1960, when he rode strongly despite crashing on both occasions, to his independent career with Falcon from 1963 to 1966. He delayed turning independent so long because he loved all forms of cycling and did not wish to restrict his racing. His best victory for Falcon was in the 1964 six-day Tour of the South-West where he led from start to finish, beating not only seasoned independents

Pete Chisman won the 1963 Milk Race with an overwhelming show of strength, then turned Independent first for Carlton then for Sun.

like Bedwell, Hitchen, Jacob and Coles, but all the star amateurs. Metcalfe, Lewis, and Chisman. The only reason that Holmes did not collect more victories than he did was his lack of a competitive finishing sprint.

Holmes's place as the Milk Race star was taken by Peter Chisman, who had risen in one season from being totally unknown outside his native County Durham, to finishing fifth in the 1961 race and thirteenth in 1962. In April 1963 he rode well to take third place in the Merseyside four-day Easter race, was sixth behind the independents in the big Tour of the South-West in May, and finished in the lead group in the Manx International. But nothing prepared anyone for the double hammer-blow with which he opened that year's Milk Race, winning the first two stages and amassing an overall lead of almost twelve minutes. This was eroded over the following ten days, but Chisman held on to win comfortably by five minutes. The race was marked by several controversial encounters between riders and British traffic laws, and it has to be said that the continental teams were often bemused and demoralised by the non-closure of the roads. Chisman's great lead on the first stage was helped by the closure of the Warrington Bridge over the Manchester ship-canal, which held up the bunch behind him for five full minutes. Over the years numerous breaks were killed off by traffic lights or by buses lumbering through narrow roads, while riders were also liable to be stopped at any time by police or race organisers to be lectured about crossing the central line in the road; this was all part of the open-road

Arthur Metcalfe, a hard, superbly talented rider who went from B.A.R. champion to Tour de France rider in less than a year.

racing of the day, and had to be accepted. After taking seventh place in the 1964 Milk Race, the second great highlight of Chisman's amateur career came in 1965 when he won a stage in Tour de l'Avenir, breaking away over the northern pave to finish alone in the famous Roubaix stadium. In fact Chisman had little in the way of a sprint, and all his victories were solo ones. In 1966 he turned professional for Raleigh-BMB and won his best pro victory in May of that year, the six-day Tour of the West, which had now become Britain's premier professional stage race. Like Holmes before him, Chisman's star status stemmed above all from the Milk Race, and their victories form an unforgettable chapter in the history of British cycling, so different from the endless string of East European winners of the 1970s.

Chisman's 1964 successor, Arthur Metcalfe, took his early lead with a tremendous show of strength on a bitterly cold wet day through the Welsh mountains, and held it to the end. Yet despite this, and despite all Metcalfe's other winning rides, the Leeds man will always be remembered for his twin victories in the national road race championship and time-trialling's B.A.R. in the same year, a feat unique in British racing history. In two successive weekends in September, tacked onto the end of his road-racing season, Metcalfe overtook all the time-triallists who had been campaigning for months. Without a superfast 50, he produced a sub four-hour 100, and with only one chance for a 12-hour ride the following week, he succeeded magnificently with a total of 270.5 miles, barely missing the competition record. It was an exploit that won him the respect of every racing man in Britain, roadmen and time-triallists alike. Just ten months later, Metcalfe was riding in the Tour de France alongside Simpson, Hoban, Denson and the others, and he made it all the way to Paris. In the 1965 Milk Race he had come in sixth behind Les West and took the King of the Mountains prize. Two weeks later the order was reversed as he and West sprinted it out together in the Manx International, Metcalfe coming out the winner. In August he and Bradley and John Woodburn broke entirely new ground when they travelled to Canada to race in the two-week Tour of St Lawrence, and Metcalfe won two successive stages. Signing for Carlton in 1967, his best professional year was 1968, for although he failed to finish in his second Tour de France, he won both the Tour of the

South West, the Isle of Man road race, and the three-race Mackeson series championship.

Gaunt, and unsmiling, Metcalfe was the image of the hard, calculating road-racer. His nickname in the peleton was "the Snake", which leads one to suspect that he was not over-popular with his fellow riders, alternately tearing them to pieces from the front, or ruthlessly sitting in behind. "I'll never forgive him for that one", muttered Colin Lewis after one race, when Metcalfe had sat on his wheel for twenty miles, then glided past on the line. In one race Metcalfe even slung punches at another rider, Peter Gordon, for allegedly not working in a break, and the fighting continued into the dressing-room. After he had scaled down his riding, Metcalfe formed the bike-building business called MKM, his partners being Wes Mason and Ron Kitching, turning out quality racing frames throughout the seventies and eighties.

In complete contrast to Metcalfe was the outstanding amateur roadman of the mid-sixties, Les West. In the five years 1964 -1968, West achieved a staggering list of multiple wins in all the biggest races in Britain: two Manx Internationals, two Milk Races, two national road-race championships, as well as a dozen other major road-race wins such as the Vaux, the Harp, and the Tour of the Cotswolds. He broke Billy Holmes's Isle of Man time-trial record in 1963, beat all the top time-triallists in 1964 to take the 50-mile championship, and on the track he broke Sheil's British hour record in 1965 with no special

The outstanding road-man of the 1960s, Les West won everything there was to win as an amateur, and narrowly missed a professional world championship medal in 1970.

preparation at all. Despite this string of titles, West's personality appeared relaxed, honest and unassuming. He always emphasised that no career consisted only of victories, and he made no secret of the struggle he had had to overcome a series of huge disappointments in those years. The first of these almost caused him to turn his back on the sport: in 1964, having been selected for both the World Championships and the Olympics, he reported a minor injury to the B.C.F. racing committee, whose response was to drop him from both teams. The sensational circumstances under which he won his first Milk Race in 1965 are well remembered: after Santamarina's disqualification, the last stage started with West lying second, almost two minutes behind the Pole Janiak, and this was just the challenge West needed, for he made good the deficit and put a further five minutes between himself and Janiak. Later in the year he won the national road-race championship, and he broke the national hour record – after which he went out and won a road-race the following day. But the season ended with a demoralising trip to the World Championships in Spain. Unable to find any form, he finished in the pack, while in the rain-soaked team time trial the British quartet (West,

Lewis, Cowley and Bettinson) was next to last. In 1966 West raced a good deal in Holland and Belgium, and this experience deterred him from moving on to a pro career on the continent, for he saw the extent to which drugs were being used and wanted no part of it. He felt that this racing in Holland had given him greater speed but had damaged his climbing form, and it was this that prevented him from getting on terms with the Poles and Russians who dominated that year's Milk Race. The greatest near-miss of his amateur career came that year in the World Championship race on the Nurburgring, when he was outsprinted for the gold medal by Dolman of Holland, his legs cramping up on the line. Had he won that sprint he would surely have had great difficulty resisting the pro con-

Wes Mason (left), Commonwealth Games road-race champion in 1962, with Keith Butler, one of the few riders to have won both the amateur and professional road titles.

tracts that would have been offered to him.

1967 saw West take his second Milk Race in the most emphatic manner possible, recovering from a seventeen minute deficit after four stages, to win by a further seventeen minutes, a margin which people said was in the style of Coppi, especially as ten of those minutes were gained during a break on the final stage, when he had not needed to attack at all. Regaining the national championship three weeks later, West was confirmed as beyond question Britain's supreme roadman. Once again the pro offers flowed in, but West had a special reason for remaining an amateur for at least one more year: he wanted to erase the memory of the 1964 Olympic

fiasco by competing in Mexico in 1968. Yet his '68 season was to be filled with bitter disappointments. A closely-marked man in the Milk Race, he lost interest, and was forced to watch as the Pettersons dominated the race. He was beaten on the line for the national championship by Pete Matthews, after towing the Liverpool man for miles. His low-point came in the Olympic race in Mexico, where he punctured after only ten miles and waited four minutes for service while the bunch vanished into the distance. In despair, he felt he had reached the end of the road in his present career, and only a complete change of direction would keep him in the sport: it came in the form of a pro contract with Holdsworth. A popular figure with a well-documented career, West is still something of an enigma: detached and humorous, he never appeared driven by passionate ambitions. If you believed his own accounts he didn't train especially hard. He admitted that he lacked confidence, particularly when it came to racing abroad - he once said he'd love to ride the Tour de France, but that he'd never have the nerve to get on the start-line. He did not perform well in the Tour de l'Avenir, feeling very unsettled away from home. Physically his build was extremely average, and he had a tendency to cramp up, which he himself believed was psychological. This Achilles heal, his modesty, and the many disappointments he suffered, somehow made him more popular. In many ways the successor of Bradley, West's talent was phenomenal, his record stands above any other roadman of those years, and the memory of his wins is a permanent part of cycling history.

The one great difference between the fifties and the late sixties was that there now existed a clear pathway to a professional career if the rider wanted to take it. The Milk Race and the Manx International were the classic proving-grounds for British amateurs, and stage wins or high places there meant not only international selection, as it had before, but a possible future with one of the professional teams. In addition to those riders already discussed - Bradley, Holmes, Chisman, Metcalfe, and West - the list of those who followed this route includes Keith Butler, Bob Addy, Wes Mason, Dick Goodman, Johnny Clarey, John Bettinson, Mike Cowley, and Hugh Porter - all of whom went on to become professionals. International selection was no longer the end of the line. One rider who could not join them however was Peter Buckley, one of the best amateurs of the sixties, who won the Commonwealth Games gold medal in 1966, the Scottish Milk Race in 1968 and the Manx International in 1969. Buckley was tragically killed at the age of 24 in a freak

Graham Webb shows off his world champion's jersey at the 1967 six-day event in London. His victory came out of the blue, and he made it look easy; he found it much harder to succeed as a pro in Europe.

accident while out training, caused when a dog dashed into his path and brought him down. Buckley's Commonwealth gold followed that of Wes Mason in 1962, Booty in 1958 and Eric Thompson in 1954: this was one international event where Britain had an excellent record. Keith Butler (son of Stan and father of Gethin) shared with Les West the distinction of winning both the amateur and professional road-race championships. Dick Goodman had been second in the amateur championship in 1962, and second twice in the Manx International in 1962 and 1963, finally hitting the top in his first pro year of 1966, winning the national championship race and the season-long award as the best pro.

It was possible to side-step the normal routes to the top however, and no one did so more spectacularly than Graham Webb. Webb had none of the usual pedigree of Milk Race or Isle of Man successes; instead he began as time-triallist who narrowly missed both competition record and the national championship at 25 miles. He was a bit of a loner and entirely self-taught, who ground out enormous training distances on a rough, heavy, old roadster. Turning to the track he broke Les West's British hour record and took the national pursuit championship in 1966, although he lost the title in 1967 by inches to Brendan McKeown. It is something of a mystery why he was chosen for the World Championship road race in Holland that year. His road-race record was thin: by far his best result was to finish third behind Les West in the national title race, but the selectors felt that his experience of racing that year in Holland and Belgium was worth more than a few victories in England. So he started in the road race, and the rest is history: he won the World Championship with an outstanding ride, going with the first break, dropping back to check on his team-mates, getting up again to the leading group, and riding away from them all in the last mile. It was incredible and totally unexpected by anyone in England. Over the years star riders like Booty, Bradley, Holmes and West had failed, while Webb, the enigmatic loner, had triumphed. He was being signed up as a professional the very next day, while he watched Merckx winning the pro race. But Webb's professional career was a failure from the first. In Poulidor's Mercier team, he suffered a run of bad luck and poor results, and found himself ostracised, with no second chance given. A transfer to a small Belgian team the following year brought no greater success, and he turned his back on the sport. In England, Webb had never been taken up and feted as a champion, partly because he chose to continue living in Belgium, and he slipped into obscurity, ignored by the press and cycling's governing bodies. In a way reminiscent of Cyril Peacock in the 1950s, Webb was a world champion who was later thought of as a failure; yet he and Simpson are still the only British men ever to win a world road-race championship.

Still another route to the top was to ignore the limitations of the British domestic scene and leave for the continent, as so many did with the achievements of Robinson and Simpson to inspire them. But to succeed alone in a foreign environment took a very special kind of personal strength, and most returned home within a year. Barry Hoban succeeded of course, and Vin Denson was another who made it, but that was after a strong career in England as a time-triallist then a Milk Race rider - Denson finished sev-

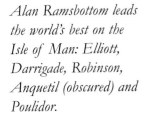

Alan Ramsbottom leads the world's best on the Isle of Man: Elliott, Darrigade, Robinson, Anquetil (obscured) and Poulidor.

enth in 1959 and fifth in 1960. Denson rode many classics, the Tour de France six times between 1961 and 1968, and in 1966 he became the first English-speaking rider to win a Giro stage. Yet a small number of riders left for the continent and made the grade without having climbed the traditional rungs of the home ladder, and the public here would suddenly learn with amazement that an Englishman was out there racing alongside Anquetil and van Looy. The classic case was Alan Ramsbottom, the Lancashire rider who looked more like a schoolboy, with his spiky hair and big spectacles. Ramsbottom had finished well up in the 1959 Milk Race, and he came second to Bradley in the amateur championship of 1960, but failed to gain any international selection, so he headed off to the Troyes region of France. Driven by a burning ambition almost equal to Simpson's own, he progressed so well that the very next year found him riding the Tour de l'Avenir alongside Bradley, Holmes and Hinds, taking a stage victory and briefly wearing the yellow jersey. He secured a pro contract with the Pellforth-Sauvage team, and after a year's apprenticeship, 1962 saw him finish the Tour de France in 45th place, including a great ride in the mountain time-trial where Simpson cracked badly, and lost his yellow jersey, beaten by Ramsbottom by almost three minutes. In 1963 Alan did even better, reaching Paris in 16th place just 30 minutes down on Anquetil. It seemed that Simpson was not unique, and an ecstatic press began to float the idea that a British team capable of winning the Tour could be built up around these two. But for

Ramsbottom this was to be the high-point: placings in the one-day classics refused to come, then an unfortunate team dispute kept him out of the 1964 Tour, and he never made it back in again. A move to Belgium, a change of teams, a series of accidents - everything went wrong for him, and in the winter of 1966 at the age of thirty he returned to England to ride briefly as a pro for Viking. Like so many British riders before him, Ramsbottom had reached a certain height and could go no further. When interviewed he exploded the idea that pro riders in France all lived like princes: he had made a bare living for five years and that was all. He returned with virtually nothing, except the fading memory of the star status he had once been given.

Brian Jolly, the "Killer", dominant amateur roadman of the late sixties.

Another English rider who made his own way to a pro contract in Europe and Tour de France rides was Derek Harrison, the Midlands man who had based himself in France in 1965, who won the Mountains jersey in the 1968 Tour of Switzerland and who finished a very creditable 32nd place in the 1969 Tour. But perhaps the strangest English star discovered overseas in the 1960s was Michael Wright. Born in Essex, but living in

Billy Bilsland just seconds away from his historic stage win in the 1967 Peace Race.

Belgium since the age of three, Wright was suddenly hailed by the press as a great British competitor on the European pro circuit. In 1965 Wright became the second Englishman, after Robinson, to win a stage of the Tour de France, and, riding for the national team in 1967, he repeated this feat. He made rare visits to race in England - for example he won the Vaux International in 1967 - but in spite of his obvious class as a rider, it was hard for the public to identify with this man who spoke not a word of English.

The existence of half a dozen pro teams in the late sixties attracted a constant stream of top amateurs, opening the way for a new wave of young riders to star in the classic amateur races. Dave Rollinson, Brian Jolly, Billy Bilsland, Doug Dailey, Geoff Wiles, Garry Crewe, Sid Barras, Phil Edwards - riders like these came to the fore in the Isle of Man and the Milk Race, and rode for Britain in the World's and the Tour de l'Avenir. The strongest and most consistent amateur of the late sixties was probably Brian Jolly, the tall powerful Sheffield rider who possessed a complete armoury of talents reminiscent of Bradley and West. He could climb, sprint or break away to win alone; he was aptly nicknamed "Killer". Already an international, with finishes in the Peace Race and the Tour de l'Avenir to his credit, 1969 was almost a miracle year for Jolly: multiple stage wins in the Milk Race, overall victory in the Scottish Milk Race, a day in the yellow jersey in the Tour de l'Avenir, and the national road race championship, where he won alone by almost two minutes in a 120-mile race run at an average speed of almost 26 m.p.h. Never was a man more certain to turn professional than Jolly, and never did a man make the transition more convincingly, winning several top races in his first pro year, including the Tour of the Peak and the Tour of the Chilterns.

Jolly's successor as national champion was Dave Rollinson, who had shared the British success in the Avenir tour, winning the stage on which Jolly took the leader's jersey. Rollinson had already won Milk Race stages, and had finished second overall to West in 1967, and taken second place in the Manx International. Moving between France and England, Rollinson hesistated about a pro career, and decided to stay an amateur for a while longer, retaining his national title in 1971. The '69 Avenir team must have been one of the best that Britain ever sent abroad, for it contained still more future champions, amateur and professional, such as Doug Dailey, Geoff Wiles and Danny Horton, and the man who had already won the Scottish championship at the age of nineteen, Billy Bilsland, who won the final stage of the race. The smiling, broad-shouldered Scot was the archetypal hard wee man from Glasgow, driven by a fierce determination to succeed on a bigger stage than home racing. All conversations with him seemed to come back to his expressive catch-phrase "Aye, it's no easy". Already a Peace Race stage winner in 1967, he settled in Paris with one of the big sponsored clubs, and achieved some great results, including victory in the 165-mile amateur classic Paris-Tours. Riders like Bilsland, Jolly,

Barras and Rollinson could take stage wins in the Milk Races of the late sixties, but the overall pattern of dominance was passing more and more to overseas teams, with victories and top placings being taken by Poland, Holland, Sweden and Czechoslovakia, and several team wins for Russia. After the years of home wins that stretched from Bradley to West, this was an ominous trend, and it would become critical in the next decade, when the Iron Curtain countries took an unshakable grip on the race. The Manx International however saw excellent wins for John Bettinson, Peter Buckley and Gary Crewe.

The leading riders in the road-racing world faced difficult choices as they tried to build their cycling careers. They could remain amateurs and enjoy winning the races of their choice, but they knew that international selection was a two-edged sword that might bring them fame, but also disappointment and a sense of failure. They could turn professional for one of the home teams, but it was clear that the home pro scene could not be made to grow by magic, to equal the continental system. There were still only three or four leading teams, perhaps twenty to thirty riders competing against each other every week, for as fast as new teams appeared, others dropped out as Condor-Mackeson had done. The development of the pro class was undoubtedly hindered by the general peception that cycling was a minority sport, lacking in glamour, for which sponsors were hard to find. Contacts with the European professionals were minimal, and the feeling was that the British pro class still remained something of a ghetto, despite containing some outstanding older riders like West, Lewis and Porter, and some brilliant newcomers like Jolly, Barras and Crewe, and the number of good testing classic races available to these men was sadly limited. The third option of living and racing on the continent remained a dream that was as hard to realise as ever. Horizons in the world of road-racing were wider than in time-trialling, the excitement was greater and the potential rewards were richer, but the road to success was a risky one, strewn with obstacles and littered with disappointments. The time-triallist just enters his race and rides, but the roadman's ambitions are bound up to a greater extent with teams, sponsors and organisers who all provide the context in which he races.

Even as the new decade was beginning, British cyclists experienced a dismaying sense of *deja vu*, when in the autumn of 1970 relations between the B.C.F. and the R.T.T.C. once again threatened to break down. The twin issues this time were the control of time trials in stage races and the control of team time trials, both of which the B.C.F. wanted to take into its own hands. The joint agreement between the two bodies, through which the sport had been run throughout the sixties, gave the R.T.T.C. power in both these areas, which they now refused to give up. It seemed that this joint agreement was about to be torn up and the sport returned to a form of warfare reminiscent of the 1950s. The R.T.T.C.

Mini-revolution: Vic Nicholson shows the speed of the new racing Moulton in 1967.

even warned that it would retaliate by running its own programme of road races. Ordinary cyclists were appalled, seeing this as a power game played by arrogant officials, irrelevant to any of the true needs of British cycling. This feedback clearly reached the B.C.F. for both the president and the racing committee chairman resigned, their successors drew back from the brink, and the joint agreement survived.

This conflict pointed to a deep fault-line which still existed in British cycling. The B.C.F. was the governing body of the sport in this country, recognised by the U.C.I. and they, together with many cyclists in the road-racing branch of the sport, could not reconcile themselves to the power held by the R.T.T.C., a body which carried no international status, and which had no objectives wider than the promotion of time-trialling at home. On their analysis, road-racing was the serious, international, forward-looking form of cycle sport, whose development in Britain was their overriding aim, an aim which must necessarily mean the weakening of the British passion for time-trialling. The time-trialling enthusiasts however, could easily point out that their sport was simply a democratic response to popular demand; it had been nurtured and efficiently run by the R.T.T.C. for many decades; it was supported each week by thousands of ordinary club riders, and no other cycling organisation had any possible right to intefere with it. They were defending a democratic, uncomplicated, voluntary sport, which had no international dimension. The excellence which time-triallists achieved was recognised by other time-triallists, and they were content with that alone. These conflicting attitudes once again revealed the forces that were at work in British cycling, pulling in different directions - towards road-racing, internationalism and professionalism; or towards time-trialling, insularity, and the satisfaction of competition in a purely amateur sport.

The new decade: Dave Rollinson leads Gary Crewe in the 1970 amateur road race championship; they finished in that order.

Time-Trialling

It would be easy to say that time-trialling in the 1960s glided serenely on, immune from the problems that seemed to swirl around in road-racing, and that the only changes to ripple the smooth surface of the sport were quaint events like the abolition of bells in races in 1965. But in fact the time-trialling scene generated a number of controversies of its own: course measurement in 1961, when records had to be rejected; following cars in 1969; arguments about advertising and amateurism, and the consequent suspension of riders; criticism of drag-strip courses, where speeds were boosted by heavy traffic flows. But all these problems, with the exception of the last one, were internal to the R.T.T.C. and the time-trialling community. Good regulation and good management should have been capable of resolving them - they were just so many storms in teacups. The drag-strip issue was another matter: first noticed in the 1960s as the traffic volumes on Britain's roads increased, it would haunt the B.A.R. competition until the present day.

But time-trialling in the 1960s was above all a period of brilliant achievement, with records taken to new heights, often in a series of quantum leaps, from Frank Colden's stunning 1962 season, to the miracle year of 1969, which brought new records at every distance from 25 miles to 24 hours. How can we explain this relentless rise in record speeds? First there were the super-fast courses, the Southend Road for the 25 and 50, and the A1 in Yorkshire for the 50 and the 100. Traffic on these dual-carriageways created a slipstream effect which, on the right day, counteracted any headwind and made even the uphill sections seem fast. Many riders saw their times improve as if by magic when they visited these courses for the first time. They were called "suck and blow courses": the traffic's slipstream sucked you out in spite of any headwind, and the tailwind blew you back to the finish. These roads encouraged the second factor, which was the use of big gears in place of the traditional fixed wheel. If you could get a 115-inch gear turning with a steady swirl of traffic flowing past you, or with a tailwind behind you, then cruising speeds of 25-28 m.p.h. became a matter of course. Third was the increased focus on training for speed, rather than the traditional formula of long, steady miles. The lesson was finally being learned that if you wanted to race at 25 m.p.h., all the training in the world at 15 m.p.h. was useless to you. This message had started with the 25-milers, Sheil, Engers, McCoy, Bonner and the others, and had filtered through to the distance men, culminating in the 12- and 24-hour records of Watson and Cromack, who were both very fast short-distance men. The final factor was probably the use of cars to get to races. It was certainly not true that all cyclists in 1960s owned a car, but most people knew someone who did, and who could drive them at least to the important races; the energy saving compared with a two-hour ride at 4 a.m. to the start of a 50 or a 100 can easily be imagined. Interestingly enough, in spite of all the rumours and suspicions about drugs in the sixties, no one ever suggested that the dramatic improvement in time-trial standards might be due to widespread drug use by competitors. Time-trialling was universally perceived as a clean sport, and no real evidence ever came to light to contradict this view.

In the galaxy of star riders who re-wrote the record books in the sixties, who was the greatest? Is it possible to compare the speed of Dungworth or Engers with the tenacity of Carline, with his unique tally of five 24-hour championship wins? In fact the choice of the outstanding rider of these years is not so difficult to make after all: in terms of total dominance by one individual over a period of time, in which the sport was taken to a new

*Beryl Burton,
unequalled in cycling
or in any other sport
for her multitude of
victories and records.*

level, the choice has to be Beryl Burton. It is as near certain as anything can be that her time-trialling record will never be beaten: 70 national championships at distances from 10 to 100 miles, 50 competition records, and 25 successive B.A.R. awards make up truly a lifetime's achievement, the rewards for a talent and a dedication that remain unequalled. How many races she won in her entire career - time-trialling, road and track - no one knows: it must have been close to a thousand. The most vivid proof of the sheer number of her victories is that she herself forgot how many world championship medals she had accumulated: she found them one day rattling around in a bag, and when she counted them, there was one more than she could remember winning. Every landmark in women's time-trialling fell to her: the first sub-hour 25, the sub two-hour 50, the first sub four-hour 100, the first 240-mile 12; it took fully twenty years for the others to catch up and equal her times. She will always be remembered as the only woman ever to break a man's record - her famous 12-hour ride of 277.25 miles in September 1967, when she caught and beat Mike McNamara even as he was beating competition record and winning the B.A.R. Yet this was no isolated case, for on numerous Sunday mornings, Beryl's winning time in the women's event was faster than that in the men's, so that she was the undisputed winner of the race. The most astonishing aspect of her career was her longevity: she began winning top-level races at the age of 18, and she was still winning them at the age of 46, for her appetite for racing and for victory never diminished. It's an interesting question whether any one individual has ever dominated any sport so completely and for so long as Beryl dominated women's cycling.

What drove her on no one really knows. After just five years in the sport she had won everything there was to win several times over, yet still she went on racing. She came from a working-class family, she had no education and no special skills, but in cycling she discovered something that she could do supremely well, and she kept on doing it - she saw no reason to stop. One does not demand of a writer or a musician that they stop writing or composing because they are too good, and for her the exercise of her talent was her life. Years before feminism was invented, she showed that a woman could achieve something outstanding in a man's world. That she drove herself too hard in her later years is probably true: she became slightly accident-prone, and she died many years before she should have. She knew that cycling was a minority sport, and she became increasingly bitter not to receive greater recognition for her achievements. Had she raced in the 1990s instead of the 1960s, she might have become a star and earned a great deal of money. In fact as the opportunities for women have improved, it is possible that with her strength of character she might have achieved success in another field completely. Within cycling she was idolised in the 1960s, although she did become slightly less popular as the years went on, perhaps because her dominance was too complete, she overshadowed her female rivals to such a degree that it almost seemed unfair, her ability seemed super-human. But she did have her failures and she did make mistakes. She never captured the track hour record, which was surely within her grasp. She lost her world pursuit title in 1961 by one tenth of a second, and experienced observers pointed out that she would have kept it had she ridden closer in to the pursuiter's line: she probably rode twenty yards further than her rival. In the historic 24 hour race of 1969, she set off at a suicidal pace, despite a troubling knee injury, and she paid the price: determined to be the first rider to top 500 miles, she covered the first half at a speed that would have given her 540 miles, before she abandoned. In the late 1970s she attracted some bad publicity when she appeared to resent the success of her daughter Denise. One has to sympathise with the many fine women riders who raced for so long under her shadow: Jo Bowers (later Killingbeck) Joan Kershaw, June Pitchford, Carol Barton and many others, some of whom enjoyed careers almost as long as Beryl's, and who were capable of winning national titles if she faltered. How did she train? Hard, but apparently no harder than hundreds of others, male and female. Her ability to see off every new challenge from each new generation was due to some inner strength of mind rather than of body. Apparently dry, down-to-earth and unimaginative, she possessed some fire that drove her on to her countless victories and records. Perhaps one day a serious biographer will explore her life and personality in greater depth, and give us some answers to explain her unique achievement.

In the elite world of the top 25-milers, competition record holder when the decade opened was Alf Engers with 55:11. But Alf was still only twenty years old, and was by no means the certain winner that he later became. Gordon Ian had beaten him for the championship in 1959 and 1960, and in 1961 a revolution hit 25-miling when John Woodburn took the championship riding on gears. Woodburn had watched the impact that gears had made on the longer distances, especially noticing Wiltcher's superiority at 50 miles. In one particular 50 in June 1960, Wiltcher had beaten Woodburn by a margin

Randy Allsopp, 50 champion in 1963, and 25 champion in 1970.

of four minutes, and Woodburn, who had felt strong and on good form, was convinced that he had been handicapped by the traditional single gear. Switching to gears he quickly recorded a personal best of 56:1, just 50 seconds outside the record, and for him the case was proved. That championship day in June 1961 was sudden-death day for the fixed wheel that had ruled British time-trialling for fifty years, for the silver medallist too, Charly McCoy, was also riding gears, and never again would any national championship - the 25 or any other - be won on fixed. Engers was twelfth that day, and he too said goodbye to the fixed wheel. Woodburn had been racing since 1954, and had been climbing into the top echelons of time-trialling, but had tended to be overshadowed by his younger Barnet clubmate Engers. Now however he looked forward to the 50 championship with confidence, having recorded the year's fastest 50 shortly before. But on a wet, puncture-strewn day Woodburn, Craven, Ian and Booty all saw their hopes vanish, and Barry Hoban was the surprise winner in a relatively slow time. More disappointment followed for Woodburn that summer, when after a super-fast 50 he was disqualified for passing the wrong side of a traffic island. Then in August he sliced 9 seconds from Wiltcher's 50 record, only for the race to fall victim to the short-course disaster of that year. The courses in question were the 25-, 30- and 50-mile E courses in Essex, where road re-alignment had shaved precious yards from the standard distances. His record was invalidated, as was the team record which he shared with Engers and Harvey. This experience was a factor in this trio's decision to turn independent for Ted Gerrard at the end of the year. This move brought some notable successes for Woodburn in the road-racing world, but it would keep him out of time-trialling for fully seven years.

Late in 1961, Charley McCoy, the 1960 Olympic track rider, coached like Norman Sheil by Eddie Soens, placed himself in the frame to succeed Engers and Woodburn by taking 10 seconds from the competition record. In the following summer he justified these expectations when he won the national 25 championship, becoming the first man since Stan Higginson in 1953 to hold the record and the title together. However this ride had an unhappy and slightly ridiculous sequel: following the appearance of McCoy's photograph in *Cycling*, a picture in which the manufacturer's name on his bike was plainly visible, McCoy was suspended for advertising. Most observers were incredulous, since they knew that such pictures featuring any number of riders appeared almost every week, and it seemed that McCoy had been singled out simply because he was the champion. It was a strange regulation in any case, for it did not seem to matter how many people *saw* the name on McCoy's bike, it was only when a picture was *printed* that an offence occurred. But was a rider responsible for what was printed in the press? No official at the start or the finish ever warned a rider that he might be doing anything wrong. It was all very tortuous and pointless, but it was typical of its era, for it sprang from the absolutely literal interpretation of the amateur rules: there was no way to defend the amateur code except to stamp ruthlessly on every imagined offence. But it seemed to some people a very strange thing that the R.T.T.C., the guardians of this stringent code, had accepted advertising inside its own handbook and indeed on its front cover for years. McCoy rode in the national championship 50 of 1962 and finished second to Frank Colden, but he never returned to top-level racing after that.

Towards the very end of the 1962 season a new star appeared on the 25-mile scene when 19-year-old Dave Bonner took more than half a minute off McCoy's record with his 54:28 ride in mid-October, in a day of fine autumn sunshine on the Essex roads, with Ken Craven second almost one minute down. Bonner duly took the national championship the following year amid a sea of new faces that included Porter, Bennett, Webb, Breedon and Cromack. Bonner could undoubtedly have gone on to further glory in the time-trialling world, and might perhaps have taken his place with the other greats of the 1960s, but he chose instead a road-racing career, and led the Condor-Mackeson team with great flair from 1964 until 1970. The 50 championship of 1963 was however one ride Bonner would prefer to forget: after a fast start on a heavy fenland course, he faded dramatically in the last quarter to finish three minutes behind Randy Allsopp. That result concealed another drama because Allsopp too had died completely in the final miles, and had freewheeled over the line, convinced he was well out of the placings. The result showed that he had edged out Ken Craven by just 2 seconds, one of Craven's closest approaches to the championship gold medal that always eluded him. Also behind Allsopp that day were Les West, Chris Munford, Paul Bennett and Peter Hill. Allsopp was a real tryer who suffered some serious illnesses, but who came back to finish sixth in the 1968 B.A.R., and then in 1970 he defeated all the top short-distance men to win the 25-mile championship; Allsopp's was a very unusual progression from B.A.R. contender to 25-mile champion.

Bas Breedon - Yorkshire's other B.B. - short-distance record-breaker and champion.

Short distance time-trialling in the mid-sixties was dominated by two riders, both Yorkshiremen, who between them won seven championships and broke six competition records: Barry Breedon and Dave Dungworth. Breedon was a tall, powerful big-gear pusher who had already become the fastest man of the year in 1964 and who started as favourite for the championship. The title race that year on a wet and windy day was very close however, and Breedon's 56:57 was just 7 seconds clear of Brian Green, with Graham Webb a further 5 seconds down. The story might have been very different if Randy Allsopp had not gone off course and lost a whole minute – enough to have won him the title. Confident and pugnacious as he was, Breedon was well beaten by Les West in the 50 championship three weeks later, collapsing at the finish with exhaustion and disappointment. This was West's miracle week, which saw him win the Manx International, the Isle of Man time-trial and the 50 championship. Second and third were the two North Londoners Hugh Smith and Chris Munford, with Breedon well back in eighth place. But Breedon's pride was restored in superb fashion when he came back in the next few weeks to break competition records at both 25 and 50 miles. First he clipped 5 seconds from Bonner's 25 record with 54:23, then he really took the 50 record into new realms with a two and a half minute beating of Frank Colden's time, only narrowly missing the 1:50 barrier with a fantastic time of 1:50:3. This race, held on the A1 in Yorkshire in August 1964 was one of the most memorable 50s ever held, for the first four riders all broke the old record: Derek Reay, Mike McNamara, and Peter Hill all in succession held the record for a matter of minutes, before Breedon put the record on the shelf for the next two years.

In the following year, 1965, Breedon demonstrated his complete superiority by taking a rare double victory in both the 25 and 50 championships. The 25 was held on the almost laney A377 in North Devon, where Breedon's 55:18 was an outstanding time, almost a minute clear of the man who would top the B.A.R. that year, Keith Stacey, with

Roy Cromack third. Graham Webb snapped a rear fork-end after 17 miles, but still finished fourth. The 50 championship was a much closer affair, with Breedon again pushing Stacey into second place, but only by 8 seconds. Revenge over West was complete, the latter having lost his speed edge in winning the Milk Race. Breedon's number one spot in the shorter distances was acknowledged, but it received a severe dent only a week later when Paul Bennett took a pretty huge chunk out of the competition record with 53:31; supported by Alan Rochford and Joe Mummery, the Barnet C.C. also took the team record. Before Bennett finished Mick Burrow had also broken the record with 54:4 in a multi-record race.

It was a well-deserved triumph for Bennett, who had travelled all the way to Devon for the championship, only to suffer gear failure immediately after starting, and he had also finished third in the 50 championship. Bennett's club, the Barnet C.C., were back to record-breaking level under the guidance of Alan Shorter, having lost Engers, Woodburn and Harvey to road-racing, and there was more to come with Hugh Smith and Trevor Morgan. The heavily-built Bennett started the 1966 season as favourite to gain the title from Breedon, whose form seemed to have slipped away a little. Yet incredibly Bennett was once again the victim of mechanical failure, his back wheel collapsing while he was on a winning ride, leaving victory to the rising star Dave Dungworth, with Trevor Morgan second and Breedon third.

Dungworth was Bennett's physical opposite: small and wiry, his legs looked disproportionately long for his body. His unusual build must have been ideal for time-trialling, for he dominated the short-distance scene for the next two years. He stormed into the record books in 1966, first with a new record time for the 30 of 1:5:21, then with a resounding victory in the 50 championship, winning by over two minutes from Pete Smith, with Breedon back in eighth. He then grabbed back the 25 record from Bennett with a time of 53:18, before reducing that dramatically at the very end of the season to 52:28. This ride was in mid-October on the Southend Road,

Dave Dungworth, prolific winner of national championships and breaker of records.

just like Bonner's in 1962, and Trevor Morgan also broke the record that day with 52:56, which stood as the record for nineteen minutes. It had been a fantastic season for Dungworth, with two championships, three competition records and 24 wins in 29 rides, and he was still only 21 years old. In 1967 Dungworth held off all challengers to win both the 25 and 50 titles again, achieving what at the time was a unique double-double, that was later repeated by Chris Boardman in 1991/92.

Trevor Morgan's ride in that record-breaking 25 was doubly upsetting for him, for while chatting to *Cycling* journalist Ken Evans afterwards, he was reported as saying that he "took as much advantage from the passing traffic as possible". This remark was seized upon by officials as an admission of paced riding, and an inquiry was ordered. Morgan denied ever making the remark, and in the end no action was taken. The episode left an unpleasant sense that this rider had been singled out and persecuted, as McCoy had been. The problem of the drag-strip courses had been put into the spotlight, for Morgan must have enjoyed exactly the same conditions as all the other riders, including Dungworth. People were beginning to ask why the R.T.T.C. permitted races on courses like this, and then found fault with the conduct and result of those races. Perhaps it was fortunate that Morgan had not finished the season as record holder, otherwise the controversy would have been much greater. In 1967 there was more official trouble at the 25 championship, which was another Dungworth-Morgan battle, Dungworth winning a hard, wind-blown fight on the A1 by just 5 seconds, with Breedon third. But the result was declared to be provisional only, while complaints about following cars were investigated. It was four weeks before the result was officially confirmed, but Morgan and three other riders were sent letters warning them about the following car rules. The issue was whether cars were available at certain points around the course to help with punctures and so on, or whether

they were in attendance the whole way, possibly pacing, and giving physical or psychological help. This problem had not existed ten years earlier, and was a side-effect of growing car-ownership. But again as in the McCoy case, why single out a few top riders? Did it not matter if slower riders received the benefit of a following car? Rightly or wrongly, there was a suspicion that officials took pleasure in cutting top riders down to size, reminding them that it was they who really ran the sport. Dungworth's 1967 season continued almost as a mirror-image of 1966, with a lowering of his own 30 record to 1:4:56, and then a tremendous victory in the 50 championship in July, leaving the new stars Pete Smith and Ant Taylor three minutes in arrears with 1:52:24. This was Dungworth's last time-trialling season for many years, as the following year saw him join Sun Cycles as a professional. The two-year reign of this diminutive but brilliant figure had been full of superlatives, and the only pity was that he never came up against Engers.

Pete Smith, first man inside 1:50 for the 50.

Among the big-gear pushers and the drag-strip courses, it's worth remembering that some enthusiasts were still fighting a rearguard action in favour of the fixed wheel. In 1966 Dennis Brown achieved a record of his own when he recorded the fastest-ever 25 on an 84-inch fixed, with a time of 54:50, while John Greatwood put up an even more amazing 1:50:36 for the 50, also on an 84-inch gear. Greatwood finished fourth in the B.A.R. with a time of 4:10:44 for the 100 and a 261-mile 12. He did not win any converts however: What would he do on gears? - that was the inevitable response.

The record which had eluded Dungworth, the 50, passed a big milestone in 1966 when Pete Smith became the first man inside 1:50. On a warm, still September morning, Smith slashed 41 seconds off Breedon's record with 1:49:22. Smith's Clifton C.C. club-mate, John Watson, then only 19 years old, was second with 1:50:11. It was a taste of what was to come from the Clifton team in the next couple of years, for with Paul Taylor on 1:54:15, the team record was pulverised by over six minutes. In July 1967, Smith reduced his record still further to 1:48:33, a ride which came in a special international invitation 50

on the Bath Road course, and which seemed to disprove claims that only the A1 could now yield record times. It was a tremendous ride by Smith: Dungworth and Breedon were at their best, but were beaten by minutes, while McNamara, Roach and Stacey were still further back. Later that year Smith went under four hours for the 100, and he missed winning the B.A.R by just 0.065 m.p.h. In fact Smith was unable to use his fastest 50 time because it had been achieved in that special invitation event, which was not a B.A.R. counter; if that time had been included, Smith would have won the B.A.R. that year. Smith was one of the best time-triallists never to win a national championship, setting a superb 100-mile record of 3:50:20 in 1969, and finishing eighth in the world road-race championship the same year; in 1970 he turned professional for Clive Stuart cycles, but continued his time-trialling by slicing 13 seconds from Earnshaw's pre-war R.R.A. 50 record, with 1:39:29.

The 1968 25-mile season seemed more open with Dungworth

Alf Engers, supreme 25-miler over a twenty-year period, from the late fifties to the late seventies.

gone, and Breedon now almost thirty years old, and moving up to the B.A.R. distances. The new factor this season was the return of Alf Engers, reinstated after his five years out of the sport. In March and still visibly overweight, Engers won his comeback race, going just inside the hour, but six weeks later he showed he was serious when he was down to a 54-minute ride, the fastest of the year, and he found himself favourite for the championship. It proved one of the closest title-races ever: Engers finished joint second with his Polytechnic C.C. club-mate Joe Mummery on 54:52, both of them beaten by one second by Midlander Ray Ward, another man making a comeback after a couple of years out of racing. Mummery was the more disappointed of the two, for he had unshipped his chain and had to stop to replace it, losing precious seconds and the title. In September 1968 Engers equalled Dungworth's 25-mile record of 52:28, but he was informed by the R.T.T.C. that his time would not receive official recognition since there could only be one record holder - a rather puzzling doctrine that makes one wonder what would have happened if Engers and Dungworth had both achieved their times in the same race?

Engers made no mistakes in 1969, for he was by now pursuing a very intensive interval-training system which he himself devised, with flat-out efforts and short recoveries, repeated over and over again in twenty- to thirty-mile sessions. He won the championship by a clear margin from Brian Hayes and Willi Moore, in an incredible performance which saw him puncture just as he launched himself off the start-line, lose at least half a minute changing the wheel, and recommence his ride with nerves and adrenalin tingling. At 29 he had become the oldest 25-mile champion ever. Engers's ambitions extended to track racing, and in July he took the national kilometre sprint title from the rising star Ian Hallam. In August he broke the 25 record with 51:59, an astonishing ten years after first taking the record. He had serious hopes of riding at the world track championships, but he found himself ruled out because he had ridden as an independent seven years before. He gave vent to his disappointment in September by lowering his own record to 51:00, where it remained for no less than nine years, until he himself shattered it. In the history of short-distance time-trialling, Engers's comeback was unique, and, although neither he nor anyone else knew it, the best was still to come.

A new dimension was added to 25-mile racing in 1969 when *Cycling* and Campagnolo jointly sponsored a new season-long points competition, using thirteen selected races around the country. Engers won the first four events, then seemed to lose interest, leaving it to Ray Ward to dominate the later stages. It was at the very end of October that Ward won the final race which would seal his overall victory, but then the following-car problem erupted once again. The result of the final event was declared provisional only, and Ward was left in limbo for no less than three months before he was cleared of any wrongdoing and awarded the Campag trophy valued at £100. The whole affair was deeply embarrassing, and it soured what should have been an innovative new competition. Nobody seriously believed that Ward had won by cheating, and once again people asked why only the winners and the stars were singled out for attention. And once again, despite a long investigation, no action was taken: it seemed that officials were good at finding problems, but had no clear idea how to deal with them.

The 10-mile competition has so far received no mention, despite the important part that it played in club-life. It was always used as a speed-training race, and as an introduction for youngsters into the world of time-trialling, but a competition record was not recognised until 1972, when Willi Moore's 20:36 was the fastest, and no national championship was held until 1994, when Rob Hayles won in 19:48. But there is one 10-mile race from 1964 that deserves special mention, a celebrity event on the Great North Road for members of the bike trade and the press, plus a few elder statesmen of the cycling world - names like Jock Wadley, Dave Duffield, Ken Bird, Alan Shorter, Alan Gayfer, Alf Hetchins, and Condor's Monty Young. In very last place that day with a time of 37:52 was Dr. Christopher Woodard, an intriguing figure in British cycling history. For the past ten years he had contributed articles to *Cycling* which claimed to offer a radical scientific approach to training. He used the pseudonym of "The Athletic Specialist", but he also published books under his own name. His writings attracted attention because he was a doctor, and because they claimed that most cyclists had absolutely no understanding of basic physiology, of what training for their sport really involved. What did Dr Woodard's scientific method consist of? Well that was the problem, because from all his writings it is impossible to extract one single concrete, practical training idea. He produced statements about body fat, diet, muscular development and psychology which were generalised and fairly obvious, but he never once set out a training schedule. He made the most bizarre statements - that a cold proved you were unfit, that drinking during a race was harmful and would make your legs and feet swell, that smoking was a useful aid to relaxation, that top cyclists like Frank Colden had badly underdeveloped physiques, and so on. Somehow Woodard made this subsidiary career for himself as a scientific expert on cycling, yet here was a man in his late forties who could not ride ten miles faster than 37:52. The truly intriguing thing is that people listened to him: his status as a doctor made him appear to be a guru in a sport that had at that time almost no theory and no scientific basis. When true physiological testing began to emerge and influence bike training in the late sixties, Woodard's mysterious ramblings were consigned to the scrap-heap.

Alf Engers announced that he would not be competing in the 1970 time-trial scene, although he did race in the late summer; this left the field open for both the national title and the Campag Trophy. The championship was won by Randy Allsopp, another comeback man who had been out of the sport and seriously ill for several years, taking the title from Malcolm Johnson and Pete Watson. The second year of the Campag Trophy belonged to a sensational newcomer, Derek Cottington, a brilliant talent, famous for his 40 miles each-way training to work and back every day. He staggered the cycling world by riding a 56-minute 25 on Christmas Eve, and already in 1970 he was talking about soon cracking the 50-minute barrier. He was widely seen as the new Engers, but although in his best year of 1971 he took both the 25 and 50 championships, Cotters was not destined to dethrone the old master for long.

The 50 record took yet more battering in 1969 when Midlander Dave Whitehouse took almost a minute off Pete Smith's time with his 1:47:38 on the Boroughbridge course. Whitehouse was third in the 1969 B.A.R. and he won the 50 championship in 1970, but the 50 mark was truly shattered in August 1970 when John Watson brought it down by

Roger Wilkings, winner of three successive 12-hour championships, 1960-62.

almost four minutes to 1:43:46, again on Boroughbridge. Three other riders were inside the old record that day - Jeff Marshall, Hugh Smith and Ian White - but only White finished before Watson, so he too stands as a brief record holder. Watson's time was equivalent to two 25s of 52:13, at a time when no one except Engers had ridden that fast even for one. This superb record resisted all attacks for thirteen years - after Cromack's 24 it was the longest-surviving competition record ever - and it made Watson a certainty for the B.A.R.

October 1969 marked two very important milestones in time-trialling. First, the joint committee of the R.T.T.C. and the B.C.F. announced that from the following season mixed male and female racing would be permitted. This did not exactly mean open racing, since events could still be designated male or female, but they could also be open to both if the promoters wished it, while separate championships and the B.A.R would still be run. Second, the reinstatement of former professionals was made much easier, for they could revert to amateur status when they reached the age of forty, or if they had not held a pro licence for five years. These were both significant steps towards a simpler and more open structure for racing in this country.

After Wiltcher's two B.A.R. titles in

1959 and 1960, victory in the 1961 competition went to Brian Kirby, a member of Ken Joy's old club, the Medway Wheelers. Kirby had shot to fame in 1960 when, aged only twenty-one, he had ended Booty's five-year reign as 100-mile champion. Kirby, short and stocky with massive thigh muscles like Rik van Looy's, was at his best over 100 miles when the going was hard: on a cold and windy day his name was sure to come to the top of the list. He was one of the army cyclists nurtured by Major Harry Keates, and he achieved his B.A.R. during his final national service year. On leaving the army and entering his family business however, his serious cycling came to an end. There were two other top-class army riders who narrowly missed topping the B.A.R. in the early sixties: Roger Wilkings and John Baylis, who were both in the six-foot plus tradition of Jowers, Booty and Wiltcher. Wilkings came close to the four-hour 100 in 1959 with a 4:1:44 ride, and he won the 12-hour championships three times in succession from 1960 to 1962, his 1960 mileage of 271.3 being just half a mile short of Owen Blower's competition record. The record books show that Baylis was the 100-mile champion in 1961, although he finished four seconds behind Keith Butler in a much talked-about result. Butler had caught Harry Middleton and John Bompas early on, but could not get away from them, and the three scrapped for a full 50 miles, first one leading then the other, before Butler finally dropped his two shadows. No other rider complained and Butler was the moral winner of the conflict, but officials had seen enough to have all three, including the unfortunate Butler, disqualified for paced riding.

    The 1961 B.A.R. had been won at the slowest average speed for seven years, but the following year's competition was the fastest ever, for 1962 was Frank Colden's miracle year, when he broke first the 50 record and then took the 100-mile record

Brian Kirby, 1961 B.A.R., who seemed to ride better on bad days.

onto a completely new level, as Booty had done before him and as Roach and Taylor would do again later in the sixties. Colden, a Guildford printer, had been racing for four or five years and was already edging into the top levels of time-trialling, finishing fifth in the 1960 B.A.R., a result which included fourth place in the 50 championship behind Wiltcher and sixth in the 100 behind Kirby. Colden took a year out in 1961 to assess where he was going, and he spent that time concentrating his mind on what lay ahead. He studied all that he could find about the world's leading athletes and cyclists, trying to discover the secrets of their success. From them he learned that there are no secrets, except burning ambition and complete dedication, and he determined to try a radical experiment, to see if he could raise himself to championship level. He switched to a part-time job to give himself more time to train, and pursued a ferocious training regime, maintained throughout the winter of 1961-62, riding between 50 and 100 miles almost every day, almost always alone, often in the dark and the cold, and always pushing himself to the limits. The mental discipline behind this regime was intense and demanding, and Colden would bargain with himself, trying to find excuses to take a day off, but his willpower prevailed. From being a very good time-triallist, he emerged in the early summer of 1962 as an athlete whom his friends and rivals scarcely recognised. His experiment had succeeded and

Frank Colden revolutionised time-trial records in just one season, then slipped out of the sport.

he later recalled that, after the purgatory of his training, the racing seemed almost easy: it seemed to him that he had a right to win after all that he had endured. In the 50-mile national title race in July, he beat all the top riders including McCoy, Bonner, Kirby, Cromack and Butler, by a huge margin, and the following month he demolished Wiltcher's competition record by more than a minute with his 1:52:38. In that race, Chris Munford also broke the old record but saw his time overtaken by Colden's.

But in between these two 50s came the ride that really put Colden in the history books. In the Bath Road 100 in August, which was also the national championship, he became the second man inside four hours, not simply bettering Ray Booty's six-year old record, but annihilating it by an incredible margin. The cycling world had long been waiting for Booty's time to be up-dated, but it was stunned by Colden's 3:54:23, more than four minutes faster than Booty. That morning was the vindication of all Colden's efforts, for he recalled almost floating in a cyclist's nirvana, without pain and virtually without effort, finishing relaxed and unruffled. He now had two championships and two national records, and was a certainty for the B.A.R. The only question remaining was by how much he would he break the 12-hour record. But here fate intervened in a bizarre fashion: a cat dashed into his path during the title race, and he crashed heavily and was unable to finish. Yet there were signs that his dominance was not so complete at this distance: having led Roger Wilkings by almost ten minutes at the 100-mile mark, his lead had been cut to three minutes at 160 miles when the crash occurred. Wilkings won his third national title, and Colden had to rest for several weeks before attempting the 12 that he needed to take the B.A.R. In this he succeeded with 260 miles in a race where he finished second to Doug Meekins. The B.A.R. was his, and the racing fraternity had all winter to digest Colden's sensational breakthrough, and to speculate on what he would do next year. In fact he did nothing, for he was at last free of his self-imposed challenge. He knew he could not go higher, and the only way off this summit was down. He could not face another winter of training and sacrifice like the one he had imposed on himself before, and he planned to slip out of the limelight. Early in 1963 however, he was told that he was being short-listed for world championship selection, and he did begin training again, but a crash spoiled his preparation, so that he never raced at the top level again, and soon quit the sport altogether. Colden's was an unusual story of a man who pushed himself to the limit to see how fast he could ride, and having done so he stepped back with a sense of freedom, without feeling driven to try again and again. He looked coolly and rationally at what he had achieved and what it had cost, and decided it was time to move on in life. His great year became part of time-trialling history, but the human story behind it is just as intriguing, raising questions about how far an individual can push himself and why, and about the place of sporting achievement in the context of one's life as a whole.

Colden's successor as B.A.R. was in his way just as sensational: Peter Hill was only eighteen years old when he took the title in 1963, and he remains to this day the youngest ever winner. 1963 was obviously the year of youth, for the aggregate age of the top three - with Ron Spencer second and Doug Meekins third - was only sixty. Hill's average speed was noticeably slower than Colden's and Wiltcher's had been, but his times would still be hard for any eighteen-year-old to beat today: 1:56:4 for the 50, 4:1:35 for the 100 and a 12 of 257.2, and moreover the competition was intense in 1963, with five men in contention on the very last day. On that last Sunday in September, Hill was camped by the start of the final 50 in Leicestershire, and when he awoke at 5 a.m. the sound of the wind already moving the treetops told him that no improvements would be possible that day, and that the title was his. He had broken no competition records and won no championships – Allsopp took the 50 title, Derek Woodings the 100, and Ron Spencer the 12 - but not surprisingly Hill was being hailed as a future world-beater. Some critics warned that he had done too much too soon, for he had risen from a novice cyclist to B.A.R. in two short seasons: incredible as it seems, he rode his first race, a 25 in 1:4 in April 1962, aged sixteen, and by September 1963 he was B.A.R. In his first season he had ridden 4:23 for the 100 and a 247-mile 12 when still only seventeen. Hill was a quiet, likeable boy, one of a large family in the South Yorkshire mining town of Askern, who lived and breathed cycling, going off on cycle-camping holidays in the middle of the racing season. He had no coach, and claimed no special secrets; he was not phenomenally fast, but he possessed an extraordinary natural strength over the longer distances. In the winter of 1963-64, Hill trained 1,000 miles per month, and in the 1964 season the sceptics were proved wrong, as he improved all his performances to take the B.A.R. for the second time in a quite decisive fashion. This time he won the 100 championship, and later became the third man inside four hours for the distance with a 3:57:12 that assured him of the B.A.R., seven minutes faster than second man Eric Moody. Hill's 50 time of 1:51:39 had stood as competition

Peter Hill, teenage sensation of 1963, still the youngest ever B.A.R. winner.

record for a few minutes in the multi-record race in which Breedon's 1:50:3 was the highlight. Only Hill's 12 of 261.2 was slower than Moody's and slower than Mike McNamara's, who was third. Hill might perhaps have gone on to dominate the B.A.R. distances for years to come, or he might have burnt out or lost interest, but in any case he had other ambitions, and he went to France early in 1965, racing very successfully as an amateur before turning pro for Peugeot alongside Simpson. He held the yellow jersey in the 1966 Tour de l'Avenir, and he twice finished in second place in the amateur Grand Prix des Nations, beating Bernard Thevenet and Luis Ocana among others. But Hill's career as a professional was a disappointment: stage racing at this level proved to be beyond him, largely because he was not a strong enough climber. He started the 1967 Tour de France, still aged only 22, but failed to finish. In 1968 he was back in England riding briefly as a pro for Bob Jackson, before returning to settle in France, although he soon retired from serious racing. Once again the European pro scene and the mirage of the Tour de France had proved the graveyard for the ambitions of a talented English rider, yet Hill retains his unique place in the record books by virtue of his outstanding rides at such a young age.

There is perhaps something slightly lacking in the B.A.R. competition if the winner breaks no records in the course of the year and wins none of the championships. Wiltcher and Colden had demonstrated their superiority beyond all doubt by doing both, but Kirby had not, nor had Hill in his first year, and the same was true of the 1965 B.A.R. Keith Stacey. But Stacey - nicknamed "the Cheshire Cat" for no apparent reason, for he was never photographed smiling although he did come from Cheshire - was only twenty years old, and had only been cycling for four years. He was certainly thought of as a short-distance rider, for he won silver medals in both the 25 and the 50 championship in 1965, and the B.A.R. target emerged almost by accident. Stacey did not even contest the national championship 100 or 12 , won respectively by Derek Woodings and Eric Matthews, and entered his 12 "just for experience". It was Stacey's three-minute margin in his 50 which gave him the B.A.R. title, for the second and third men, Chris Holloway and Mike McNamara, had virtually identical 100s and 12s. Just as Hill had done, Stacey raised his game in the following year by improving both his 50 and his 100 (though not his 12) and winning the 100 championship, but unfortunately none of this brought him a second title, for, having led the B.A.R. tables from the start, he came up against Arthur Metcalfe's concentrated late challenge which gave him his unique victory just weeks after winning the road-race championship. Metcalfe was way ahead in his 100 time - he was only the fourth to get inside four hours - and his 12 narrowly missed Blower's competition record. Only his 50 was slower, inevitably, than all those who had ridden in the late 50 on Boroughbridge when Pete Smith set his competition record time of 1:49:22.

Metcalfe's epic performance in 1966 has provided ammunition ever since for roadmen who claim that time-trialling is unreal, a second-best form of racing. How else, they ask, could a roadman take the top time-trialling award in the country with such contemptuous ease in just three straight rides? A good question, but it would have more point if it had ever been done again, which it hasn't. There never has been another Arthur Metcalfe - a B.A.R. who was riding and finishing the Tour de France six months after receiving his trophy. Nevertheless Metcalfe himself, having won the award, joined the growing number of B.A.R. critics, pointing out its basic flaw that those who compete in it do not necessarily race against each other in the same events - surely a very odd form of competition. Metcalfe too had won no championships and broken no records, yet he had ended the season with the title of best all-round time-triallist: did that really make sense? Metcalfe suggested instead a move away from the emphasis on pure speed to a format where a dozen or so races

Keith Stacey B.A.R. in 1965, looked set to repeat his win in 1966 until Arthur Metcalfe sensationally invaded the world of time-trialling.

each year, including some hilly events, should be designated as the B.A.R. counters. He argued that this would bring all the contending riders face to face and give a truer result. Many others have suggested similar plans, and such competitions have come into being, but the B.A.R. in its classic form still survives.

Metcalfe's B.A.R. was won at a record average speed, and indeed he inaugurated a glorious period of five years in which the record was taken higher every year. He was not a contender for the B.A.R. in 1967 and the title went to one of the most durable riders of the time, Mike McNamara, who finished in the top twelve every year from 1964 until 1971, and who came back yet once more in 1974 to finish second to Phil Griffiths. McNamara's B.A.R. year included a very fast 100 of 3:58, and at last a decisive beating of Blower's nine-year-old 12-hour record, with 276.5 miles. But it was Mac's misfortune that his ride that day was overshadowed, and always will be, by Beryl Burton, who went three quarters of a mile further. The story of Beryl catching Mac and offering him a liquorice allsort as she went past has deservedly entered time-trialling legend. Compared with Hill and Stacey, Mac, who was thirty-two years old, seemed almost a veteran, but had been building strength and steadily improving for fifteen years, and had taken the national 12-hour championship the year before. In 1967 he formed the ambition of taking the B.A.R. average speed over 25 m.p.h. for the first time, and failed by only the narrowest of margins with 24.955 m.p.h. Behind McNamara in the B.A.R. in second, third and fourth places were the all-powerful Clifton C.C. trio of Pete Smith, 50-mile record-holder, Roy Cromack, that year's 12-hour champion, and John Watson the 100-mile champion.

In 1968 the B.A.R. trophy went south, and with it the distinction of reaching the magic 25 m.p.h. average. In winning the title that year, Martyn Roach demonstrated his complete superiority by taking two national championships and two competition records. In the 50 championship Roach became the second rider to go inside 1:50, with his time

of 1:49:56, almost two minutes ahead of Roy Cromack, and this time not on the magical Boroughbridge course but on the Bath Road, with a headwind finish. The 100 championship three weeks later was even better, an epic battle on the A1 with John Watson, in which Watson was leading by over one minute from Roach with just eight miles to go, with both men on record-breaking schedule. But in the last five miles it was Watson who cracked, and Roach who pulled back the deficit and stormed home to win by a slender seven seconds, and take almost three minutes from Colden's 1962 record, with 3:51:41. The third man, Alan Boden, was four minutes behind the pair, and four riders had gone inside four hours in one event for the first time. This was the first R.T.T.C. championship at which drug-testing was introduced. Few people seriously believed that drugs were being used by time-triallists, but in the climate of the time it was probably a necessary step. At the end of 1967 the B.C.F. racing committee chairman had stated, almost in passing, that he knew drug-taking to be rife in time-trialling as well as in road-racing. The R.T.T.C. was incensed and challenged him to produce evidence for this statement, but none was ever forthcoming. It was evidently an unguarded remark, based on rumour and hearsay, but one which reflected the atmosphere of suspicion sur-

Martyn Roach, B.A.R. in 1968, prolific winner of championships, and formidable roadman too.

rounding the drugs issue.

Roach looked a near-certainty for the B.A.R. but he made absolutely sure by improving on McNamara's 12-hour record with a ride of 277.17, although this missed beating Beryl's 12-hour mark by about 150 yards. Roach's rewards were first a massive beating of the 25 m.p.h. average with 25.428 m.p.h., and second comparisons with Frank Colden, for no one had taken the B.A.R. in such grand style since Colden's miraculous 1962 campaign. There was a direct link with Colden's victory, for Kevin Fairhead, who with Jeff Marshall was a member of Roach's winning Hounslow team, had also been the third counter in Colden's Camberley team. Roach was just twenty-one years old, and although he would not win the B.A.R. again, he raced at the top level for another ten years, becoming national 50-mile champion in 1969 and 1972, 100-mile champion in 1976, and 12-hour champion in 1971, 1975 and 1976. In the 50 title race of 1972, Engers was chasing the elusive 25 and 50 double, but was convincingly beaten into second place by Roach. Roach was also a feared roadman, capable of riding away from a bunch and time-trialling to victory, as he did in the 1969 Harp G.P., which he won by four minutes after a sixty-mile lone break. He rode in three Milk Races, his best finish being eighth overall in 1972.

Probably the only tax-inspector ever to become a champion cyclist, Roach was blunt and outspoken in his views on the sport, and made himself unpopular more than once during his career. He poured scorn on the ultra-fast times achieved on the Boroughbridge courses; he disapproved of amateur cyclists who gave up full-time work in order to train; and he asked what purpose was served when British amateurs travelled to world or Olympic championships to get slaughtered. Roach was most unwilling to go to the Mexico Olympics because of the altitude, and his own dislike of flying, but his statements provoked a good deal of criticism, and the counter-claim that to represent one's country at the Olympics should be the highest goal of any sportsman. In the following year he was a member of the team-trial-trial squad at the world championships in Czechoslovakia, where our very strong team of Watson, Smith, Dailey and Roach was tenth, nine minutes behind the winning Swedes. This was in fact the best British TTT result of the decade, and in the 1970 World Championships at Leicester Britain's team of Roach, Marshall, Taylor and Tooby was back to 16th place, again nine minutes down on the Russians; perhaps Roach's point had been proved.

John Watson, B.A.R. in 1970, who set 50-mile and 12-hour records that withstood all attacks for a decade.

Given the soaring of time-trial speeds in this period, logic would suggest that the margin of improvement would become smaller and smaller, that records were now so fast that only seconds would be nibbled off here and there; yet nothing of the kind happened. Watson's 50 record in 1970 was a phenomenal improvement of almost four minutes, but it had been preceded by another quantum leap - the 1969 100-mile record by Anthony Taylor. Roach's record of 3:51:41 had already been brought down by Pete Smith to 3:50:20, but this time was only three weeks old when Taylor smashed it to pieces with his 3:46:37, the first ride inside 3:50, and inside by a massive margin. Conditions were good on the Boroughbridge course, but Taylor was out on his own that day, with riders of the calibre of Phil Griffiths, Jeff Marshall, Mike McNamara and Martyn Roach beaten by between eight and eighteen minutes, and there was a stunned feeling that a record so recently set could be shattered by so much. On the same day the Bath Road 100 was won by Bob Porter in a time of 4:11:1, the slowest time for the event since 1951, making a poignant contrast between the old classic and the A1 course which now obviously held the key to all B.A.R. ambitions. Only weeks before his new record, Taylor had won the national championship on the Bath Road course in a time of 3:54:8, with Roach in second place. Even Taylor himself admitted that the dominance of the Boroughbridge course was unhealthy, that rides there could sometimes be unreal, unlike anything that could happen anywhere else. Taylor was an interesting rider, who had been second to Roach in the 1968 B.A.R. He may have been one of those frowned on by Roach for giving up work in order to race, but Taylor reasoned that you have only

one chance to reach the top in any sport, and he determined to sacrifice everything to that goal while he was young and at the peak of his strength. Rugged, muscular and crew-cut, he looked rather tough and forbidding, but he was a thoughtful rider, with his own advanced ideas on diet, emphasising cereals and salads, and in his training he was an exception to the growing vogue for interval training, for he had reverted to the long steady-state ideas that most others riders were now abandoning: his weekly total was 500 miles or more, with individual rides of up to 200 miles, and it clearly worked for him.

Taylor rode 277.7 miles in the national 12-hour championship, good enough to add half a mile to Roach's competition record, but still only good enough for second place, for John Watson was pounding to the title and

Anthony Taylor, B.A.R. in 1969, who exploded the 100 record with his 3:46 ride.

a new record of 281.8 miles. This was the first of Watson's two phenomenal records, this one staying on the shelf for ten full years. Taylor did not contest the B.A.R. in 1970, having plans to switch to road-racing which however did not materialise. He was a member of Britain's TTT team in the 1970 world's at Leicester, where he finished demoralised in a state of total collapse, and announced that he would never race again, and soon afterwards he vanished from the sport as suddenly and completely as Frank Colden had. In his absence, and with Pete Smith now a professional, Watson convincingly headed the B.A.R in 1970, his stunning 50 record being the key to his success, but his 100 of 3:53:38 and his 12 of 279.4 were also the fastest of the year by a long way. His winning average speed was now 0.042 m.p.h. short of 26 .m.p.h., just two years after Roach had become the first to top 25 .m.p.h. But Watson, a six-foottall builder from a family that had cycling in its blood, now decided that he had achieved all that he wanted to: marriage and the family business took him out of the sport at the age of just 24. The almost simultaneous departure of Taylor, Watson, Cromack and Pete Smith, signalled the end of a glorious period in time-trialling, when it seemed that anything could happen, that records could be beaten by inconceivable margins by any one of a number of riders.

In the world of straight-out R.R.A. records, the sixties saw far less activity that the fifties had, but one outstanding milestone was passed in June 1965 when Dick Poole took the End-to-End record inside two days for the first time, with a time of 1:23:46:35. Poole was an experienced 24-hour rider, not in the championship class of Carline, Matthews or Smith, but he had nurtured a lifetime's ambition to take this record, and it was a perfectly-judged ride, a triumph of perseverance. It began badly enough however when he crashed and injured himself after 130 miles, and lost half an hour on his schedule. Not until Perth at 600 miles was he up on the existing record of Reg Randall, and not until more than 800 miles had passed did he catch up with his own schedule. Over the last difficult climbs in Caithness however, he was moving at an unprecedented speed, sensing that the 48-hour target could be his. After a brief rest at John O'Groats, he set off to add the 1,000 mile record, which he achieved by well over two hours. Sadly, when the whole route was later re-measured, it proved to be just over a mile short of the distance, and Poole was deprived of the second part of his triumph. The tandem End-to-End was brought closer to the solo time in two stages by two virtually unknown club pairs. In 1960 Jim Bailey and Jack Forrest brought the old time down to 2:4:48, and then in 1966 Pete Swinden and John Withers beat that time convincingly with their 2:2:14, a superb record which still stands and which is more than an hour better than the mixed tandem record put up in 2000 by a very star pair of distance riders - Andy Wilkinson and Lynne Taylor. There were some other memorable R.T.T.C. competition records too. Dave Crook became the first tricyclist to go under the hour with his 59:58 in 1966, while in 1965 Martin Perks and Eric Beauchamp up-dated the Joy-Bearsdmore tandem 100 record with a flying 3:36:54.

Perhaps the ultimate record-breaking ride of this extraordinary period was the 24-hour, which fell to the third man of the great Clifton C.C. trio, Roy Cromack. Incredibly this was Cromack's only ride at the distance, for he was not a 24-hour man in the traditional mould, and yet he entered cycling history as the first man to top 500 miles, and he placed the record out of reach for an unprecedented 28 years. The way to the 500-mile 24 had perhaps been prepared by the announcement of a special

Dick Poole, the man who brought the End-to-End record inside two days in 1965.

medal for the feat by *Cycling*, and by the progress of the record, first with Eric Matthews's topping 490 miles in 1964, and then by Nim Carline's 496 miles in 1966, which brought the magic distance within sight. Carline, friend, employer and training partner of Beryl Burton, was the phenomenon of 24-hour riding in the sixties, winning the championship an unequalled five times, and starting his own revolution in his riding at this distance, pushing big gears and powering through the first 100-150 miles at full blast, attempting to demoralise his rivals. It worked pretty often for him, but sometimes he blew up and had to quit, as he did in the race with Cromack. Carline had also pulled out of an End-to-End record attempt in 1966 after a fast start which saw him well up on Poole's schedule. Perhaps the ultimate 24-hour master was London's Cliff Smith, who won the championship just once in 1964 at the age of 44, but whose chief claim to fame lay in his having won no less than eighteen 24s. Smith was the totally dedicated, old-style distance man: thin and bald, riding a hub-gear machine even in 1970, he looked anything but an athlete, yet nothing would ever make him give up, and he was never photographed without a big grin on his face. Perhaps he was entitled to smile, because some years before Smith had suffered appalling injuries as a result of his army service with the artillery, and had spent years recovering, being warned that he might never even walk again. Smith also took one memorable R.R.A. record in 1965, the Edinburgh-London, in which he broke Cyril Heppleston's pre-war time with his 18:49 on a bitterly cold November day. These men trained by clocking up their huge distances, Carline for example thinking little of a 200-

Roy Cromack, first to break the 500-mile barrier for the 24, setting a record that stood for 28 years.

mile run from Leeds through to the Lake District and back on a Sunday.

This was where Cromack differed from the rest, for he had started as a short-distance time-triallist and track-pursuiter, switching to road-racing and riding for Britain in the Peace Race and the Olympic team time-trial in 1968. He had won the national 12-hour championship in 1967, but was certainly not thought of as a stayer like Matthews, Carline or Smith, for he was a 54-minute 25-miler and had gone inside four hours for the 100. The idea of the 500-mile 24 appealed to him as a special challenge, and he reasoned that, if he were mentally determined enough, speed training should be perfectly adequate to prepare for the required 20.8 m.p.h. target speed. Immensely long distances would, he believed, drag the body down instead of building it up. He therefore completed just one 120-mile night-ride for the experience, and all his training followed his normal pattern, rarely more than 50 miles but very fast; the rest was concentration and scheduling, which he enjoyed for he was a mathematician by profession. In the Mersey R.C. National Championship at the end of July, his theories were brilliantly vindicated. He kept his gears down, and allowed himself to be caught and dropped by Beryl Burton after little more than 100 miles, as she flew ahead to a lead of 20 minutes and more. Cromack coolly stuck to his schedule however, and at 250 miles he had caught the faster-starting Carline, and fifty miles later he had the satisfaction of re-passing Beryl, who packed soon after. It was not only Cromack who received this news with some joy, but Christine Moody, who went on to finish and set a new women's competition record of 427 miles. Inevitably overshadowed by Cromack's ride, Christine's fine record was itself to stand for fourteen years. Cromack was cheered by the crowd on the finishing circuit, who knew that they were witnessing a historic time-trialling achievement, until he flashed passed the 500-mile mark, then eased off for a further twenty minutes or so, until he finally rolled onto the grass with 507 miles accomplished in his first and last 24. Eric Matthews was second with 492 miles, and Cliff Smith fourth with 473.

In a matter of months in this summer of 1969 we had seen Enger's 25 record, Taylor's 100, Watson's 12 and Cromack's 24, and in the following year Watson's 50 would complete this miraculous period of record-breaking. All records are there to be broken, and of course these would eventually go the way of all others, but they survived well into the next decade, far longer than most records before or since. There was no doubt that something revolutionary had happened in the late sixties, that some kind of limit had been reached, and that a few years consolidation must follow before the next leap forward.

Hill-climbing in the sixties saw repeated battles between the same handful of specialists who emerged every October to humble the much bigger names from time-trialling and road-racing. The decade opened with two fantastically close wins for Pete Graham from Russell Foster, first on Yorks Hill in Kent in 1961 and then on Nick O'Pendle in 1962; incredibly both these races were decided by one fifth of a second, surely at the very limit of timing accuracy. In the 1962 event, one fifth of a second also separated the third and fourth men, Dave Patten and Barry Shelley. Hill-climbers are noted for the length of their careers, none more so than Granville Sydney of Huddersfield, who first won the title on Winnats in 1963, won again on Dover's Hill in 1965, then collected three bronze medals before returning to his winning ways in 1969 and 1970. Sydney, known as "the

Beard", was often supported by his younger brother Graham, also a talented climber. The Beard had amassed a dozen hill-climb medals by the end of the sixties, and he went on to two more victories in 1972 and 1973, a record six hill-climb titles never subsequently equalled. Sydney later suffered from depression, and tragically he took his own life. The hill-climb title during these years was very much a northern possession, with Pete Greenhalgh from Nottingham being the nearest approach to a southern winner in 1966. Londoner Claude Kearley did take a silver medal in 1969, but that race at Llywel in South Wales was one of two occasions when there was a dead-heat for second place: Kearley had exactly the same time as Ralph Wilson, while in 1965 Pete Graham and Ron Martin also dead-heated for the silver medal on Dover's Hill.

Granville Sydney -"The Beard"- winner of six hill-climb titles between 1963 and 1973.

Cyclo-Cross

Cyclo-cross was another continental import - at least the name was, for a similar form of racing had existed in Britain for many years. International cyclo-cross events had taken place in France from the 1920s onwards, and a U.C.I. world championship was inaugurated in 1950, won by Jean Robic, the first post-war Tour de France winner in 1947. The equivalent British events were called scrambles, such as the famous Bagshot Scramble, and they often involved conditions as extreme as any seen later in cyclo-cross proper; crashes, hospitalisation and wrecked bikes were common. Searing starts, back-breaking gradients, wild descents, bumping over heathland or ploughing inches-deep in mire, vaulting styles, pedalling, running, and often sprawling in the mud - this was the traditional scramble. It was a highly entertaining form of racing, but for a different crowd of spectators from the six-day audiences. Slightly less extreme were the winter "roughriders" time-trials, which used narrow lanes and tracks. These were both a form of off-season competition, not taken too seriously by some of the riders. It was the upsurge of interest following that first world championship that led to more events, a new name and a more organised approach. Regional cyclo-cross associations were formed, all in the south and the midlands at this stage, and these came together in November 1954 to become the British Cyclo-

John Atkins, multi-champion in cyclo-cross in the 60s and 70s, and (below) one of his chief rivals, Keith Mernickle.

Cross Association. This was not an initiative from the N.C.U., but very much a grass-roots movement, as the B.L.R.C. had been, and the really interesting thing is that cyclo-cross in Britain and on the continent was classless, open to all riders, with no licensing and no labelling of amateur or professional. The idea was to keep things simple, keep the element of fun, but to build up cyclo-cross as a worthwhile branch of the sport. In 1954 the N.C.U. noticed the rise of this new-style winter sport, and responded by inviting applicants to put their names forward for the world championships that were to take place in Italy, mentioning however that riders would have to pay their own expenses; were they surprised when there were no takers?

The first B.C.C.A. national championship was run at Welwyn in February 1955, and from a field of almost 100 the race was won by south Londoner Alan Jackson, who later took the bronze medal in the 1956 Olympic road race. There was a general belief that gears would foul up, so Jackson rode a single freewheel of 59 inches, while some competitors even favoured a fixed wheel. Jackson was one of the top roadmen in the southern area, and a leading figure in forming the Southern C.C.A. and his presence showed the seriousness with which cyclo-cross was now being regarded. He led a British team to the 1955 world championships in Saarbrucken, but they were well beaten, and no further teams were sent during the 1950s. Continental courses were generally drier and faster than British ones. Jackson retained his title in 1956, from midlanders Don Smith and Mick Weston, with Billy Holmes in fifth place. Jackson was succeeded in 1957 and 58 by another double champion from south London, Don Stone, now riding gears like most of the others. One striking thing about these early years of cyclo-cross, as well as the roughriders events, is the primitive ideas about winter clothing: photographs of January and February races show riders struggling over snow-covered hillsides and splashing through icy puddles wearing shorts, sleeveless jerseys and no hats; did they think it was a sign of weakness to protect themselves from the cold?

In 1959 the title went away from London for the first time and became thereafter a possession of the midlands: Bill Spence won in 1959, Dave Briggs in 1960, and in 1961 the 18 year-old John Atkins began his remarkable career that would take him to a dozen national titles over fifteen years. 1961 was also the year when Britain began sending regular teams to the world championships, Atkins, Briggs, Paddy Hoban and Bill Radford travelling to Hanover, but although cyclo-cross was an open sport, most of the continental competitors were professional roadmen, and the class difference was too great for the British amateurs to bridge. In the mid-sixties the first phase of Atkins's reign was interrupted by illness and by Percy Stallard's son Mick, who took the national championship in 1963, 64 and 65. By this time the independent idea

had spread to cyclo-cross, and Keith Mernickle, riding for E.G.Bates, rivalled Stallard as the country's top crossman. In 1964 Mernickle, aged only 19, had been unlucky to lose the championship to Stallard after crashing, and he put up one of the best-ever British performances at the world championships in Belgium to finish eleventh. Atkins came back in 1966, the year in which the independents became professionals. After a dozen years of open sport, it was felt that two titles must now be awarded, although in this first year they were still competed for in one race. Stallard had signed for Falcon by this time, but he was fourth in the title race, won by Atkins, still an amateur. The slightly-built Atkins was to prove almost unbeatable over the next few years, especially when the going was wet and rough and called for a great deal of running; he took the professional title in 1969, 70 and 71, and in 1968 he achieved his best-ever fifth place in the world championships in Luxembourg, finishing just 14 seconds behind the winner, de Vlaeminck. More pros like Dave Nie, Mick Ives and Roger Claridge were taking a serious interest in cyclo-cross, while Barry Moss, Ollie Nagle and Daryll Brassington were now the top amateurs.

Above, extreme cyclo-cross, 1950's style. Below, Chris Wreghitt, winner of five national titles in succession, 1978-1982.

By the end of the sixties, cyclo-cross was firmly established both as off-season training and as a serious form of competition in its own right. The "roughriders" events were a thing of the past, transformed into the more conventional "hardriders" hilly time-trials, but many of the scrambles had survived, merged into the newer cyclo-cross programme. From its original base in the south and the midlands, cyclo-cross spread to all the regions, the first Scottish star being Andy Kerr, who won his national title three times from 1960 to 1962. Cyclo-cross was used as training by many roadmen, but few cyclo-cross champions seem to have crossed over to become top-flight roadmen. One who might have done so successfully was Chris Wreghitt, enormously powerful in the early 80s, but whose career was halted by injury just as he secured a professional contract to ride in Europe.

Track Racing

Track racing in Britain in the sixties suffered perhaps even more than road-racing from a lack of stars able to win at international level. The track, as an arena where spectators can see the top riders in action at close quarters, needs such stars to maintain its hold on both public and riders alike - witness the excitement when Simpson came back for one of his guest appearances. Nevertheless domestic track racing provided a tremendous spring-board for some great British riders, such as Hoban, Webb, Porter and Hallam, and it did create stars of its own who gave enormous pleasure to the crowds at Herne Hill, Manchester, Nottingham, Coventry or Portsmouth. There are also enough famous names in the list of champions to show how important the track was as a school for road-racing and time-trialling: Clarey, 5-mile champion in 1962; Woodburn, pro pursuit champion in 1962; Cromack, 10-mile champion in 1964; Engers kilo champion in 1969; McCoy's Melling Wheelers team pursuit win in 1960, Bonner's Old Portlians' in 1962, and Webb's Solihull in 1965 and 1966. As in the 1950s, there was still no collective national championship meeting, instead the individual titles were allocated to various meetings throughout the season. Even in 1970, with the Leicester track re-surfaced for the world championships that summer, the idea of a bringing together a two-day or three-day championship meeting did not seem to occur to anyone.

The outstanding track personality as the decade opened was undoubtedly Lloyd Binch, who seemed to embody the enigma of success and failure in British racing. A courageous and entertaining sprinter, his career had begun in the early fifties in the days of Harris and Peacock, and it was in 1955 that he won the first of his seven successive national sprint titles. Binch retained the Harris-Peacock connection between Raleigh and track-racing, riding Raleigh bikes and working for them as a bike-tester - this job was either a pure fiction or it was the amateur cyclist's dream. Yet as the years passed, frustration

The track as arena for the stars: Coppi comes to Herne Hill in September 1958; Robinson leads the bunch. The day of this meeting was the very-day that Russell Mockridge was killed in Australia.

began to build up, for although Binch won a good number of international matches on the tracks of Europe, he could never bring back a single medal of any kind from any world or Olympic championship, although he did win the bronze medal at the 1958 Empire Games in Cardiff. It might have been nerves, so important in the sudden-death world of track sprinting, or it might have been technical mishaps, but whatever the reason Binch, who won trophy after trophy around the tracks at home, was always dogged by his reputation as a failure on the really big occasions. In 1961 he was named by the B.C.F. to go to the world championships in Zurich, but only if he travelled at his own expense, a mean insult to a rider who had given so much to the sport for almost ten years and who had by then been six times national champion. Perhaps Binch was aware of his vulnerability on big occasions, for he never seriously considered turning professional.

Binch's long career at the top was achieved at the expense of two other fine sprinters, Dave Handley and Karl Barton. It was Barton who reached the final of the Empire Games sprint in 1958, losing the gold medal to Dick Ploog of Australia, and it was Barton who finally drew a line under the Binch era by taking the national sprint championship in September 1962. But the end came in a unfortunate fashion, with Binch crashing badly in the last of their three-match semi-finals, leaving Barton to defeat Handley in two straight rounds in the final. Barton had been racing for nine years, constantly in Binch's shadow, and he now came into his own, keeping his national crown for three years, and repeating his silver medal win in the Commonwealth Games of 1962, before a serious crash in 1965 ended his racing career. Dave Handley was another long-term sprint rival to Binch and Barton, but he did what the others could not do, namely bring home a medal from a world championship, a bronze in 1960. Handley had come into track-racing via cycle speedway, and he struggled for years to gain international selection, and like all the sprinters of this time his career was punctuated by crashes and some horrific injuries, which they always seemed able to shrug off. But Handley did stand on the podium as national champion year after year in that most heart-stopping event, the tandem sprint, in which finishing speeds of 45 m.p.h. were common. Handley was the steersman, and with four different partners including Eric Thompson and Geoff Cooke, his reign in this event was just as long as Binch's in the solo sprint, beginning in 1957 and continuing for six full years. Perhaps even more remarkable was Thompson's graduation from stoker to steersman when Handley retired, for he then teamed up with Geoff Cooke for a further championship-winning period. This was the same Eric Thompson who had won the Empire Games gold medal in Vancouver in 1954, and who had partnered Pete Brotherton to tandem victories in the early fifties; Thompson ended with a total of nine national tandem titles spread over a period of fourteen years. The tandem sprint has since been abolished as a championship and as an international event because it is considered too dangerous. These remarkable long reigns of the sprint champions had ended by 1965, for after that the younger riders Roger Whitfield and Reg Barnett both won the title twice and Fred Booker once, Booker's best year being 1966 when he also won the kilo sprint.

Dave Handley rides cross-bar to Lloyd Binch, while heir-apparent Karl Barton looks on.

Lloyd Binch, six times national sprint champion.

After Sheil's departure to the professionals, the pursuit crown passed to a youthful Barry Hoban, who beat Alf Engers in the 1960 final and Harry Jackson in 1961. Jackson's turn came in 1963, but Jackson was an all-round trackie, capable of winning 5- and 10-mile events and even a 50-mile madison, rather than a specialist pursuiter, unlike his successor Hugh Porter, who completely dominated the scene for the next three years, and then took the professional title for another three. Porter also won the Commonwealth Games title in 1966 in Jamaica, where Ian Alsop took a gold medal in the 10-mile race, and Fred Booker the sprint silver. After Porter came Graham Webb and Brendan McKeown, before a great new talent emerged at the end of the decade: Ian Hallam's two pursuit championships in 1969 and 1970 and his gold medal at the Commonwealth Games in Edinburgh were preludes to his magnificent silver medal in the world championships at Leicester, ending years of disappointment for British trackmen at this level of racing. Hallam went on to many more honours and to become the spearhead of a new generation of British team pursuiters in the 1970s.

International track racing of a rather different kind came to England in the 1960s in the form of the Skol-sponsored six-day race, first at Earl's Court in 1967, and thereafter at Wembley. These events brought specialist riders from Belgium, Holland, Denmark and Germany, who would dominate the racing, but they were teamed with British pairs with whom the crowd could identify. Preceding the Madison sessions which made up the main race, there would be a programme of supporting events in which the crowds could look forward to seeing guest riders, especially if they were newly-crowned world champions, as Graham Webb was in 1967. Some of these supporting races produced memorable moments, like the one when Peter Post, giant of the six-day world, was beaten in an invitation pursuit by none other than Alf Engers. For the British competitors in the main event this new form of competition was tense, exhausting and dangerous. It was really the beginning of a learning process almost as radical as that of the 1950s, when British pioneers went to learn the road-racing scene in Europe. Whirling round the tiny, steeply-banked track at 30 m.p.h. in a group of twenty riders was a new and nerve-racking experience. The demands on the rider's concentration and skill were just as great as the physical demands, and just to survive the six days without crashing out was an achievement. Between 1967 and 1970 the British riders who got the chance to enter this challenging arena included Dave Bonner, Billy Holmes, Hugh Porter, Norman Hill, George Halls, Trevor Bull, Johnny Clarey, Albert Hitchen, and above all Tony Gowland. Gowland was a good professional roadman with Carlton, but not a big winner, yet he took brilliantly to this new discipline and went on to become a winner in the 1970s, partnering the top names in this field, including Patrick Sercu. Six-day racing was a spectacle very different from any other form of racing: it was glitzy and continental, taking place from the late evening until past midnight, as the spectators wined and dined in the track centre. The riders played to the gallery, the top men carefully orchestrating the racing to give the crowds what they wanted, even if it sometimes verged on fixing. It had its own set of complex rules, and its own stars with their very special skills. From the British point of view it was almost irrelevant who won the Skol sixes: it was the experience and the spectacle which mattered.

The Scottish Scene

Racing in Scotland, while overlapping with that in England, has always had its own identity. The few years after 1945 saw political conflicts that were perhaps even more confusing than those in England. There were two governing bodies established since the early 1930s: the Scottish Amateur Cycling Association controlled time-trials, and its rules were almost identical to those of the R.T.T.C. The other body, the National Cyclists' Union Scottish Section, promoted massed-start racing on closed circuits and track racing; in 1946 this body changed its name to the Scottish National Cyclists' Union, affiliated to the N.C.U. but still an independent entity. In 1934 the N.C.U. Scotland had promoted the Glasgow-Dunoon road race on open roads, and, for reasons which no one can now explain, there was no controversy and no objections by anybody, and this technically illegal race established itself as a classic. By 1945 the B.L.R.C. revolution had reached into Scotland, and several clubs became affiliated to it, and began a road-racing programme. Both the S.A.C.A and the Scottish N.C.U. dissociated themselves from this movement, and a split opened up exactly like that in England.

In 1947 the Scottish section of the B.L.R.C. adopted the name Scottish Cyclists' Union, an autonomous body but affiliated to the B.L.R.C. It was not long however before good sense prevailed, and for the good of the sport these three bodies moved towards amalgamation, accomplished in 1952 with the birth of the Scottish Cyclists' Union. This amalgamation was triggered by the S.A.C.A.'s decision in 1951 to promote its own road races on open roads, just as the N.C.U. would do in England in 1952. Interestingly enough, one of the main doubts preceding this decision concerned its implication for Anglo-Scots relations: would not any Scot riding a road-race immediately be barred from racing in England in both the N.C.U. and R.T.T.C. events, and would he not also be barred from international selection in British teams? It was clear that the move to open-road racing must be followed by special arrangements with the English authorities to ensure that this did not happen. It was equally obvious that there was now no reason not to move to a single

Jock Allison, Scottish champion and winner of the B.B.A.R. in 1945, still the only Scot ever to win the national title.

governing body in Scotland. The comparative ease with which the new S.C.U. was born suggests once again that the perpetuation of the split in England was due to obstinacy and personal hostility between the rival officials. The S.C.U. entered into agreements with all the English bodies, which led to the bizarre situation where Scottish riders could ride in any events in England, while English riders still could not. Initially open-road road-racing in Scotland had to take place on quiet roads, on Sundays only, and start by 8 a.m.

Some friction arose in 1955 about B.A.R. eligibility: if Scottish riders could take part in, and win, the national B.B.A.R., could not English or Welsh riders travel to Scotland to compete in the B.A.R. there? At first it seemed that they probably could, although in practice none did. But relations between the S.C.U. and the R.T.T.C. soon became strained, mainly over the issue of national championships, following Janet Sutherland's victory in the women's 100 championship in 1954. It all stemmed from a rather comic confusion between English and British, and again when Janet Sutherland claimed her 25 time as a British record, the R.T.T.C. replied that there was no such thing as a British record, only R.T.T.C., Scottish, Welsh and Irish records. For many years both bodies adopted the position that their own championships must be native championships, a rule changed only in 1989. The B.B.A.R. was different, for if it were not open to all, it could evidently not be termed the British B.A.R. The rule here was that counting events for the English (British?) and Scottish B.A.R.'s had to be ridden in those countries. This could lead to some curious situations, as it did in 1957 when E.V. Mitchell won the Scots B.A.R with Ken Laidlaw second, but Laidlaw finished above Mitchell in the national B.B.A.R., based on the times he achieved in England.

For geographical reasons Scottish racing was naturally concentrated into the three main areas of population: the Glasgow-Ayr region in the west, Edinburgh and Dundee in the east, but there were clubs and a fair amount of racing in Fife and Aberdeen, and some

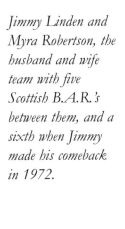

Jimmy Linden and Myra Robertson, the husband and wife team with five Scottish B.A.R.'s between them, and a sixth when Jimmy made his comeback in 1972.

in the Borders too. Glasgow riders have tended to dominate the scene because there are more of them, and the tradition of competitive cycling there is very strong; however the number of champions and record-breakers from eastern clubs is scarcely less than those from the west. As in England, cycling was predominantly a working-class sport, a sport of miners, factory workers and technicians. Scottish cyclists always felt, probably rightly, that their sport received scant coverage in the pages of *Cycling*, but there was never a big enough market to support their own magazine. One feature of Scottish racing which had no parallel in England was the grass-track circuit contested by unlicensed professionals. At the village games mainly in the agricultural districts in the east of the country, dozens of these riders turned out each weekend to race for cash prizes, alongside the runners, the shot-putters and the tug-of-war teams. It was an intriguing form of grass-roots cycling, utterly divorced from the S.C.U. or the B.C.F. and their rules and regulations. Many of these riders were farm workers, and they prepared themselves by a form of cyclo-cross training on fields and paths. This was a type of competition that was rooted in local communities, a link with the carefree pre-war days, when anyone with a sporting talent was free to use it to earn himself a little pocket-money, with no thought of rules and regulations, or of progressing to national or international selection.

Gordon McNaught, road-racing star who took the 1962 Scottish B.A.R. in three straight rides.

Although it was normally quite isolated from the English scene, Scottish racing in the post-war years started with a bang through the triumph in 1945 in the national B.A.R. competition of Jock Allison. It was an unprecedented Scottish victory over all the top English riders, Overton, Derbyshire, Heppleston, Maitland and Harding, made all the more impressive because Allison was only one of four Scots in the top twelve: Dave Scott was third, Tom Love seventh and Jim Walker twelfth. All their rides were achieved in Scotland, on courses normally reckoned slower than the better English courses, although this idea may have been mere supposition, since few riders if any raced on both sides of the border. Allison was just twenty years old, an Edinburgh miner, whose rather unusual hobby was sunbathing. Allison's three B.A.R. rides were all Scottish records, and he had undoubtedly set new standards for Scottish time-trial-lists to aim at. In 1946 Allison was again the best Scot, but finished fourth overall in the B.B.A.R., with times that were slightly slower than those of 1945, except the 12-hour, in which he narrowly improved his own record, becoming the first Scottish rider to top 250 miles. Tom Love was close behind in the B.B.A.R. in fifth place. Strangely perhaps, Allison never won a Scottish time-trial championship in the years 1945 or 46, but he did win the road-race title in 1947, and he had won the classic Tour de Trossachs mountain time-trial in 1945. From 1947 to 1955 inclusive, no Scottish time-trial championships were held, although there was a Scottish B.A.R award each year; the championships were revived by the S.C.U. in 1956. One record which Allison never took however was the 25: it had been taken below the hour in 1944 by Dave Scott with his 59:55, but another eight

Fraser Connell, versatile road-race and time-trail champion.

years were to elapse before the first 58 minute ride, and then it was the visiting English champion, Stan Higginson, who did it. In between, the record had been skimmed by seconds here and there, by Scott's own brother James among others. There was a third Scott brother, Will, who had held the 25 record before the war; remarkably, one or other of these three brothers held the 25 record for eleven years. The outstanding short-distance man of the late fifties was Hyslop Dickson, three times 25-mile champion in 1959-61, and 50-mile champ and record-breaker in 1959.

Allison was not the only pace-setter in Scottish time-trialling in the 1940s, for in 1949 and 1950 the first star of women's racing, Isobel Adams (later Campbell) won the first two women's B.A.R. competitions at 10, 25 and 50 miles, and set every record in the book, including the first sub-five hour 100, which she achieved in 1949. Isobel was the first of a long line of women riders who seemed able to dominate the racing scene in Scotland for four or five years in succession. In the absence of individual women's titles before the 1980s, the B.A.R. was the one big prize in women's racing, and Isobel's successor, Janet Sutherland, headed the list each year from 1951 to 1954. She took the 50 record down from 2:20 to 2:13, and her 25 record of 1:3:54 of 1953 was faster than the English record at that time, and it lasted until Beryl Burton smashed it in 1969. Serious women cyclists were pretty rare in Scotland, and after Janet Sutherland it has to be admitted that there was little progress in records or B.A.R. speeds, even during the long championship reign of Sheelagh Fraser in the late 1960s. Rita Jones and Grace Brierley, both of the same Glasgow club, the Johnstone Wheelers, alternated for the B.A.R. in the 1950s, and Rita set a fine 100 record of 4:41:40 in 1958, which survived for more than twenty years. Mixed male-female racing was introduced into Scottish time-trialling in 1964, five years before it arrived in England.

The 1948 season was marked by ferocious winds in Scotland, and the B.A.R. was won in a slowish time by Doug Murphy, a man known as the star of bad mornings. In 1949 the rider emerged who placed the Allison era firmly in the past: Jim Hamilton, the Ayrshire miner who went on to win the B.A.R. three times and who in 1949 wiped out Allison's Scottish 50 and 100 records. He was forced to take a year out in 1950, having crashed during the Empire Games in New Zealand, breaking his wrist badly, and the B.A.R. was won by Willie Shewan. Hamilton was back in 1951 to take his second B.A.R. in a dramatic final-day 50, lifting himself from fourth to first position, with a very narrow victory over Bob Scott, the man he had beaten in 1949. Hamilton's third trophy came in 1952, when he once again lowered the 100 record and added the 12 record to his tally. Hamilton could surely have become the first four-times winner of the B.A.R. had he not emigrated to New Zealand in 1953. After Hamilton, the B.A.R. went east for four years, with Tom Blakely, a stonemason from Hawick, and Ben Balneaves, the R.A.F. man from Forfar, both winning two titles, and improving the Scottish records from 50 miles to 12 hours. A major milestone was passed in 1954 when Ernie Mitchell - "E.V." as he was always known - took the Scottish 50 record inside two hours with his 1:59:53, beating Balneaves's month-old figures of 2:0:39. This ride came on the same July weekend when Eileen Sheridan and Crimes and Arnold were setting their historic End-to-End records. Mitchell went on to probably his best year in 1957, when he brought the Scottish 25 record back home, by skimming 2 seconds off Dave Keeler's 1952 time with 58:9, and he won the B.A.R. trophy, a very unusual feat for a record-breaking 25-miler. The 1955 result was one of the closest ever recorded, with Blakely regaining his title by just 0.005 m.p.h. from Joe Millar, Balneaves's Forfar club-mate, with Balneaves himself now in third place. Millar had featured in the B.A.R. tables for eight years, was second three times, but finally took the top spot in 1958, his rides including a new Scottish 100 record of 4:10:24.

In third place in 1958 was the man who was to dominate the B.A.R. for the next three years and set a new series of Scottish records, Jimmy Linden. By 1959 Linden was head and shoulders above his rivals in Scotland, but he improved still further in 1960 and 1961, moving up to take ninth place in the British B.A.R. in both years. His superiority was the reward for his famous twice-daily training routine: an hour every morning before breakfast, and then the main session in the evening. Interestingly, his occasional trips south to English courses did not seem to result in faster times, and he himself maintained that the difference between English and Scottish times did not lie in the courses, but in the competition. Linden was a teacher of engineering by profession, and in 1961 he married Myra Robertson, twice winner of the women's B.A.R. Linden's reign was ended in 1962 in a sensational fashion, by the rising young road-race star, Gordon McNaught, who invaded the time-trialling scene as dramatically as Metcalfe did in England in 1966. But not only was McNaught's victory achieved in three straight rides, but, incredibly, each one was his first attempt at the distance. He had never competed in time-trials other than 25s before, yet he finished tenth in the B.B.A.R. while Linden was an unlucky thirteenth, beaten in both the 50 and the 100, but salvaging a one-mile margin in the 12-hour. Linden's strength really told at the longer distance, and his 12-hour record of 264.7 set in 1960 lasted for twenty years. The twenty-one year old McNaught looked a brilliant prospect for the 1962 Empire Games in Australia, but his luck deserted him towards the end of the season and a broken ankle halted his racing for a while, and, although he did come back to racing, he never fulfilled the promise of that sensational 1962 season. Linden on the other hand made a magnificent comeback a full ten years later to take the 1972 B.A.R.

The Linden era was succeeded by a run of B.A.R. champions who held the trophy for just one year each: Alan McGibbon, Jim Greig, Lionel Wylie, Bert McLennan and John McMillan. The big name missing in the early sixties is that of Fraser Connell, record-breaker at 50 miles and 100 miles and road-race champion. Faster than McGibbon in the 1963 season, Connell's bugbear was always the 12-hour event, which he could rarely finish, but without which he could not take the B.A.R. John McMillan was another top-class roadman, who finished second in the 1966 Scottish Milk Race, and who also had the speed of an elite 25-miler, having broken the Scottish record no less than four times: his final mark of 55:33 was to stand for nineteen years, until the Dave Hannah era. McMillan later

Joe Christison, star of the early Tours of Britain, who missed out on a successful pro career.

Ken Laidlaw, time-trial champion who became the first Scot to ride the Tour de France in 1961.

moved to the London area and raced very successfully against the top southern riders. The last two B.A.R.s of the decade were won by Jock Ritchie, who might have gone on to even greater things had he not emigrated to Australia in 1970. One of the most consistent time-triallists of the sixties was Andy Kirk, who took half a dozen championships at 50-miles, 100-miles and the 12, but never clinched the BA.R. until 1974, after more years of trying even than Joe Miller.

Interestingly, many of the top time-triallists of the sixties, such as McGibbon, Greig and Wylie, still favoured the 84- or 85-inch fixed wheel, several years after it had been almost completely abandoned in England. Whether this was a contributing factor or not, it has to be admitted that by the late sixties time-trialling in Scotland was pretty static. Where men like Hamilton, Balneaves and Linden had finished well up in the top twelve of the B.B.A.R., the gap between Scottish and English times had now widened alarmingly: John Watson took the 1970 B.B.A.R. with a speed .042 short of 26 m.p.h while Dennis Mitchell's winning speed in Scotland was 23.042. No Scottish B.A.R. winner ever went to the R.T.T.C. prize-giving now as one of the country's leading riders. A study of the S.C.U. record tables shows that record-breaking had apparently died out as a national pastime, and that nothing remotely like the explosion of speed by the English time-triallists occurred in Scotland. It would be easy to argue that Scotland lacked high-speed dragstrips such as Boroughbridge, and few courses in England still included a level crossing like the one west of Dundee. But the fact is that England saw an overall improvement of standards in the sixties that was quite dramatic, while Scottish B.A.R. times showed no advance at all between 1960 and 1980. Sheelagh Fraser scored an outstanding series of victories in the women's B.A.R. competition for five successive years from 1966 to 1970, yet her times were slower than Janet Sutherland's had been in the early fifties. Linden's comeback in 1972 was a personal triumph for him, but it should not have been possible if the level of racing had been higher. Perhaps the only significant new record in Scotland in these years was George Berwick's 24-hour ride of 448.7 miles in 1967, and this, rather incredibly, still stands thirty-seven years later. Club membership was generally falling, and serious cycling had apparently suffered in Scotland even more than in England from social factors such as growing car ownership and the lure of television. The traditional recruiting grounds of the club-run and the youth hostelling weekend probably seemed dull to sixties teenagers, and the dominance of football as the national game was even more intense than in England. The decline in standards in Scotland in these years was reflected in the pages of *Cycling*: each year throughout the forties and fifties, a review of the year in Scotland had appeared as a winter feature, but by the mid-sixties this was quietly dropped. In the Commonwealth Games in Edinburgh in the summer of 1970, six cycling gold medals were on offer, of which Australia and New Zealand scooped four, England was left with one, while Scotland took one silver through Brian Temple, three times 25-mile champion, in the ten-mile track event.

In some ways road racing was stronger in Scotland than time-trialling, where the competition was man against man, rather than man against the clock. Every few years it seemed that an outstanding roadman would emerge who was not content with victories at home, but had bigger ambitions, and was prepared to travel to achieve them. In the fifties, after Ian Steel, there was Joe Christison and Ken Laidlaw, and in the sixties it was Billy Bilsland who become the inspiration for young Scottish riders seeking wider horizons. Christison, road champion in 1953, became one of the top professionals of the early fifties, riding in several Tours of Britain, finishing fourth in 1954 and fifth in 1955. With Ian Steel he went to the Vuelta in 1955 and was shelled out in the heat and the mountains, and later that year he became a casualty of the collapse of the pro teams in Britain. After a year out he was reinstated as an amateur and took third place in the 1957 B.A.R. Christison was one of those roadmen who could ride an exceptional time-trial – in 1954 he set a record in the Tour de Trossachs which stood for ten years. In 1958 he took fifth place in the Manx International and looked set for a strong ride in the Empire Games road race in Cardiff, until officialdom intervened. His status as a former independent came to light at the last minute and he was barred from riding. Many cyclists would have given up the sport in disgust, but Christison came back in 1959 to ride and finish the Peace Race, before bowing out of racing. He was obviously an immensely strong rider who, with better luck and better career-management, might have gained very high honours. It was left to Ken Laidlaw to reach the highest pinnacle, for he had the distinction of being the first Scots rider in the Tour de France: in 1961 he rode confidently to finish not far behind Robinson and Elliott. In 1957 Laidlaw had been both road-race champion and 100-mile champion in a record time, in a memorable race in which Joe Christison and Ernie Scally both beat the old record before Laidlaw came home in the fastest time of all. In the Bradley-dominated Milk Race of 1960, Laidlaw took eighth place, only narrowly losing the Welsh mountain stage to Bradley himself. But the '61 Tour de France proved to be the high-point: in '62 the Tour was back to trade teams, so that only the continental pros could ride, and Laidlaw was one of several British riders of this time who, having aimed at the very top, felt himself out of place in domestic racing, and quit the sport.

The inauguration of the Scottish Milk Race in 1965 was a major event, bringing international riders to Scotland and capturing public attention for the sport. The first race saw the home riders frankly outclassed by the Czechs and the English, with no stage wins and Jim Leitch the best finisher in fourth place. The following year saw a miraculous transformation, with home riders taking the top three places, Andy McGhee winning by a small margin from John McMillan and Billy Bilsland, the latter scoring a fine solo stage win. Perhaps the presence of Norman Sheil as Scots team manager had something to do with this success. Sadly it was not to be repeated, as victory in the 67, 68 and 69 editions went to Pijnen of Holland, then Peter Buckley and Brian Jolly, before the race fell victim, like its English counterpart, to a succession of winners from Eastern Europe. Andy McGhee made a big impact on the Scottish road-racing scene, twice winning the national championship in 1966 and 1968, although in the Commonwealth Games of 1970 before his home crowd he finished a disappointed ninth, six minutes behind the winner Bruce Biddle of New Zealand.

After the excitement of the 1950s, when both road-racing and time-trialling had produced Scottish riders of national and international quality, there was undeniably something of a lull by the mid and late sixties. Billy Bilsland decided early that as a serious rider he had to look abroad, and he moved first to England and then to France in search of competition. Only in the late 1970s would we see virtually a new era of racing standards in Scotland, with Sandy Gilchrist and Dave Hannah the stars, but always challenged by riders like Drew Brunton, John Clark, Dave Miller and Rab McCleod.

Retrospect

The sixties had opened with the bike industry in pessimistic mood, and many manufacturers and shops failed to last out the decade. Condor survived through its commitment to cycle-sport, its reputation boosted by the publicity which its racing team brought with it. But there was one positive revolution in the bike trade in the early sixties, which helped Condor and many others dealers enormously: the Moulton, which for a few years changed the image of cycling and reached out to thousands of new customers who would otherwise never have be seen on a bike. Cambridge-educated engineer Alex Moulton had made his reputation by designing the hydrolastic suspension for the Mini,

John Woodburn proves the Moulton's speed potential by breaking the Cardiff-London record in December 1962.

before he turned his attention to the bicycle. He felt strongly that it was time to challenge the diamond frame from the perspective of engineering principles. He instinctively objected to the large wheels with the high centre of gravity, the rigid ride and the poor luggage capacity. All these could be corrected by using small wheels, except the bumpy ride, which would become worse. Moulton's stroke of genius was to see that the frame must be sprung, which he achieved through a spring and rubber suspension unit in the extended head tube, and a swinging arm on the rear wheel, like that of a motor-bike. The resulting machine gave a brilliant ride and fast acceleration. It was manufactured in one size with an instantly adjustable saddle, it was unisex, and it included a large luggage-carrier. It was a revolutionary design that really worked, and above all it looked new and exciting. It exactly captured the mood of the time: the Mini car the mini-skirt and now the mini-bike. Launched at the Earl's Court cycle show in November 1962, it created immense press interest, hundreds of orders were taken on the spot, and celebrities were soon pictured with their Moultons: actresses, peers of the realm, company directors, pop singers - all people who would never have bought a bike now had to have one. The Condor shop was one of Moulton's main London outlets, and one of Monty Young's first customers was Giles Wilson, son of the Prime Minister, his model being personally delivered to Downing Street. It was a tremendous gift to the trade, and production at Moulton's works soon reached 1,000 per week. In three years 100,000 models were sold at around £35 - that's £3.5 million injected into an ailing industry by one new idea. Of course Moulton's rivals were falling over themselves to copy it, but the way was blocked by Moulton's cunning patents. Their only course was to imitate the small frame concept without the crucial springing, and this meant fitting wide balloon tyres, which rendered their machines sluggish.

Moulton was intent on proving that his design could be not merely a popular success, but that it was the equal of the conventional racing bike. He built a lightweight drop-handlebar model, and in December 1962 John Woodburn rode it and smashed the R.R.A. Cardiff-London record by a big margin, bringing it down to 6:43:29 for the 158 miles. This record stood for five years until it went back to a conventional bike, ridden by Brian Catt, who improved it by ten minutes, but he had saved ten miles by using the new Severn Bridge. Only three months later Moulton's own rider, Vic Nicholson, responded by winning back the record with a magnificent time of 6:14:57. The Moulton's credentials as a serious racing machine were established. A touring model, the Safari, was also launched and it immediately gained a high reputation among serious international tourists. But fashion is fickle, and the Moulton's problem was that it became so closely identified with its time that it became too quickly outmoded. There was also the problem that people bought the imitation models which were less effective, were slightly disappointed with them, and the Moultons shared their displeasure. By 1967 the boom was over, Moulton was ready to sell to Raleigh, and the small-wheeled bike took its place as just another model in a range of mass-market machines. But the financial boost which the Moulton had given to the bike shops was invaluable.

What of the road environment, which had been so deadly to cyclists in the forties and fifties - had it begun to improve? Dual-carriageway roads were taking the heavy traffic, leaving the minor roads somewhat safer for cyclists, and car design was improving. A new, tougher Highway Code was published in 1955, M.O.T. tests were introduced in 1958, and breath-tests for motorists in 1961. There was some slight evidence that a feeling of guilt and responsibility was at last emerging about the slaughter on Britain's roads, but it was admittedly very slight. In the late forties the cycling press had been full of cases like that in August 1949, when two members of the Easterly C.C. had been hit head-on by a car on Stag's Hill, Barnet, and killed. At the inquest, it transpired that the car driver had pulled out to overtake a bus going up the hill, and had ploughed into the cyclists while on completely the wrong side of the road. The driver elected not to give evidence, and the inquest verdict was accidental death, in line with attitudes at the time: if a cyclist was killed in a collision with a car it was, by definition, an accident. The inquest jury also saw fit to warn cyclists to take greater care to ride well in to the left. Twelve years later, in December 1961 in Horsham, Sussex, members of the Clarence Wheelers were out on a club run

They'd never seen anything like it: Condor's window when the Moulton was launched in the winter of 1962-63.

when a car veered across the road without warning and smashed into them. Nine cyclists were seriously hurt, and two, both teenage boys, died of their injuries. This time the police charged the car-driver with careless driving. In court he could give no explanation of what had happened. He was 81 years old, his car was sixteen years old, and he had never taken a driving test because he had been driving since before tests were introduced in the 1930s. He was fined £10 and ordered to take the driving test. Perhaps attitudes were changing, but it was a slow business.

It may not be unduly pessimistic to see a link between incidents like these and the status of cycling as a whole: it offered enormous personal and social rewards, yet it seemed doomed always to remain a minority sport, incomprehensible to those outside. The sporting achievements of British cyclists in the sixties had been brilliant, but they themselves were troubled by doubts about their ability to compete at the international level. The World Championships at Leicester in some ways crowned the decade. They were a huge success as a spectacle, pitting British riders against the world's stars here in England, but our haul of medals was undeniably thin. Even Hugh Porter's admirers could not disguise the fact that his gold was won against undistinguished opposition, since the times put up by the pro pursuiters - except Porter himself - would not even have qualified them for the amateur finals. The team time-trial, where four of our fastest riders were badly beaten on their home roads, led to a new round of despair about the sport. As an out-of-the-blue hero, the crowds and the press feted the Australian Gordie Johnson, winner of the sprint title just weeks after turning pro, on the principle that any English-speaking winner was better than a European one. The most abiding memory of Leicester was probably Les West's ride of a lifetime in the pro road race, missing a medal by yards.

In the months after Leicester, cycling's two governing bodies were once again embroiled in conflict, as the B.C.F. planned to assert its authority over the R.T.T.C. It was unsuccessful of course, because the R.T.T.C. was an independent body serving its own self-contained sporting community. The R.T.T.C.'s sole aim was the promotion of time-trialling in this country, and this, its critics argued, led to pure complacency. This political ill-feeling was further evidence of the persistent belief that time-trialling was somehow linked to our continuing international failure, and that British cycling had to be guided out of its insularity. The process of rapprochement between British and continental cycling was a long, slow one, which threw up its heroes and which claimed its victims, and it was still far from complete.

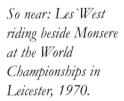

So near: Les West riding beside Monsere at the World Championships in Leicester, 1970.

Chapter Three

Breaking With the Past

In cycling, as in British society as a whole, while the 1970s continued many of the patterns of the 1960s, the 1980s was definitely a time for shedding old skins and breaking old forms. The work patterns, the leisure patterns, the fabric of social life and the whole psychology of the nation seemed then to shift into a new phase of non-stop innovation. Technical change, organisational change, the electronics revolution, the impact of the media, consumer choice, free-market ideas, participation, alternative cultures, minority rights, environmental awareness - our lives were revolutionised by all these things on an unprecedented scale, both in the home and in the work-place. Whether people wanted these changes or whether they were imposed from the outside is a matter for debate, but they became inescapable. This process of accelerated change could be a painful one, in two senses: first it created social conflict and destroyed old values, and second it brought disillusionment when high expectations were not met.

In the sphere of British cycle sport the central questions were still these: were we fully part of the international scene or not; why could British riders not bring home major victories and medals like other nations; could we compete in the traditional amateur way in a world of sophisticated professionalism? Money in one form or another now seemed to be central to all these questions: money from sponsorship, money from governing bodies, money to get the media attention which would lift the sport out of the shadows into the professional age. To secure financial backing for the sport, and to channel it to the best riders was a management task which would demand new thinking and take years to accomplish. The dissolving of the professional-amateur categories came about slowly, from about 1980 to 1995, and it amounted to a re-structuring of the sport, in the same way that so many other organisations were re-structured in that period. While it was hap-

The shape of things to come: Condor track bikes at the National Championships at Leicester, 1986.

pening, an impassioned dialogue was conducted about the sport's problems and future, a dialogue in which everyone - riders, coaches, officials, sponsors and journalists - had his opinion on what was wrong and how to put it right. In a round-table discussion in 1975, three leading figures - Reg Harris, Ian Hallam and Doug Dailey - all stated quite bluntly that in Britain no structure, no official system existed for finding and developing future champions: if a rider had talent and ambition, he had to find his own way and do it himself, it was as simple as that. This was a damning criticism of the governing bodies which had supposedly been directing the sport for many decades. It has always been easy to blame the committees of the B.C.F. or the R.T.T.C. for whatever was wrong in cycling, in the same way that we like to blame governments for deeper social changes over which they really have no control. Yet when figures like Harris and Hallam, whose careers were separated by thirty years, agreed about the weakness of central direction in the sport, then this had to be taken seriously. The gulf in expertise, energy and vision between riders and officials was a problem that seemed to be endemic in cycling.

In the bike trade between 1970 and 1990 there was good news and bad. Cycling reflected the drastic decline in British manufacturing industry which brought a rising tide of imports. For the first time British riders began to desert their traditional frame-builders in favour of Peugeot, Bianchi, Colnago, Gitane, Superia, and the rest. Then a style revolution really hit cycling in the 80s: it came from abroad and it took three forms: aerodynamics, mountain bikes, and new frame materials. All these things appealed to an increasingly sophisticated market, and foreign design and flair proved irresistible to the British buyers - of bikes as well as cars, hi-fis, food and fashion: it suited their new lifestyle - itself the classic buzzword of the eighties.

That lifestyle had been profoundly influenced by the oil crisis of 1973, which brought western nations face to face with the ecological boundaries of their lives, ignored for so long. From that crisis there flowed an entirely new wave of environmental awareness, in which cycling, long regarded as a marginal activity, now came to be seen as both logical and smart. Increasingly vocal cycle campaign groups pointed out that cycling answered so many problems, from energy conservation to personal health and the appalling congestion in our cities. So the new bike styles, health consciousness and the new ecological awareness all combined to put cycling back in fashion again, and the eighties saw a boom-time in bike retailing. Condor had survived the thin years of the sixties, and, with its reputation for quality and commitment, was now well placed to capitalise on the new demand. Monty Young's son Grant became joint manager with his father in 1980, a move which ensured the future of the firm. Of the many

"The New Cult of the Body": the health- exercise culture of the 1980s hits the headlines. Even continental magazines borrowed Condors for their photographs. It is interesting to compare this picture with the one on page 76.

small specialist bike-building shops which were once to be found all over London, the vast majority closed when the founder retired or died, and Condor was one of the few which continued into a second generation. By contrast the critical decline in British bike manufacturing was marked in 1987 when Raleigh, the biggest brand-name in the industry, was sold by its parent company Tube Investments to an unknown American consortium. In the previous five years Raleigh had lost £30 million pounds, and both its production and its sales were sinking remorselessly. The vogue for cycling was to benefit overseas manufacturers far more than British ones.

The cynic might point out that the new-wave riders of the 80s and 90s were merely rediscovering what the clubmen of the 40s and 50s had always known - that cycling meant freedom, and that it meant health in its widest sense, both personal and social. Cycling had then played a central role in a far simpler lifestyle; perhaps it could once again find an important place in a more sophisticated age. New forms of cycling emerged to enrich the sport: audax, mountain biking, and triathlon. They came not from above, not from the governing bodies, but from the grass-roots, and from contact with cyclists overseas. As a consequence some traditional forms of the sport declined: long-distance time-trialling was one obvious sufferer, for the sort of people who might once have ridden 12s and 24s were now attracted to audax events of 200 or 300 kilometres, or even longer. Any sport evolves with the society around it, and these changing patterns of life and leisure form the essential background to cycling in these years.

Road-Racing

The British road-racing scene was enlivened by a succession of strong, sometimes brilliant riders, who were often uncertain how to fulfil that brilliance - what goals to aim at, and how to handle their successes and their failures. A string of star amateur riders notched up single-day victories and Milk Race stage wins, then faced the big choice whether to turn professional, or stick with what they knew, and if they did become professionals, should they aim for the top on the continent or try to build a pro class at home ? The pro scene in Britain sometimes seemed to resemble a game of snakes and ladders, with the launch of new teams, promises of more pro racing and an imminent breakthrough into European competition, only to be followed by withdrawal a couple of years later, leaving riders unemployed and disillusioned.

The great event in the amateur road-racing year was of course the Milk Race, and it was here that the British problems came into sharpest focus. After Les West's convincing win in 1967, with Dave Rollinson in second place, eight years followed in which the victory went abroad, mainly to Dutch riders - den Hertog, Kuiper, van Katwijk and Schuiten - but also to the Swedes Petterson and Johansson, and to Mainus of Czechoslovakia, with the Poles always a factor. Without wishing to denigrate the strength of these foreign riders, the cycling public could be excused for being put off by result-sheets filled day after day with names like Mikolajczyk, Pollipanov, Kaczmarek, Zwirko or Gorgensson, most of whom could not speak a word of English. And it wasn't just that a

Phil Edwards, the top British rider in the Milk Races of the early 70s.

foreigner always won, but that the British (after Buckley in 1969) were never even seen on the podium, they never won the team prize or the mountains prize, and even stage wins became a rarity. In part this was a tribute to the Milk Race itself: it was regarded as one of the best amateur races in Europe, and all the strongest nations wanted to compete in it. On the other hand it was run on our own roads, and the home riders should therefore have enjoyed an immense advantage.

Throughout these lean years, Britain's leading rider was Phil Edwards, the big Bristolian who had won the national junior title in 1967. Between 1970 and 1973 Edwards finished the Milk Race in 6th, 7th, 4th and 5th position. His tally of stage wins was not huge, but he was clearly a strong, consistent stage-race rider, and he carried most of the British hopes for overall victory. Perhaps this was a burden for him, for Edwards seemed to display problems of temperament, and often found himself at odds with fellow riders and officials. These tensions came to a head at the world championships at Mendrisio in 1971, when Edwards dropped out of the team time-trial after only five miles, leaving the British team unable to finish, the worst result in a long series of disasters in this event. Incredibly, the same thing happened a year later at the Munich Olympics, when once again he was tailed off by Lloyd, Dailey and Bayton, who continued to finish 13th. It is hard to believe that there was a physical cause, since Edwards recovered just a few days later to produce a fine ride in the Olympic road race, where he closed a gap on the leading group in the final miles and finished 6th, half a minute down on the lone winner, Hennie Kuiper. After the Olympics Edwards stayed on in Europe and rode the Tour de l'Avenir, taking 9th overall, and then settled in Italy (he was half-Italian by birth) where he became a professional. For five years Edwards rode successfully in Moser's Sanson team, his most memorable return to England being in June 1977 when he won the pro road-race championship, run that year as a rather bizarre marathon up the A1 from London to York. He rode all the classics and the Giro in support of Moser, and although he never became a star, he carved out a very happy niche for himself in Italy and earned good money. His only regret was not making the move sooner, and he was to say later that he considered amateur racing in Britain - after a certain point - to be a waste of time, useful only as a stepping-stone to a pro career.

This was an extreme statement of one point of view, summing up the dilemma of Britain's other top amateurs who rode well in the Milk Race - Barras, Lloyd, Bayton, Clewarth, Corley, and Dailey. A few of these remained amateurs and continued to ride the one-day classics - the Essex GP, the Tour of the Cotswolds, the Manx International, the Tour of the Peak and so on - as well as representing Britain internationally, itself a pretty thankless task given the disappointments and the criticisms which they invariably faced when they returned. Dailey was rewarded with two national championships, the first in 1972 and the second four years later in 1976, by which time, at the age of 32, he was respected as a kind of elder statesman of British road-racing. In 1972 he was most unlucky not to ride the Olympic road-race, having crashed in training shortly before the Games. Dailey was an extremely tough but popular rider, one of many who worked and saved during the winter months in order to ride full-time in the summer. The leading spirit in the strong Kirkby C.C., it was no secret that he and many other riders were totally at odds with the B.C.F. national team director, Tom Pinnington, from the rival Merseyside club the Liverpool Mercury. Pinnington was not a cyclist himself, and many of the internationals with whom he worked found him ineffectual in matters of coaching, rider psychology and team management. International results during his years were thin in the extreme, and he was pushed into resignation in 1978. Under his successor, Jim Hendry, Dailey was brought in as national road manager, and he then worked with all the top riders of the eighties. This conflict and Dailey's role in it are interesting not just as a piece of gossip, but because it underlines how unusual it then was for star riders to go on to national coaching and management posts. So many great riders - Harris, Booty, Robinson, Bradley, West, Porter, Hoban - were lost to the sport when they finished racing: apparently they were never asked to coach young riders, and their experience and inspirational role were never sought by the B.C.F. The sole exception was Norman Sheil, national coach from 1965 to 1973, but Sheil had applied for an advertised post, he was not invited into the job. For reasons best known

Bill Nickson in the race-leader's jersey, Milk Race 1976. Paul Carbutt on the right. Nickson was the sole British winner in 19 years.

to themselves, the ruling body always seemed to prefer the career official, the backroom boy, the man in the blazer, to the proven champion who had actually made it to the top. Did they feel threatened by all these ex-champions, who obviously knew so much more about cycling than they did?

The long bleak years of foreign domination in the Milk Race were famously ended in 1976 by Bill Nickson and Joe Waugh, although the promise was already there in the previous year, when these two riders finished 6th and 7th, barely two minutes down on the winner, Bernt Johansson. That year Britain took multiple stage wins, was second in the team competition, and Waugh won the King of the Mountains, easily the best home result for many years. Nickson and Waugh had ridden their first Milk Race in 1973 before departing for a season's racing in France. Nickson had really impressed during 1974, winning the national road-race championship and the first of his two Manx International victories. There was some idea at first that he was Scottish, having lived in Edinburgh for a few years, and having ridden internationally for Scotland, but he was of course a Merseysider. Waugh, with his mane of flowing hair, was a phenomenal climber from Tyneside, who had taken the national hill-climb title in 1974 and finished seventh in the B.A.R. One week before the 1976 Milk Race, Nickson and Waugh warmed up by taking first and second in the Lincoln G.P., and the big race opened brilliantly for Britain with Ian Hallam's prologue win. The pattern of the race was set on the fourth stage through the Welsh mountains, when Nickson and Waugh spearheaded the vital break that gained

Joe Waugh, sharer in the 1976 Milk Race triumph, just 5 seconds behind Nickson at the finish.

four minutes on the field, and ended with Nickson in the yellow jersey and Waugh just five seconds behind him. That was the lead that was defended to the finish by the exceptionally well-organised GB team of Downs, Griffiths, Carbutt and Hayton. Waugh rode selflessly for Nickson, even backing off from his campaign to win a second mountains title. Nickson generously acknowledged Waugh's ride, insisting that they should be regarded as equal firsts.

After this victory, the sense of euphoria was almost palpable: it seemed that a new era had dawned for British riders, and that medals at the Olympics were a real possibility. But in Montreal both Nickson and Waugh were crash victims, the former failing even to finish. By the end of the year Nickson had signed as a pro for Raleigh in their continental team, where he spent an unhappy twelve months under the stern management of Peter Post. He rode the 1977 Tour de France and survived well until the Alpe d'Huez stage in the last week. He soon returned to England and joined the Falcon team, his pro record being less brilliant than his amateur career, with its highlight the national pro championship in 1981. Waugh never joined the pro ranks but added to his achievements by taking a second hill-climb title in 1976, and two successive Manx International victories in 1981 and 1982. He rode the Milk Race again several times and won stages, but he never came so close to overall victory as that slender five seconds which he had allowed Nickson to hold on to in 1976.

Meanwhile the Milk Race itself over the next six years escaped from the Dutch and Swedish stranglehold only to fall into the iron grip of the Russians: the names on the result-sheets became even stranger, and the big home loser in consequence was now Bob Downs. From schoolboy champion, the Essex rider had matured to become one of the most respected roadmen on the circuit. Although a prolific winner, his critics could point out that he seemed to miss the top spot in the really important races, leading him to miss out on international selection. His forte was stage racing, where his consistency and recovery powers served him well. He rode six Milk Races, finishing third in 1978, and fourth on three other occasions, all during the years of Russian domination. Without the Russian presence, and with a reasonable team around him, Downs would surely have taken the big prize at least once during this period. His persistence was rewarded in 1980 by a convincing win in the 5-day Sealink International, supported by team-mates John Herety, Steve Poulter and Des Fretwell. He was one of the gold medal winning quartet in the 1982 Commonwealth Games TTT in Brisbane. His 1983 Milk Race appearance was less happy: he was ill and finished well down, almost an hour behind

Bob Downs, kept out of the Milk Race honours for so many years by the all-powerful Russians.

the first American winner, Matt Eaton - who was however born in Guildford. A long-time customer then an employee at Condor Cycles, Downs finally turned professional in 1984, riding as the founder member of the Bilton-Condor team, and he celebrated his new career by winning the major pro-am Tour of Ireland. These Milk Race years did witness a few British triumphs, the most memorable being Ray Lewis's epic ride on the last stage of the 1979 event. Lewis had been penalised five minutes on his overall time on the penultimate day for taking a tow during mechanical service. So he started the final day with a big point to make - that he wasn't a cheat and didn't need help - and he made it in dramatic fashion. Two miles after the start he jumped clear of the bunch, and he stayed clear all day throughout a 90-mile lone time-trial across the Pennines, holding off the speeding peleton all the way, to finish in Blackpool 23 seconds clear, after a ride that will always remain part of Milk Race history.

Downs's constant companion and rival in the Milk Races and throughout these years was the man at the centre of so much racing activity in the seventies, Phil Griffiths. Colourful, controversial, outspoken - all these words were used to describe him, but a more scientific description might be hyperactive. He was never content to let his legs do the talking, but for almost ten years provided a non-stop commentary on his aims and achievements, telling riders, officials, journalists and anyone who would listen what had happened in his races and why. When he stopped talking, his class was undeniable: he wore the yellow jersey in the 1973 Peace race, took the silver medal in the Commonwealth Games road race in 1974, won the season-long star trophy competition in 1975, and his

Monty at the start of the 1976 Milk Race with Bob Thom, Phil Griffiths and Bill Nickson.

leadership was a big factor in the British team in the triumphant 1976 Milk Race. He was twice second in the national road-race championship, and in the Montreal Olympics he was one of the British quartet which finished sixth in the TTT, our best ever result. Griffiths never turned professional, and he would probably be remembered as a personality rather than as a big winner, if he had not also been an outstanding time-triallist, who dominated the B.A.R. distances for many years. He founded the GS Strada racing team, where he steered riders like Paul Carbutt, Eddie Adkins, Joe Waugh, Bob Downs, Sandy Gilchrist and Ian Cammish to so many victories in the national team time-trial championship. Yet ironically it was through the team time-trial that his international career came to a bizarre end, when he was accused of disrupting a world championship training event in 1979, and was told he would never represent Britain again.

For many other top amateurs, high placings in the Milk Race were just a prelude to a pro career, Dave Lloyd, Phil Bayton and Sid Barras among them. Of these perhaps the one with the most burning ambition was Lloyd, the slightly-built Welsh-born Merseysider coached by Eddie Soens. After spending his teenage years enjoying the delights of Liverpool in the sixties, Lloyd was introduced to cycling by a work-mate, and soon revealed a quite exceptional ability as a time-triallist, first hitting the headlines in the 1971 Isle of Man week, when he won both the open 25 and the mountain trial, breaking Les West's long-standing record. In that year's Milk Race he grew stronger as the days passed, finishing 7th, and he made his final preparations for the Olympics determined to break through into the top level. His morale was enormously boosted when he won the William Tell Grand Prix, a six-stage international race in Switzerland, just one week before the Munich Games. But Lloyd's Olympic hopes ended in bitter disappointment when he and John Clewarth were victims of a crash at the halfway point. He salvaged his pride in

October by taking second place in the amateur Grand Prix des Nations in 1972, so often the graveyard of British hopes, and by the end of the year he had signed as a professional for the Raleigh team, alongside Bayton, Jolly, Bilsland and Rollinson. Over the next two years he showed his speed on the track by winning the national pro pursuit championship, and on the road when he broke the RRA 50 record with a scintillating 1:35:45, a time which no one dared to attack until Ian Cammish sixteen years later. In 1975 Lloyd was one of the British riders chosen for Raleigh's European squad, and he was the only one to survive Peter Post's steely management style. He rode classics like Paris-Roubaix and he was the only British finisher in that year's world pro road championship in Belgium. The following year would have seen his debut in the Tour de France, but in spring 1976 disaster struck: after health problems in training he was diagnosed as having rare heart condition, which was not life-threatening but which obviously ruled out the extreme demands of continental pro racing. The shattered Lloyd returned to England and set about rebuilding his

Keith Lambert looks across at Phil Bayton, wondering if he is suffering as much he seems to be.

life, and having done so he made a triumphant return to amateur racing in the early 1980s, becoming an unbeatable short-distance time-trial champion. The Lloyd we saw then was all fire, nerve and energy, which he was able to channel into a concentrated solo effort of just an hour or more, and it is strange to recall that he was on the verge of a very different career as a Tour de France rider when his life suddenly changed direction.

Lloyd's friend and rival in the early seventies was the man who became known as the firebrand of the bunches, Phil Bayton, with his constant attacks, his head-down-and-away style of racing. It seemed that Bayton could not help himself, he simply could not roll along in the bunch, he had to go with every break, and if there was no break he had to make one - and then another and then another. His role in driving along a race earned him his nickname "The Engine". He served his apprenticeship in the Milk Race of 1971, took 5th in the Manx International and a string of second places in classic events like the Lincoln G.P. and the Tour of Cotswolds, and was then second to Rollinson in the national championship. In 1972 he crashed out of the Milk Race, but for Bayton as for so many other riders, 1972 really meant the Munich Olympics, and there he produced one of the rides of his life, to finish fifth, the best Briton just seconds away from a medal; he was later promoted to fourth when the bronze medalist, Huelamo of Spain, was disqualified. No British rider since has come closer to an Olympic road-race medal. After this watershed, Bayton turned pro, first for Raleigh in Europe, where he and Lloyd captured the limelight in a long two-up break in the 1973 Milan-San Remo, then in Britain for a succession of home teams including Bantel, Dawes, Holdsworth and Viscount. He didn't win as often as he would have liked, but he was always a tremendous presence in the pro bunch. He was easy to criticise because many of his attacks were suicidal, but his answer to his critics was intriguing for a professional: he said it was the style of racing that mattered to him, that too much emphasis was placed on winning, that cycling was a sport, and that true cyclists should promote the sport as a contest and a spectacle; sitting in the bunch,

SuperSid looking pleased with life, probably heading towards yet another win.

calculating tactics and letting others lead was simply of no interest to him. After some sixteen years in the pro scene, Bayton finally retired in 1989, and perhaps it was typical of the man that he could still say that the Olympic race of 1972, that glorious failure, had been the greatest moment of his life. Bayton had finished that race ahead of Francesco Moser and Freddy Maertens; the subsequent careers of these three riders surely point up the stark contrast between the racing scenes in Britain, Italy and Belgium.

Although their pro careers coincided almost exactly for nearly twenty years, there could scarcely be a greater contrast between Phil Bayton and Sid Barras: Bayton the headstrong attacker and gallant loser, Barras the watchful tactician, invincible sprinter and perennial winner. When Barras scored his 100th professional victory in April 1977, it was considered phenomenal; what no one knew was that he would score almost another 100 wins in his distinguished career. As a measure of his brilliance in finishing, it's useful to recall that the legendary Les West scored some 30 wins in his nine years as a professional. A fine amateur record with dozens of wins in the late sixties and a fifth place in the 1968 Milk Race failed to gain Barras international selection, and in frustration he turned pro for Bantel at the age of 21. It was his Bantel team-mate, Hugh Porter, who christened Barras "Super-Sid", and together they made a formidable combination. For all his speed Barras was never "just a sprinter": he could climb, he could drive a break along as well as anybody, and in order to win a sprint you have to be there at the end, even after a race as long as London-Holyhead. Like Albert Hitchen before him, Barras won this event twice, in 1970 as a first-year pro, outsprinting a powerful lead group including Brian Jolly, Colin Lewis and Hugh Porter, and again in 1977. That was a vintage year for Barras, with a total of 24 victories, including the five-day pro-am Scottish Milk Race, where, helped only by Porter, he triumphed over the top riders from Poland and Czechoslovakia, as well as pro teams from Switzerland and Holland. Any idea that Barras was just a big fish in a small pond had already been dispelled back in 1973 when he took a trip to the Tour of Switzerland and won the first road stage, outsprinting van Springel, Moser and Sercu; when he donned the yellow jersey that day everyone was asking who Barras was and why he didn't race on the continent. This was indeed the big question for him, and the following year he was signed as a member of Raleigh's European squad, but he was not the man to endure the bullying management style of Peter Post, or one to find happiness living in a cellar in Ghent, and he returned to try to build up the pro class in Britain. Despite his superiority at home from 1970 onwards, one persistent failure nagged him: for one reason or another the professional road-race championship eluded him year after year. He finally broke the jinx in 1979, in a killing, rain-soaked 150-mile epic, outsprinting Barry Hoban, Dudley Hayton and Phil Edwards in a bruising finish that saw Hoban refuse to come to the podium. For good measure Barras took the national criterium championship a few weeks later. Barras continued to race and win well into the eighties, calling a halt when he realised that he could not give away ten years and more to the new generation of sprinters - Joughin, Elliott and Phil Thomas - and still expect to win.

Once every year attention shifted from the road to the track as the British professionals clashed with Europe's best at the Wembley Six, sponsored by Skol. Throughout the seventies the British star was Tony Gowland, co-sponsored by Condor for many years, and winner with Patrick Sercu of the 1972 event. The Wembley Six was a tremendous meeting-place for the cycling world, where manufacturers, riders, race promoters, sponsors and media men came together to exchange plans, and its demise after 1980 left a big gap in the British bike scene.

If Barras took most of the headlines in the 1970s, he had a small group of committed rivals who always made him work for his wins, and who so often kept the champion's jersey off his shoulders. Chief among them were Keith Lambert, known as "Legs Lambert" by virtue of his massive thigh muscles, champion in 1974 and again in 1980, Geoff

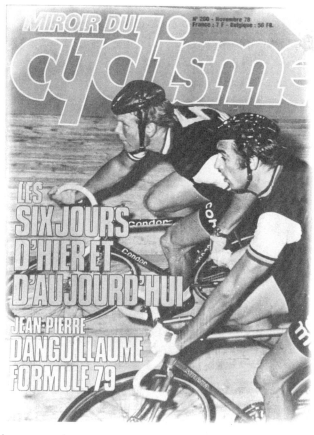

Wiles and Phil Corley, title winners in 1976 and 1978. These three were the successors to Les West, Colin Lewis and Gary Crewe in the powerful Holdsworth team, managed by Roy Thame. One of the trio's highlights came in April 1977 when they all rode in Paris-Roubaix, finishing well down on the winner, de Vlaeminck, but having the distinction of finishing the world's toughest classic. Lambert must have had a secret passion for

Tony Gowland, home favourite of the Wembley Sixes. Below, Grant Young with Gowland.

endurance events, for in November 1985, he and Dudley Hayton rode a 500 mile race in Texas, in which the pair finished second and third in the superb time of 25 hours 11 minutes. The other dominant team, Bantel, was dissolved in 1977 following the loss of Barras, who was head-hunted along with Lambert to join a new super-team fielded by Viking, the bike manufacturer from the 1950s, now reborn as a completely new company in Northern Ireland with government subsidies. The two big-named riders were joined by Paul Carbutt, and much was expected of them, under the direction of coach Eddie Soens. But the dream-team on paper did not work out so well on the road, and a year later Soens was out and Barras moved on, replaced by Dudley Hayton and Mick Bennett. Bennett was one of the many trackmen who turned pro after the Montreal Olympics, along with Robin Crocker, Ian Hallam and Ian Banbury.

The Sixes were the place to meet all the best people: Grant Young with Merckx and Sercu.

The pro scene was never static, there were always new riders, new sponsors with big ambitions and new alliances, although none of these components in the system could guarantee results. Many fine amateur riders did not make the transition to the pro racing scene, company finances could change quickly, and egos could clash, so that more than a few teams pulled out after only a year or two. Events themselves were equally vulnerable: the professional governing body, the BPCRA - later the PCA - had the task of securing sponsors for races and prizes, and nothing was guaranteed. The lack of long, tough one-day events, and still more of stage races, was a big factor in the British pros' lack of competitiveness when they went abroad to world championships, where the distance invariably defeated them.

History was made in July 1974 when the Tour de France came to England, but the choice for the course on this one-stage visit was distinctly odd: the field raced up and down a short stretch of by-pass on the A38 east of Plymouth. Nobody seemed to think it was a good idea, for it had little of the character of the real Tour, and it attracted few spectators. A far more successful occasion came in June 1977, when boxing and motor-racing promoter Mike Barrett entered the sport of cycling and brought a clutch of top continental stars, headed by Merckx, Sercu, Poulidor and Ocana, to ride a criterium at London's Eastway circuit. The two-hour race was a dream come true for British fans, as they saw Barras, Lambert and Bayton finish in the first five, along with Merckx and the winner Thurau. In the following year the criterium switched to Crystal Palace, with Thevenet and Gimondi the stars and world champion Gerrie Knetemann the winner in the final sprint from Paul Carbutt. Barrett brought continental racing to Britain again in August in the Raleigh Tour of Britain, run over five days between Glasgow and London. It was a memorable race, with long hard stages reminiscent of the early Tours of Britain. Overall winner was the Dutchman van de Velde, with Reg Smith of the Carlton team a very close second. Barras and Ian Hallam both suffered crashes, but Ian Banbury won a high-speed prologue, while Les West took the mountains prize - in his final pro year. Sadly, there was to be no repeat of the stage race and no further instalments in the criterium series, as Barrett pulled out of cycling. An even sadder milestone was passed in June 1979 when Dave Broadbent became the first pro cyclist to be killed in Britain, after suffering head injuries in a race, despite wearing the helmet that had been compulsory since 1973; before that date it had been common to see a field of riders hurtling downhill at 50 m.p.h. or thundering up a finishing straight bear-headed.

The Holdsworth team, who had produced six national champions in nine years, was disbanded at the end of 1978. Carlton followed in 1979, a victim of parent-company Raleigh's economic troubles, in spite of their excellent results under Barras's leadership. At the end of 1980, no less than three teams - Viking, Elswick-Falcon and Weinmann - all pulled out within one month. TI-Raleigh were widely criticised for their on-off approach to sponsorship, and still more for their decision to spend six-figure sums each year on their continental team while neglecting the home racing scene. Back in the early eighties, Doug Dailey had rejected the idea of turning pro for the simple reason that he loved racing, and he knew he could race far more often

as amateur and with far greater variety of events. Despite the strength and class of the individual riders, the commercial vulnerability of British pro racing seemed to be unending problem, and discussions on the subject of open racing now took place among the governing bodies. There could be no question yet of an open licence, with the distinction between pros and amateurs abolished, for such a move could only take place by international consent, but open racing would ensure a full programme for the pros - championships excluded of course - while still allowing them to sell their services to commercial sponsors. It was both surprising and encouraging that the R.T.T.C. sought to help this development by permitting professionals to take part in its time trials from 1981 onwards, again excluding championships and the B.A.R. In view of the Council's long-standing views on pure amateurism, this was an historic move, and it showed how far cyclists' attitudes were changing with their changing environment.

String of pros at Eastway: Barras, Joughin, Bayton, Nickson, Elliott, and Downs. Below: Paul Sherwen who leap-frogged the usual hurdles to an early pro career.

As Edwards, Lloyd, Nickson, Bayton and Carbutt joined the pro ranks, a new wave of ambitious amateurs came through to replace them: Paul Sherwen, Steve Lawrence, Graham Jones, Robert Millar and Steve Joughin. For Sherwen everything happened incredibly quickly: he burst on the scene as a nineteen year old in 1976, when he outsprinted Carbutt and Downs to win the Pernod GP. Carbutt was again his victim in June when he added the Manx International to his growing list of victories. He was offered a place in the Milk Race, but declined because of pressure of college work. No Milk Race ride meant no Olympic selection, which Sherwen understood quite well, but he compensated by going on to win the season-long Pernod Star Trophy, the road-man's equivalent to the B.A.R. In the following spring he retained his Pernod laurels in brilliant fashion with a solo win by almost three minutes, after which, his final exams over, he set off for France where he joined the well-known Paris club, the ACBB, the lure for so many ambitious British riders. He scored wins and high places in a number of the French amateur classics, return-

Steve Lawrence, brilliant one-day rider and double national champion. Behind him Alf Engers makes a rare road-race appearance.

ing to England in August to contest the road-race championship, where he was beaten in the final sprint by Steve Lawrence, a defeat which rankled badly because he attributed it to a muffed gear change at the crucial moment. But his record in France had taken him to the top of the amateur scene there, and before the year was out he had signed as a professional with the Fiat team. From being just another amateur rider in England two years before, he rode into Paris in July 1978 at the end of his first Tour de France, an incredible progress which had cut out the usual years of apprenticeship in the Milk Race and selection for World Championships. Intelligent and out-going, Sherwen was to ride the classics and six more Tours, in which he never became a star rider, but where he laid the foundations for his later career as a commentator.

Sherwen's great rival was a very different personality: Steve Lawrence had been dedicated to cycling and racing since he was fifteen, but silence and concentration were his hallmarks. He rode the Milk Race four times and won stages, but he knew that stage-racing was not his forte. He was slightly moody and inconsistent, but he could produce brilliant flashes of form which made him the best one-day rider of his era. He would never accept that Sherwen had lost the 1977 championship through bad luck with his gear change: Lawrence felt certain throughout the race that he was the strongest, in fact he had vowed to take the title back in January, and had built his season around that aim. In the following year he won the Manx International ahead of Robert Millar, but their positions were reversed two weeks later in the national championship, when Millar became the first Scot to take the title in a decisive sprint. Lawrence won other classics - the Lincoln GP in 1978 and the Tour of the Cotswolds in 1979, but illness ruined his chances of selection for the 1980 Olympics. This misfortune was only a prelude to his greatest triumph however, as he set out to recover his very best form and regain the national championship, which he did with an inspired ride on the Isle of Man, where he set out to catch the lone leader, Neil Martin, in the closing miles, and stormed past him to win. He achieved this great come-back through some intense training routines, the secrets of which he would never reveal, thus adding considerably to his mystique. Lawrence went on to take fourth place behind Malcolm Elliott in the Commonwealth Games road-race in Brisbane in 1982, and he was a member of the TTT squad which took gold. Lawrence never seriously considered turning professional, sensing correctly that it was not the life for him, and after ten years of dedicated racing, his brilliant career ended very strangely, a victim to his mood-swings. Riding in the Lincoln GP in 1983 in pouring rain, something inside him snapped, and he suddenly knew that he had had enough. He climbed off half-way through the race, drove back home, and never touched his bike again, ever.

It was partly Sherwen's example which inspired a string of other riders to seek out the sponsored clubs in France, and none had a more brilliant career than Graham Jones, a year after Sherwen. In 1977 Jones had won the Essex GP alone in grand style, and departed for France immediately afterwards. Over the next eighteen months he won an unprecedented series of amateur classics, including Paris-Troyes, the GP de France and the amateur Grand Prix des Nations, making himself probably the best amateur in France. Jones was a phenomenal climber but he was not selected for the world championships that year at the Nurburgring - a very hilly circuit which would have suited him perfectly - because the selectors in England did not appreciate the quality of his victories in France. But like Sherwen he was rewarded with a pro contract with Peugeot, rode his first Tour in 1980, and finished a magnificent 20th in 1981 . Later he would be 9th in the 1982 Paris-Nice and second in Het Volk the same year. But bad luck dogged him in the form of accidents and illnesses, he found himself still playing the role of domestique in his team, and

Robert Millar leads Steve Lawrence in the 1978 championship race; they finished in that order.

his motivation suffered. For reasons that seemed to have little to do with his ability on the bike, Jones never fulfilled his immense potential, and his career faded away. In complete contrast, Sean Yates's talents developed slowly and steadily after he too had followed the trail to the famous ACBB club in Paris at the same time as Jones. Several unrewarding years as a domestique passed before Yates realised his great potential in the late eighties, at the time when Jones was saying goodbye to the sport. Jones and so many other British exiles had found that whatever your talents as a rider, success in the continental teams requires other strengths which few possess.

One who did possess them was the most successful of all the British colony in France - Robert Millar. His rise to the top level in the amateur ranks was as rapid as Sherwen's had been: from a sixteen year-old novice rider with the Glasgow Wheelers, he became Scottish junior road-race champion in 1976, hill climb champion in 1977, and British road champion in 1978 at the age of nineteen. The bicycle had been the means of escape for the teenager from the streets of Glasgow, and it led him into a different world altogether, for the difference between Millar and most other Scottish riders at this time was his decision to travel south regularly to compete in the top events in England. His first Milk Race in 1978 saw him get stronger each day and finish 21st, giving him the strength to contest the Manx International with Steve Lawrence and finish second. In the national championship two weeks later, Millar found the edge in an uphill sprint to take the title. He secured sponsorship money, abandoned both his engineering career and the domestic racing scene, and headed for France. In 1979 he rode brilliantly in the French amateur classics, returned to England to retain his national title by outsprinting Joe Waugh, and took fourth place in the world championships in Holland, only seconds behind the winner, but bitterly disappointed, such were the high standards he had set himself. A contract with Peugeot showed Millar how hard was the transition to the professional class: his only outstanding ride in his first year came in the world championship race on the murderous Sallanches circuit, where he remained with the leading group until the final ten miles, finishing eleventh. Two frustrating years followed during which Millar was denied a start in the big races, finally making his Tour de France debut in the most sensational way in 1983 with victory in the big Pyrennean

Steve Joughin, master sprinter, wins the Bournemouth stage of the 1981 Milk Race.

stage and in the King of the Mountains classification. It is a matter of history that Millar went on to become the most successful rider in the great national Tours that Britain has ever produced, with fourth place in the 1984 Tour de France, second in the Giro in 1987, twice second in the Vuelta, in 1985 and 1986, as well as second in the Tour de l'Avenir in 1982. In the Lemond-Roche-Delgado generation, Millar was up there with the world's best. Yet Millar was a difficult character who took few pains to make friends, and stories about the grimness of his Glasgow upbringing and his acerbic personality were legion. He refused to conceal how harsh, competitive and unfriendly the world of continental racing could be. He made no pretence to glamour, sportsmanship or even enjoyment in his chosen life. Years ago he had had no desire to be merely the best rider in Scotland, and now he seemed to have no overwhelming desire to be the best in Europe either: cycling was just a job, which he was very good at, but which he seemed to have no love for. He had been an outsider as a child in Glasgow, and he was an outsider still, a very successful one, but always a restless, unsatisfied and enigmatic personality.

A totally different personality was Steve Joughin - nicknamed "Jockey" for his size and speed, in fact his first job on leaving school had actually been in a riding stable. Outgoing, highly sociable and five foot three in height, Joughin was inevitably compared to Dave Bedwell and Dennis Tarr for his phenomenal sprinting powers. Raised on the Isle of Man, he began riding at fourteen and started making regular racing trips to the Merseyside region, taking the national junior road-race championship in 1977. In 1979 he became the first ever home winner of the Manx International, and the time had come to settle on the mainland and compete in all the leading events. 1980 saw him take the season-long Pernod competition, with victories in the Essex G.P. and the Lincoln G.P. His reputation as a sprinter was by now a fearsome one, with no less riders than Barry Hoban and Sid Barras falling victim to his speed in the pro-am Elswick centennial race at Easter; later conquests would include Abdujaparov and Kelly. But Joughin was no sit-in sprinter: he was an attacking rider who had built his power through long sessions behind a motor-bike around the mountain course on his native island, covering the course in around 1:15. He could time-trial too, for it was on that course that he came within seconds of Dave Lloyd in his record-breaking ride in 1981. In that year he rode his first Milk Race, taking an early stage win and with it the yellow jersey. But he knew he was at his best as a single-day rider, and he was proved right with further amateur classic victories such as the Tour of the Cotswolds and the Pernod G.P. He had tried a spell of living and racing in France, but could not settle and returned to the racing and the social life he knew, turning professional for Moducel in 1983. He crowned his career in 1984 when he beat Bill

Nickson and Malcom Elliott to win the national pro road-race championship, again before his home crowd on the Isle of Man. One of the most successful and best-liked riders of the eighties, Joughin later played a leading role in the Bilton and Ever Ready teams, winning his second national title in 1988.

In one important respect the life of the leading amateur roadmen of the late seventies was becoming very different from that of a decade or so earlier, for almost all of them belonged to sponsored clubs. For some years a change in attitudes to amateurism and sponsorship had been speading throughout the cycling world, and this received official blessing in 1971 when the B.C.F. agreed to permit the commercial sponsorship of clubs, with the attendant change of name and advertising functions. There had in fact been a brief experiment in club sponsorship before, between 1964 and 1967, but it was probably ahead of its time then, and made little impact. In the seventies however it was a different story, for, from modest beginnings, the practice spread until it had effectively changed the lives of scores of ambitious riders. Some of this sponsorship came from

Two Condor-sponsored clubs: Gerry Taylor (above) leading rider in the early years of Team Haverhill, and Gary Baker (below) of Olympia Sport, on the Milk Race with Monty in 1987.

within the bike trade, and Condor began a long association first with Team Haverhill and then with Olympia Sport and its successor, Anglia Sport. But it was striking to see how much sponsorship also came from outside cycling: builders, car dealers, brewers, insurers, newspaper publishers all now lined up to donate money in return for seeing their name in the local or national press. The terms of the sponsorship, the contract between sponsor and club, were in theory regulated and transparent, with all transactions authorised by a club sponsorship committee. The best riders in the club were provided with clothing, equipment and transport to races. This removed most of the outright expenses of racing without making the riders into paid professionals. But over time the rewards of sponsorship

Simon Lillistone, one of the Team Haverhill-Condor star riders of the late 1980s.

became more enticing: riders were provided with complete bikes, they were given cash fees and win bonuses. In some cases there were rumours of cars and even houses being provided, and part-time managers being paid to look after the team riders. With this kind of help it became possible for young riders to live without working, at least through the summer months, when they could also receive welfare payments, while they worked and saved through the winter. If they had understanding parents, even this became unnecessary, and a few riders admitted that they had never worked since leaving school. Some clubs would negotiate with leading riders to persuade them to join, in the knowledge that more wins would keep the sponsor happy and elicit more cash. The B.C.F. held on to the rule that sponsored amateurs could not be featured directly in advertisements for the sponsor, otherwise it was hard to define any distinction between them and the professionals.

By far the best-known sponsored club was the Manchester Wheelers, a very old and distinguished club (its most famous son being Reg Harris) which now secured substantial backing from Trumann's Steel, and signed up riders from all over England to race in their colours. The Wheelers became the elite among clubs: fees were paid to riders on joining, like a soccer star's transfer fee. Money on this scale had never been seen in amateur cycling before: there were stories of nights in classy hotels before races, and champagne from the cooler in the car on the journey home afterwards. The sponsorship of clubs had become the sponsorship of an elite team of individuals: in effect, a new semi-professional class had been established almost accidentally, not through a planned strategy by the B.C.F. or the B.P.C.R.A., but by market forces, from the grass-roots up. The man behind this particular sponsorship was Jack Fletcher, boss of Trumann's Steel, who could claim to have been one the most influential figures in British cycling. His approach was entirely typical of the 1980s, in the sense that he introduced market forces into sport, or, to put it more bluntly, he showed that success could be bought. He showed that the ideas of an individual could make a decisive difference to the ethos of a sport, always provided that those ideas were backed up with money and action. In this respect he offered a striking contrast to the officials of the governing bodies, who seemed to move slowly and uncertainly, and who always lacked the vision or the resources to initiate radical changes.

What were the implications of this innovative approach? Firstly a number of people were extremely unhappy at the apparent death of the amateur ideal, which had rested on the principle of fairness, and the idea that taking part was more important than winning at all costs. In the process the social basis of club life was being discarded too, as these elite clubs came to resemble a professional team. Not a few of these critics resigned in protest when their own clubs became involved in commercial sponsorship. Another unhappy group were the professionals themselves, who felt that money which should be building a genuinely professional class was being wasted on "shamateurs". This point was underlined when a number of top amateurs were reported as saying that they had no incentive to turn pro now because they were already so well looked after.

But others applauded this development as the only way forward for the sport, pointing out that the traditional amateur could no longer compete internationally with the state-sponsored athletes from the eastern bloc, or from many other countries where state or private money was given to develop sporting talent. They pointed out that the much-envied clubs of France which put Sherwen, Jones, Millar and others on the route to stardom, were all sponsored. In the case of ACBB, it was municipal money deliberately aimed at nurturing future medal-winners for France, and nobody criticised these riders for seeking the benefits which those clubs offered. In 1980 the director of the Sealink International, John Burns, had refused to accept a Russian team in the race because their ill-disguised professionalism had already stifled the Milk Race; the only true competition in that race would come when it was opened to professionals from 1983 onwards. Meanwhile there was no longer much pretence that the country's leading riders were amateurs in the way that Bill Bradley, Les West, or Arthur Metcalfe had been: it was simply no longer possible to reach that level on evening training rides after work. Time-triallists could still win domestic championships on that kind of regime, but the road-racing competition, not to mention the time taken up by the races themselves, made it impossible.

Paul Curran, nearly unbeatable in one-day races in the mid 80s.

So now the long-established lines between amateur and professional were becoming blurred, apparently by common consent. The transition to full open racing could not be made yet, for the whole international racing structure was still based on the pro-am distinction, and in Britain as everywhere else you had either a pro or an amateur licence, and this decided which events you might ride. But what you did with your life, how you earned your living, who bought you your equipment, who drove you to a race and what name was on your jersey - all this seemed to matter less and less in Britain, as it had ceased to matter long ago in France, Belgium, Italy and most other places. The important thing now was results, and it seemed that the sponsorship route might be the answer to the debate that had been going on for years about how British riders could compete for international honours, for British riders of the eighties certainly seemed to be achieving things in Europe as never before. It was also the answer to securing greater media attention for the sport, and the eighties would see some high-profile sponsorship for both city-centre and stage-racing, which in turn stimulated the true professional class, and benefited the next wave of riders including Yates, Doyle, Joughin, Elliott, McLoughlin and Curran. Throughout the 1970s the entire national track championships at Leicester were sponsored by the watch manufacturers Newmark. This new age of sponsorship suited the new context of cyling generally in the eighties: cycling was smart, it was physically challenging, it was eco-friendly, and it made good television.

This was a revolution which had crept up quietly and unexpectedly, and the eighties would see it gather pace and momentum. It reflected two forces which were emerging in British society: first, the fashion for deregulation, for breaking down artificial controls and letting market forces produce winners and losers; it was in effect the first stage in the re-structuring of British cycling, a process that would eventually lead to the dissolving of the amateur-professional divide. Second, it reflected the movement against discrimination, against classifying people because they were male or female, black or white, old or young, fit or disabled, Oxford-educated or educationally sub-normal. What mattered now was what you could actually achieve, not what pigeon-holes people put you in. In this atmosphere, the old labels of amateur and professional could not long survive. Whatever was felt about sponsored clubs at the time, it now seems clear in retrospect that they were an important bridge into the new environment of fully-commercialised sport. This new environment was officially acknowledged by the mid eighties, when state grants, through bodies such as the Sport Aid Foundation, and finance from private sponsors began to be allocated quite openly to cyclists and other amateur sportsmen, specifically to enable them to prepare for major competitions, the Olympics above all. The first Centres of Excellence were started in 1979, as an initiative from the Sports Council, and they were in a sense the B.C.F.'s answer to the sponsored clubs: an elite racing team with its sponsor - this time a state-funded body - its coaches, and its goals.

For most of the 1980s it seemed that the Manchester Wheelers was a multi-headed monster, with one of the team invariably turning up to win every big race in the programme - road, track, time-trial, team and individual. Bob Downs, Jeff Williams and his brother Mike, Steve Joughin, Dave Lloyd, Pete Longbottom, Mark Bell, Deno Davie, Darryl Webster, Malcolm Elliott, Sandy Gilchrist, Paul Curran, the Gornall brothers Alan and Mark, Pete Sanders - the list went on and on as the blue and white jerseys amassed national championships, Star Trophy wins, hill-climb titles and international selections. With riders like these living and racing as virtual professionals, the standard of amateur riding was elevated to a new level. Among the strongest of all these on his day was Mark Bell, one of the elite group of riders who have won both the amateur and professional road titles, the second of these victories scored in 1986 with a memorable lone break and a three-minute winning margin, almost unique in the annals of the pro championship.

For sheer speed however, the outstanding rider was Darryl Webster, as he proved with his untouchable time-trialling, taking

The 1989 Kelloggs Tour: Curran in the centre between Elliott and Anderson.

over where Lloyd left off, but he admitted that he sometimes lacked tactical sense. Nevertheless he was a constant presence in all the top road-races, and he won a number of classics such as the Lincoln G.P. in 1985 and the Manx International in 1987. Like his coach Eddie Soens, Webster was a stormy petrel of British racing, with a natural genius for upsetting everybody with whom he came into contact. He never bothered to keep his opinions to himself, and diplomacy was unknown to him. His natural speed and athletic ability saw him take countless individual track and time-trial titles at home, but his refusal to cooperate with officialdom meant that he never brought home the international hon-ours of which he was undoubtedly capable. Paul Curran started his career as a track rider and won numerous national medals in the points, Madison and team pursuit events, before turning seriously to the road. Only slightly bigger in stature than Steve Joughin, Curran proved almost unstoppable: he topped the season-long Star Trophy competition an unprecedented three years running from 1985-87, during which time every amateur clas-sic fell to him: the Essex, the Lincoln, the Manx, the Cotswolds and the Peak, while he was national road-race champion in 1987. In the Commonwealth Games in Edinburgh in 1986 Curran was one of the winning team time-trial squad, and he added a second gold medal with his courageous solo performance in the road-race. Neither Curran nor

Malcolm Elliott, whose years in the ill-fated ANC team launched his continental career.

Webster made any apology for being full-time riders: their spon-sorship existed to get the best out of them, and they used it to good purpose. When they did turn pro, they had both left it too late, and injuries and team problems meant that both these high-achieving riders would be remembered for their amateur victo-ries, although in Curran's case his career had another twist to come. Disillusioned with the pro scene, he returned to the ama-teur ranks in 1991, again with great success, until a very serious crash in 1996 almost cost him his life and finally put him out of bike racing for ever.

    Two of the most significant pointers to the future came in 1983, first with the televised series of city-centre races spon-sored by Kelloggs, and second with the opening of the Milk Race to professionals and amateurs together. The Kelloggs series was the brain-child of promoter Alan Rushton, who succeeded in bringing cycling into the television age with races in the cen-tre of Bristol, Glasgow, Nottingham, Manchester and Birmingham. The philosophy was to bring road-racing down off the hilltops and into the cities where people could see it, and where the glamour of television would attract a live audience too. Foreign stars invited included Moser, Kelly, Anderson and Raas, but the end of the series saw Phil Thomas of the Falcon team crowned with overall victory. The series boosted the fortunes of the pros and the identity of bike racing, and it was repeated the following year, with Thomas's phenomenal sprinting power once again bringing him the series win. Over the next two years, vic-tory went to Australian Shane Sutton and Malcom Elliott. The

Sights that would have been unimaginable twenty years earlier: London and Blackpool city centres closed for the Milk Race in 1989.

final race in 1986 was in the heart of London, where Tony Doyle, newly crowned as world pursuit champion, showed off his rainbow jersey with a winning ride. The Kelloggs races were not the only criterium events: Michelin sponsored a Spring Cup series and a number of other televised city-centre races followed in the eighties. By 1987 however Alan Rushton's race plans had matured into a five-day professional Tour of Britain. It was run from Glasgow to London, and included some massive 150-mile stages that were reminiscent of the old Tours of the 1950s. Highlights of the race were televised each day, and large crowds at the roadside saw Joey McLoughlin hold on for a tense victory over Tour de France star climber Steven Rooks. In 1988 it was Malcolm Elliott's turn to take top place on the podium after a race-long battle with McLoughlin, both now riding for continental teams, and in 1989 Robert Millar continued the pattern by returning to Britain to win the event, again by a matter of seconds. In 1990 the Belgian Michel Dernies became the race's first foreign winner, when a crash within sight of the finish snatched certain second victory from Millar's grasp. The Kelloggs criteriums and then the Tour had established themselves as one of the high points of the racing year, bringing continental stars to Britain, and preparing both the television companies and the public for the televising of the Tour de France.

The 1983 Milk Race was the biggest of a number of races being opened to pro-am competition, and with the Russians not invited it was felt to be the best chance for a home win for many years. The professionals - Barras, Doyle, Yates, Lambert, Bayton and Steve Jones - were in a composite grouping drawn from different trade teams, and they made a stronger replacement for the more familiar British "B" or regional teams, with Arthur Metcalfe as team manager. Barras and Bayton won stages, and Yates briefly held the yellow jersey, but the undoubted star of the race was the phenomenal Malcolm Elliott, who won no less than six stages, a record unapproached even in the days of Bradley or West or by the all-conquering Russians. Elliott had been racing as a sponsored amateur both in France and then in England as a member of the elite Manchester Wheelers, and the successes of both the amateurs and the professionals demonstrated that no great gulf existed between the two classes any longer: it had been a genuinely open race, and Arthur Metcalfe was the first to admit how much standards had changed since his day, with amateurs and pros competing on an equal footing. Just as remarkable as Elliott's performance was the fact that the overall winner was the American, Matt Eaton. The American cycling boom had been talked about during the past few years, but this result really drove the fact home to the British public. Eaton's team-mates included Andy Hampsten, the future Giro winner, and Alexi Grewal, who would be Olympic road-race champion in the following year. It was in 1983 too that Lemond stunned the world of European cycling when he won his world title, while in Los Angeles in 1984 the Americans would easily top the table of cycling medals, admittedly in a Games boycotted by the communist countries. The Americans had no state aid, no central coaching system, indeed almost no recent tradition of bike racing at all, yet in a few short years they had lifted themselves to world-beating level, through their natural enthusiasm and self-confidence, their refusal to be overawed by any barriers or traditions. The rise of American racing caused a great deal of heart-searching in Britain, as did the new wave of star riders emerging from Ireland, a country with a population less than that of London.

The '83 Milk Race confirmed Malcolm Elliott's status as Britain's top amateur. A prolific winner since his junior days, he was a member of the 1980 Olympic team pursuit squad, returning from Moscow to win the national hill-climb championship. In the 1982 Commonwealth Games in Brisbane he took the road-race gold medal, outsprinting Steve Bauer, and he joined Waugh, Downs and Lawrence in a second gold-medal victory in the TTT, beating the Australians by the narrowest of margins. His Milk Race performance and his season-long Star Trophy triumph made him the most sought-after signing for the pro teams, and he joined Raleigh for the 1984 season, snatching victory in the Sealink International by one second from Tony Doyle, winning the national criterium championship, and taking the pro pursuit title during a rare excursion onto the track in 1985. For a couple of years Elliott appeared to hesitate between domestic racing and occasional forays into Europe, but even so he commanded tremendous admiration, becoming probably the only British cyclist to have his own fan-club, and it was not unusual to find "Malcy" chalked on the road before his races, in the continental fashion. Then in 1987 everything changed for him when he became part of the ANC-Halfords set-up, run by Tony Capper, head of the ANC distribution company. This team had grown from small beginnings in 1984 when Mick Morrison was its only rider, to become the biggest pro team ever seen in Britain, with a budget of a quarter of a million pounds, a compliment of more than a dozen riders, and the avowed aim of breaking into the Tour de France. It was while riding for ANC that Elliott led the Milk Race from start to finish in 1987, and it was also in ANC colours that he and Adrian Timmis went on to complete the Tour de France that year, the first British trade team to do so. Elliott described the Tour as three weeks of mental and physical torture, but soon afterwards he was beating the world's best sprinters in the Nissan Classic, where he won three of the five stages.

The other star rider whose name will always be associated with ANC was Joey McLoughlin, the Merseysider who shot to prominence in 1984 when he was first over the line in the amateur road-race championship, but was relegated to third place for switching, giving the victory to Neil Martin. McLoughlin was always to remain a wild, desperate sprinter, and no stranger to controversy. In 1985, at the age of twenty and in his first pro year with ANC, he won the Sealink International, now nine stages long and open to pros and amateurs alike, ranking second only to the Milk Race in the British road season. This sensational debut and his teaming with Elliott prepared cycling fans for the possibility of a British win in the Milk Race, for after Matt Eaton victory had again gone abroad, to

Russia and then to Belgium, and we were in the same position as we had been in the mid-1970s - ten years without a home win. McLoughlin fulfilled those hopes brilliantly, taking the lead at the halfway point of the race, with a lone break through the Welsh hills that became part of Milk Race history, as securely as the exploits of Bradley, West, Nickson or Lewis. McLoughlin kept until the end most of the four minutes he gained that day, and with Elliott second overall and stage wins going to Joughin, Martin and Yates, there was nothing that even the Russians could do to prevent a magnificent sense of euphoria in the British camp as the race came to a triumphant end with a criterium in central London. But McLoughlin did not have an easy relationship with his team, and he seemed injury-prone:

Joey McLoughlin, whose brilliant career ended all too briefly.

these factors kept him out of both the Milk Race and the Tour de France in 1987, but he made a great return to win the Kelloggs Tour in August. Yet even as this race was in progress came the shock news that the plug had been pulled on the ANC team: the riders claimed they were sacked during the race.

The inside story of what went on in the team - the schemes, the finances, the personalities, the conflicts and the final collapse - would fill most of a book, but the simple fact was that all the big plans were now finished, and some of Britain's top riders suddenly found themselves without a team. However ANC had undoubtedly launched several riders into continental careers. McLoughlin and Elliott both took the plunge into European racing, McLoughlin signing for Z-Peugeot and Elliott joining Roche and Millar at Fagor. Elliott went on to build a solid and lucrative career with Spanish and later American teams, and he left behind two enduring impressions: first that he was possibly the classiest roadman Britain ever produced, and second that he might have achieved even more with better luck and better career management. McLoughlin's later career was less happy: he did score some successes on the continent, but for three years he was also dogged by mysterious injuries and spent more time in rest and in treatment than he did racing. He returned to race for a while in England, before calling it a day in 1991, while still in his mid-twenties, leaving behind the memory of a brief but brilliant career. McLoughlin's sister, Vicky (herself an international rider) married another Merseyside road-sprinter with a canon-ball finish, Phil Thomas, who had won the Manx International in 1977, pushing into second place Pascal Simon, the man who was to hold the yellow jersey for a week in the 1983 Tour de France. Thomas's later pro career with its multitude of wins, especially in criteriums, really signalled the end of Sid Barras's domination of the pro sprints. Thomas's great year was 1983, when he topped the Kelloggs city-centre series, beating all the continental stars as well as the home pros, and took the national professional championship. Thomas was an outspoken and combative roadman, often accused of being a sit-in sprinter, and he was no stranger to the boos of the crowd. His reply to his critics was logical and to the point: if others thought they were stronger, then it was their job to get rid of him before the final sprint, and if they couldn't, that was their problem.

It was in the mid-eighties that Condor re-entered the world of pro team racing, and it came about through Bob Downs. Downs had been riding Milk Races and Star Trophy events, and had been travelling the world with British teams for some eight years, and felt that the time had come to wind down his career. A long-standing customer at Condor's shop, he had taken a job there in 1980, and by 1983 he felt that his serious racing days were probably over. He happened to mention this fact to one of his regular customers, adding that the only thing that might change his mind was a serious professional sponsorship deal. The customer was Ron Groom, chief executive of a successful London

Bob Downs after winning the pro-am Tour of Ireland in 1984, between Barras and Nickson.

building and civil engineering firm, and he promptly replied that he would sponsor Bob through his company, Percy Bilton Ltd. Condor was the natural choice as the trade co-sponsor to provide Downs with a bike and equipment. The shop was doing well in the cycling boom of the eighties, and Monty Young was delighted to put the Condor name back in the racing news after a lapse of a dozen years, although his involvement with the new team was to be briefer than with the Condor-Mackeson team of the 1960s. When the 1984 season opened Downs was racing in solitary splendour in the bright yellow and red of the Percy Bilton-Condor team. This move re-awakened his motivation, and in May he had the best possible opening to his new career when he took the Tour of Ireland, a seven-stage pro-am race in which Downs held off world pursuit champion, Hans Henrik Oersted, to win by 5 seconds overall. The decisive move had come on the second stage when Downs and Oersted took a massive seven minutes out of the bunch through the Wicklow Mountains, and Downs's bonus for the sprint win was the margin which he held to the end. This victory gave Downs great hopes for the Milk Race, in which he was part of a composite GB pro team, but illness caused him to abandon at the half-way stage. In any case nothing would have stopped the Russians, invited back after a break in 1983. Downs failed to win any further races that season, but a string of high placings prompted the Bilton management to double the budget and give him full support in 1985 by enlarging the team to three. The riders chosen were Glen Mitchell and Neil Martin, the former a top-flight trackman and the latter national amateur road-race champion and now eager to turn professional.

But the high hopes for 1985 were not fulfilled. Bob Downs was injured in April and was sidelined for most of the season. Martin and Mitchell were relatively inexperienced in pro terms and the pair were unable to make much of an impact against the more powerful teams - ANC, Falcon, Moducel and Raleigh. There were no important wins in '85, but there were some good placings, and at the end of the year the sponsors were still enthusiastic and set about strengthening the team still further. No half-measures were used, instead their numbers were doubled, by bringing in John Herety, Mark Walsham and Pete Sanders. Herety was the probably biggest catch: a 1980 Olympic and Peace Race rider

John Herety who finished second to Elliott in the 1986 Kelloggs city-centre series.

and Manx International winner, he had spent two years in France with ACBB before turning pro for Mercier. In 1982 he outwitted all the big names - Yates, Sherwen, Doyle, Nickson and Thomas - to seize the home professional championship. Illness laid him low the following season, and he found himself out of his depth in Europe, returning home to sign for the Ever-Ready team. Walsham's amateur career was almost as good, having won the G.P. Pernod and the Manx International, before turning pro for Raleigh. Sanders was one of the elite in the Manchester Wheelers squad, winner of the Wincanton Classic in 1985, placed 14th overall in that year's Milk Race; this was his first pro season.

The results in 1986 quickly justified the renewed investment in the team, with Mark Walsham outsprinting Joughin, Thomas and Doyle to win the opening event of the season, the Merseyside G.P. Two weeks later it was Sanders's turn to score his first professional win in the Eastbourne-London race at the expense of his breakaway companion Dave Lloyd. In a two-day stage race at Easter, which was lashed by wind and rain, Downs showed all his familiar strength to finish 8th, one minute down on the winner, McLoughlin. At the end of April it was Sanders again in a hotly-disputed sprint with McLoughlin in the Worcester Road Race. The high point of the early season came for the team in the Tour of Delyn in May, a gruelling 120 miles through the Welsh mountains, in which Neil Martin and John Herety finished first and second. The Bilton-Condor riders had now established themselves as among the strongest of the home teams, and they went to the Milk Race determined to contribute to the action. Neil Martin took a fine stage win on the Sheffield-Chester stage, after the climbs of Winnats and Cat and Fiddle, and he went on to finish 33rd overall. Downs was in front of him in 25th position, a great deal lower than he had hoped. The outstanding result however came from Pete Sanders, who had moved up the classification by being in the lead group during McLoughlin's great stage in South Wales, and he held his position to finish 9th overall, just three minutes down on the victorious McLoughlin.

Glen Mitchell had so far not shown as well as the others, but he made amends in the national track championships in August by winning the pro omnium title. In the pro pursuit, Sanders recorded the second fastest time in the series, and was the losing finalist in the inevitable Doyle victory. In the Kelloggs city-centre criterium races all the team rode above themselves against top international competition, and at the end of the televised series Herety finished in second place overall behind Malcolm Elliott, with Mark Walsham seventh and Downs eighth. For good measure Herety won the last pro event of the season, the Wolverhampton road-race in October, to balance Walsham's first win in March. It had been a very satisfying season: all the riders had had their moments of triumph and the future looked good.

But the world of the pro racing teams had always been a strange one, with partnerships and alliances liable to break down suddenly for no very good reason. In the winter of 1986-87 the Bilton company had new plans to sign still more riders for the team, requiring more bikes both for road and track, more equipment, more servicing and more travelling. The result was Monty Young's decision to withdraw from the partnership. He had always been happiest sponsoring a small goup of riders whom he had known as friends and customers, people like Dave Bonner, Tony Gowland, Bob Downs or John Pritchard. Condor was after all still just one shop, running at full capacity in the bike retailing boom of the eighties, and the additional pressures of servicing the proposed eight-man professional team both in road and track events was just too much. So the Bilton organisation was free to find another bike supplier, and their choice fell upon Holdsworth, once a leading player in pro sponsorship, but out of the picture since 1978. The new team was announced for 1987 as Bilton-Holdsworth, but fate intervened when Holdsworth was taken over to become part of the Falcon empire. The Bilton team never rode Holdsworths, but instead they ordered a fleet of bikes from a small workshop and branded them   with their own name. Steve Joughin and Dave LeGrys joined the team, now called simply Percy Bilton, and they raced for three more seasons, until they were dissolved very suddenly in 1989, leaving new pro Paul Curran and several others high and dry.

Glen Mitchell, leading amateur trackman then professional with Bilton-Condor

        After the break with Bilton, Monty returned with some relief to concentrate on the shop, and to the slightly less demanding sponsorship of clubs, in which Condor was involved for many years with Team Haverhill, Olympia Sport and Anglia Sport. The co-sponsor behind the first of these, Team Haverhill, was Taylor's Foundries, owned by Eddie Taylor, whose son Gerry became one of its leading riders. It was from Team Haverhill in the late 1980s that riders of the calibre of Colin Sturgess, Simon Lillistone, Rob Hayles, Bryan Steel and Bradley Wiggins emerged, riders equally at home on road or track. To these riders, Eddie Taylor became virtually the Jack Fletcher of the south, and Condor's co-sponsorship kept them at the heart of the racing scene. John Pritchard established an outpost of Anglia Sport in South Wales, which included Welsh champion Colin Wallace and John's son Ceri, national junior time-trial champion in 1996.

        The 1980s had been an exciting time in British road-racing. The internationalisation of British cycling had once meant British riders going abroad in search of fame and fortune, but now the foreign stars were coming here for the Kelloggs criteriums, the Kelloggs Tour, the open Milk Race and the Nissan Classic in Ireland. The Milk Race was no longer just a war of attrition against the Dutch or the Russians, but was contested by global teams, with winners coming from America, Canada, Ireland and Australia. In all these major races, the professionals and the sponsored amateurs raced side by side and shared in the publicity and the rewards. But in the early 1990s, the sport was overtaken by

Bradley Wiggins, future Olympic and World Champion, sponsored by Condor in 1997.

a series of changes that no one could have predicted. The economic recession of those years hit small and medium-sized businesses very hard, and these were exactly the companies which had been sponsoring sports teams. There was also a growing political conflict within the professional ranks, with the television sponsorship companies and the teams each suspicious that the other side had too much power and was taking all the profits. The televised races had brought money and publicity to the sport, but now riders, promoters and sponsors began quarrelling about the spoils. These quarrels plus the recession meant that by 1992 the pro class in Britain had virtually ceased to exist, and the future appeared to lie with sponsored clubs. In this, Condor's experience once again mirrored the structural and commercial changes that had overtaken the sport.

In this uncertain climate the Manchester velodrome, Britain's first modern, world-class indoor track, was opened in 1994, having been built in the context of the city's unsuccessful bid to host the 2000 Olympics. It was the major legacy of Ian Emmerson, the B.C.F. president ousted in the Tony Doyle affair of 1996. It was to become the jewel in the crown of the new B.C.F. drive for international honours, yet many early meetings took place before smaller crowds than had been hoped for, some high-profile meetings were even cancelled for lack of support, and public money had to be given to keep the stadium functioning. The reason was that, although thousands of new riders were coming into cycling, they were not necessarily coming into the traditional disciplines, instead they were attracted to mountain biking, triathlon or audax, which had their own clubs and associations. The rather closed culture of the traditional cycling-club world held little appeal for many of this new generation. There was a competitive market for cyclists now, in a way that there had never been in the past. This fluid situation existed in Europe too, where leisure cycling boomed while trade teams folded, sending many pros, including Malcolm Elliott, to America to find new teams. An earlier sign of this internal market in cycling had appeared back in 1982, when the League International was founded in protest against the B.C.F.'s failure to provide road racing for veterans. The League quickly built up its own successful race programme, and only after years of opposition did the B.C.F. admit the case for such racing. In a second radical move in 1986, the L.V.R.C. - the League of Veteran Racing Cyclists - broke away in its turn when the League International proposed to open its programme to non-vets. At first sight, these splits seemed to be cases of history repeating itself, recalling the days of the breakaway B.L.R.C. in the 1940s. The difference was that no one now spoke of the sport as being at war with itself: instead it was seen as a natural exercise in democracy, a proof of diversity in the sport. The B.C.F. struggled to keep pace with these changes: it was never able to develop a strategy for the sport's future because for one thing it never had any money. Its staging of the 1982 world championships had left a financial hangover that took years to dispell. Cyclists became increasingly critical of their governing body, while the new forms of the sport created their own associations without reference to it.

A symbolic blow to the British cycling tradition came in the winter of 1993-94, when the Milk Marketing Board warned that, after 36 years, it had sponsored its last Milk Race. Chris Lillywhite's narrow victory that year over Norwegians, Czechs, Russians and Belgians signalled the end of a chapter in cycling history, for the B.C.F. was unable to find a new backer. 1994 saw the last Kelloggs professional Tour of Britain, but the public's attention was already elsewhere, riveted on Chris Boardman's sensational debut in the Tour de France. The "Boardman effect" - his Olympic gold medal, his space-age bike, his world hour record, and then the dream start to his continental career - was undoubtedly the biggest publicity boost which the sport had ever received. Reg Harris's name had been a household word in the 1950s, but that was pre-television, and his image was not flashed around the world as Boardman's was. Boardman had progressed through sponsored clubs, and it was now an accepted fact that victory at these levels could not be achieved by the traditional amateur training in his spare time. The move towards open racing was becoming inevitable and it was international, guided by the U.C.I. In 1993 the long-established Star Trophy competiton for amateur roadmen was replaced by the Premier Calendar Series, open to professionals and amateurs, and in 1995 it was announced that fully open racing would become universal. The old terms amateur and professional would be dead, and even the Olympic Games would be open to Tour de France riders. When Robert Millar and Simon Bray respectively won the national professional and amateur road-race

Memories of a past era: Phil Edwards takes off at Westerdale ford in the 1971 Milk Race.

Gary Baker of Olympia Sport-Condor winning the 1996 Archer Grand Prix. Former pro Baker returend to amateur ranks to become the country's top-ranked roadman of 1996.

championships in 1995, they entered the record books as the last holders of those titles, while in the following year Dave Rand became the first open British champion. In this fast-changing and competitive world, criticisms of the B.C.F. became stronger than ever before - that it was out of touch and lacked a modern vision for the sport - and the organisation was rocked by a series of internal crises which brought it to the edge of disaster. It was forced to re-build itself under a completely new management to meet the challenges of the new era. The truth was that cycling was evolving as rapidly as the society around it, and that the established governing bodies were running as fast as they could just to stay in the same place. It would take a revolution in management, and above all a revolution in funding, to prepare the B.C.F. for the new century.

This came through the award in 1999 of £2 million of National Lottery money to support the World Class Performance Plan. Never before had such a gigantic sum of money been invested in amateur cycling, and it marked the beginning of a new era for the national team. It was to be spent on facilties, coaching, equipment, travel and direct cash subsidies given to the riders to free them for full-time training and racing. The Plan was a spin-off from the work of Boardman and Keen, for it was based on the conviction that the coaching and support of elite riders could be brought to an exact science, whose rewards would be Olympic medals. These methods were all geared to the controlled environment of the track, for no such success could be guaranteed in the tough, tactical, unpredictable sphere of road-racing. So almost exactly forty years after its foundation, after all the uncertainties about where British cycling was going, the B.C.F. at last had a master plan, a type of sports-academy concept, which had existed in other countries for forty years, but which no one could have predicted would emerge here. It was professionalism by another name, and it worked brilliantly, bringing home Olympic medals from Sydney and Athens. So the process of internationalisation that had begun in the sport a lifetime before, had reached its culmination, although in track racing rather than road racing. The sport had been comprehensively re-structured, like so much else in British society. As a result, British cycling had at last found a way into that world of international success which it had begun to search for in the 1950s, when it emerged from the world of fixed wheels and saddle-bags and time-trials. Whether it is a better world is an interesting question, but it seems to be the only one available.

Time-Trialling

After the explosion of speed in the 1960s, record-breaking became less common in the 70s and 80s. When records came, they tended to come infrequently, as shock-waves, sent out when outstanding individuals took times to unpredictable new levels. In between these waves, records might last for a decade or more, and many riders who were good enough to win championships were not good enough to get near the records. From the late 80s onwards, time-trialling was caught up in a whirlwind of technical change. After nearly three decades in which the set-up of the racing bike had remained essentially static, the search for aerodynamic efficiency now produced a stream of radical new designs for the frame, the wheels, the handlebars and other components, and for racing clothing. But the interesting thing is that none of the record-breaking rides in these years can be directly related to these changes. They may have improved performances generally, but they did not in themselves cause records to tumble. Even tri-bars, the most important of all these technical innvoations, did not have the effect of immediately tearing up everything in the record-books when they were introduced into time-trials in 1991. There was huge controversy about what was happening on the design front, especially about these bars and disk-wheels, but the truth is that they were less important than the brilliance of the half-dozen riders of genius who dominated the 70s and the 80s.

Of this small group, none captured the imagination of the cycling world more completely than Alf Engers. Holder of the 25-mile competiton record as long ago as 1959, he was in and out of the sport for some years, but came back in 1969 to win the championship and set a new record of 51:00, which resisted all assaults year after year. Once again Engers took a break from racing, but returned for a five-year period in the 70s in which his dominance became absolute, taking an unprecedented five national 25-mile titles in succession when in his mid-thirties, and winning many of his races by two or even three minutes, margins which were huge in short-distance terms. But alongside this brilliant riding, there was another side to Engers's career: the authorities simply didn't like him. They always denied it, but the evidence that he was being victimised seems overwhelming. He was watched, reported, warned, and suspended more than any other time-triallist. Having a following car, dangerous riding, taking pace, being a professional - these were some of the offences of which he was accused. What was behind it all is difficult to say. Engers was a showman, a cockney wit, a flashy dresser - it was all just harmless fun, but somehow it didn't fit in with the official time-trialling culture. The dual-carriageway courses in Essex were his kingdom, and by his own admission, Engers took his own line on the road. His commitment was absolute, and when racing he planted himself in the middle of the carriageway, he swept downhill at 45 m.p.h. or more, and if there was slow-moving traffic in his way, he overtook it. This may have been the core of the problem: the R.T.T.C. continued to promote events on these high-speed roads, but they did not like the consequences when committed riders like Engers played the courses for all they were worth. The combination of his brilliant riding and his conflicts with authority made him a gift to the press and a hero to thousands of club cyclists. He did not conceal the fact that he had help from unofficial sponsors: Alan Shorter for example built him a series of ultra-light bikes, which Engers had on loan only. But he worked for his living all his life,

Riding into history: Alf Engers minutes away from finishing the first sub-50-minute 25 in 1978.

he never made money out of the sport, and he was, by any reasonable test, a pure amateur. And for all his flamboyance, Engers could never be accused of arrogance: he never boasted about what he had done or was going to do, he never put other riders down, he was always willing to discuss training and racing techniques if anyone asked him, and the confrontations with the R.T.T.C. were never of his making.

Engers's public image in fact hid a serious purpose, a single-minded determination to make cycling history, and the target he chose was the 30 m.p.h. 25. As a teenager, Engers had been a runner, and had dreamed of being a four-minute miler, following in the footsteps of Bannister, Ibbotson and Elliott, until an accident smashed his right kneecap, after which he transferred his ambitions to cycling. Beneath the humour, Engers had a tremendous self-belief, and both in training and in racing he drove himself as few others riders could, always chasing the elusive 30 m.p.h target. He had no interest in the longer distances, it was the out-and-out speed and pain barriers which fascinated him. By the mid 1970s he was getting to an age when logic suggested that short-distance speed should be slipping away from him, but still he persisted. He came closest to the magic figures in July 1976, when he was on schedule for a 48-minute ride, but was stopped by a police patrol, who were astounded to see a cyclist topping 50 m.p.h. on a descent. For this he was banned from racing, initially for two years, but reduced to one year, a blow which might easily have ended his career.

It is a matter of history that he served his suspension and came back in 1978 to achieve his dream. The morning of 5 August on the Essex roads was nothing special - slightly damp and slightly windy - and Engers didn't feel especially strong, but when he started he realised that he was flying. The wind was there, but he seemed able to cut through it, cruising at over 30 m.p.h. with no feeling of blowing up. Only in the last couple of miles did pain overtake him, and although slowing now, he managed to hold on to the finish. Eddie Adkins finished with a time of 50:50, finally breaking Engers's nine-year old record by 10 seconds. Then someone ran up to Adkins saying that Alf had "done a 49". Adkins thought this meant 50:49, and that he had been beaten by one second, but then he heard the rest: Engers had recorded 49:24, beating his own record by an incredible margin. Ten years of trying, of single-minded dedication and of bitter disappointment, were over at last, and he had taken the record to a new height, where it would remain for twelve years. With the exception of Adkins's few minutes that morning, Engers would have held the 25 record from 1969 to 1990. As always when he raced, there were mutterings about his riding, and the record was held on ice for almost three months before it was finally ratified, and Engers's place in cycling history was assured. It is often said that he never raced again after that day, but he did make periodic comebacks, riding a short 52 in 1982, before he switched to triathlon competition. Today Engers is relaxed, witty as ever, and still a showman. He doesn't ride much any more, but he has a strong sense of the history of the sport in which he played such a unique role. Part of him however still wishes he could have been a four-minute miler, taking on Herb Elliott and the other greats of running. With his self-belief, who would say he couldn't have done it?

Probably the most consistent of Engers's rivals was Eddie Adkins, who won over 500 races in his long career. He won the first of his three consecutive 25-mile championships in 1977, during one of Engers's periods of suspension. He defeated Engers for the title in 1978, won again in 1979, and in 1980 he lost to Sean Yates by a mere 7 seconds. For many years Adkins shared Engers's dedication to the 25, but in the mid 1980s he moved up the distances, and finished second in the 1987 B.A.R.. He too had the satisfaction of beating 50 minutes, getting down to 49:39, and to 19:26 for the 10, and he went under 50 minutes again during Boardman's record ride in 1993. But Adkins entered the history books in his own right in September 1991 when he set a superb new competition record of 59:22 in the 30-mile event. The honour of being the first under the hour belonged to Gary Empson in the same race, who came home with 59:56, and enjoyed a euphoric thirty minutes until Adkins snatched the record from him, to become the only veteran ever to break a competition record. Another who was capable of beating Engers on occasion, although never in a championship, was Pete Wells, the tall lean rider who had a reputation for outclassing any field if it was wet and windy. Like Adkins, he moved up from being a super-fast 25-miler, and his victory in the 1978 100 championship has become something of a legend, for Wells sped through non-stop wind and rain to a time of 3:52:59, beating Roach, Bradshaw, Cammish, Longland, McNamara and everyone else. Wells had already won the 50 title in 1974, also in drenching rain, and in 1979 he broke the 12-hour record with 286 miles. Wells became discouraged at finishing second in the B.A.R. three times in succession from 1977-79, and

Eddie Adkins, prolific winner, constant rival to Engers, and 30-mile record breaker with his 59:22 in 1991.

Pete Wells (above) who moved up from 25-miling to become 12-hour champion, and Derek Cottington, who scored a rare double championship victory in 1971.

he took a long break from racing, but made a magnificent comeback ten years later to win the 12 championship in 1988.

Before the rise of Adkins, the short-distance star of the early 70s had been Derek Cottington, who collected a rare championship double in 1971, winning both the 25 and the 50. He had set the first R.R.A. 25 record at 47:55 in 1970, and there was a widespread belief that he would be the one to break Engers's competiton record and with it the 50-minute barrier. It turned out to be harder than anyone expected, and the closest he came was in an ill-fated event in September 1971, when he stormed to a time of 50:47. Sadly for Cotters this was disallowed as a record through no fault of his own, but because Phil Bayton, having been caught by Cotters, sat virtually on his wheel for almost ten miles to finish in 51:49. The rules on solo riding had obviously been broken, and Cotters paid the price. It was a tremendous blow to his morale, and although he continued racing for many years, he never did breach the magic 50 minutes. Another rider who broke Engers's 1969 time but who was never officially record-holder was Martin Pyne, who rode 50:43 in a private trial, although this was in any case in July 1978, just two weeks before Engers's own historic ride. Pyne did break the 10 record in 1981 at 19:41, but again this was short-lived, because Dave Lloyd took a a further half-minute off six weeks later with his 19:11. Pyne also won the 25 championship that year, although there was a suspicion that he might not have done so had Lloyd been riding: as an ex-professional Lloyd was barred from the championship.

The 10 record had been recognised only since 1972, when Willi Moore set the mark at 20:36. History was made at this distance in August 1980, when first Dave Akam and then Sean Yates broke through the 20-minute barrier. Akam's ride of 19:50 was all the more remarkable as he was competing with a hairline hip fracture, which had kept him out of the Olympic squad. The race was run in a thundery atmosphere, with low prressure and heavy rain but a total absence of wind. Yates did go to Moscow to ride the pursuit, and on his return two weeks after Akam's ride, he took back the record with 19:44.

Akam and Yates were barely twenty, but the year 1980 saw a remarkable comeback by star rider of the past now twice their age. Paul Bennett, 25-mile record-holder in 1965 who had twice missed out on championship honours because of mechanical failures, had been out of the sport for fifteen years. He had worked in the drinks industry, and like many others he had fallen victim to the temptations it offered. Having left the sport, he began drinking to the extent that his life ran completely onto the rocks and he was warned that he was courting death. At this point Bennett summoned up the determination he had gained during his cycling career, and pulled himself back from the edge. He stopped drinking, began riding again and rebuilt his lfe. His return to racing, at over forty years of age, saw him clock up some tremendous times, going faster than he had twenty years before by quite a long way, getting down to a 52-minute 25 and 1:49 for the 50. Bennett stated candidly that cycling had saved his life, and he now felt that the fifteen wasted years had been

wiped out. In his case cycling had meant literally the re-cre-
ation of his personality. It would be hard to think of a higher tribute to the sport, and now, more than twenty years on,
Bennett is still racing and still winning his own private battle.
Another amazing comeback man late in the 1980s was Dave
Dungworth, and he too went faster than he had when he set
his records, getting down to 50:50 at the age of 45.

    Bennett's comeback was a personal triumph which
did not really change the national time-trialling landscape, but
there was another comeback man in the early eighties who re-
wrote the record-books in no uncertain fashion. Dave Lloyd's
mystery heart complaint which halted his pro career in 1976
had not worsened, and as he built up his retail business he
ventured out more and more often, testing both his bikes and
himself. By 1979 he was ready for competition again, and he
embarked on a four-year spree in which he won some 130

*Two very different come-
back men: Paul Bennett
(above) and Dave
Lloyd, who both
returned to the sport
after traumatic health
problems.*

events and was beaten only a handful of times. He avoided the dragstrip courses, showing a roadman's preference for hilly events, and scored multiple wins in classics like the
Isle of Man Mountain Trial, the Circuit of the Dales, the Birkenhead Mountain Trial and
the Merseyside Wheelers Hilly. In these, as in most of his other races, it seemed that every
time he climbed on a bike, a course or event record had to fall, and his winning margin
was rarely less than two or three full minutes. On these courses he was always in a class of
his own, never more so than on the Isle of Man, where in 1980, his margin of victory over
the second man was seven minutes in the 37 miles, and that second man happened to
be Laurent Fignon, the future Tour de France winner. He didn't break the record on that
occasion, but it fell to him the following year when he went inside 1:30 for the first time.
In 1981 he won a much-heralded confrontation with Phil Griffiths in the Birkenhead
event by more than three minutes. In 1982 he smashed the early-season classic Anfield
100 record by more than 10 minutes, with a 3:47:10 ride. He defeated Sean Yates and
took the 10-mile record in 1981. A confirmed opponent of dragstrip courses, he cham-
pioned the Holdsworthy Classic League competition, run in the early 80s as a new alternative to the B.A.R., and won it by a big margin in 1982 and 1983. But he proved that
he could ride fast on dragstrips too when in 1983 on Boroughbridge he finally smashed
John Watson's long-standing 50 record with a time of 1:40:52, even though this ride
ended with one of his rare defeats, when Ian Cammish stormed home twenty minutes
later in 1:39:51, to achieve the first 30 m.p.h. 50. Lloyd tried his hand at a straight-out
record too, recording a staggering 42:37 for the R.R.A. 25 in 1983, and he set new
national track records including the hour, at 45.5 kilometres.

    Lloyd was a perfectionist, who thought deeply about his preparation and his
equipment. He pioneered the awareness of aerodynamics in Britain, favouring the smaller front wheel, and especially the new clothing styles - the skinsuit and the skullcap. It
was Lloyd's presence on the time-trialling scene which induced the R.T.T.C. to change
their rules and allow ex-professionals to compete for championships, and as a thank-you
to them he took the 25 title in 1982 and again in 1983. His secret was his intensity, his

fanaticism: he rode on nervous energy and pushed himself to the limit every time. In the end this probably took its toll, because the one thing he could not cope with was being beaten: like Merckx, when he raced he had to win, and if he didn't it was a tragedy. When Darryl Webster began to challenge Lloyd's invincibility in 1983, some of Lloyd's enthusiasm began to ebb away, even though he had the beating of Webster on more than one occasion. Lloyd stopped racing in the mid eighties after a winning run that was probably unique in the annals of time-trialling. But despite all his victories he would often say that to him all this was second-best, because the thing he wanted most of all was to ride the Tour de France. Lloyd remains convinced that he could have made it to the top on the continent, and seeing what he did to Fignon in 1980, who would argue with him ?

If there was something slightly demonic about Lloyd, then his successor as the king of short-distance time-trialling had even more of that quality about him. The main achievement of Darryl Webster's career is well-known: he was 25 champion four times in a row from 1984 to 1987, a record then excelled only by Engers himself, and he added the 50 title in 1985. But this winning run alone does not do justice to Webster's dazzling all-round talent. He was hill-climb champion four times too, from 1983-86, in fact he was the first rider ever to join the hill-climb title with the 25 mile title, although Boardman did

One of the few riders ever to get the better of Lloyd was Darryl Webster prolific collector of championships on road and track

it after him. He was also one of the star roadmen of his day, winning many one-day classics, and he was an outstanding trackman and pursuiter. Strangely perhaps, he never broke a competition record. In his miracle year of 1985 he won no less than seven national championship gold medals: the 25, the 50, the individual pursuit, the team pursuit, the hill-climb, and both the R.T.T.C. and B.C.F. versions of the team trial championships. If there had been a 10-mile championship at that time, it is certain he would have taken that too, for as a short-distance speedman, the greyhound-like Webster, who had been under the hour at the age of fourteen, was in a class of his own. But although the speed may have been physically easy for him to achieve, it wasn't easy mentally: he suffered intense stress and anxiety before competition, and he made himself a reputation as a trouble-maker. The point was however that he knew his own worth, but found himself surrounded by lesser talents, especially the officials who were supposed to be managing the teams and the events, and these were the people he was most often at odds with, and by whom he found himself so often excluded from international selection. Yes he was a difficult character, but it must stand as a reproach to the governing bodies that no coach, mentor or manager could be found to harness fully his extraordinary gifts. Webster turned professional late in his career, but with no outstanding results. In fact it is clear that time-trialling was the perfect vehicle for the expression of his intense, lonely personality, and he could, if he had chosen to concentrate on it, have won even more honours over an even longer period.

After the Webster era, the 25-mile championship was won by a man who was racing before Webster was born. In complete contrast to Webster's youthfull brilliance, John Pritchard's racing had been progressing steadily for twenty years, and in 1988 he took over a minute and a half out of second man Martin Pyne, to win the title he had dreamed of since 1968, and in doing so became the first veteran ever to win the championship. Probably the best time-triallist ever to come out of Wales, Pritchard was an RAF physical education instructor by profession, so that much of his racing was done when stationed outside Wales. In the following year Pritchard was devastated to lose his title by a big margin to the young Chris Boardman, and he blamed himself for peaking too early: the week before he had won on the championship course in a time which would have given him the victory. However he made amends a few weeks later when he won the 50 cham-

John Pritchard, a competitor for thirty years, still the only veteran ever to win the 25- and 50-mile championships. John's son Ceri became the national junior 10 and 25 champion in 1996.

pionship, and had the satisfaction of catching Boardman for four minutes in the process. Once again Pritchard had made a little slice of history, because it was the first time the 50 championship had gone to a veteran. Time-trialling was of course no stranger to fast veterans, but Pritchard's two victories in national open championships, especially the ultra-competitive 25, were unique achievements.

Super-vets were usually expected to target the longer distances, and the rider who more than fulfilled these expectations was John Woodburn. A leading 25-miler from the late 1950s, and champion in 1961, Woodburn was out of the sport for a few years waiting for reinstatement after riding as an independent. His serious comeback to top-level racing really got under way in the mid 1970s, when he was approaching forty. In 1975 he was second in the B.A.R. but then he got himself suspended, so the following year he teamed up on a tandem with John Patston, who was also serving a suspension, and set about up-dating some R.R.A. place-to-place records. Back in competition, Woodburn made history in 1978 by becoming the first vet ever to win the B.A.R., and with a record average speed of over 26 m.p.h. All three of Woodburn's rides that year came desperately close to the existing competition records. It is interesting to recall that Woodburn had

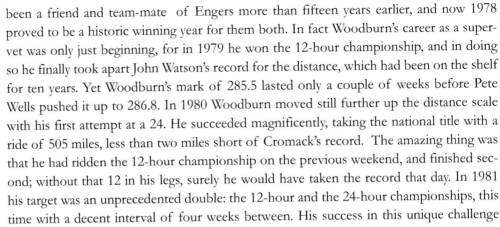

Two contrasting End-to-End record-breakers: John Woodburn, the supervet and 24-hour champion, and opposite Paul Carbutt, a roadman who had never ridden beyond 12 hours in his life.

been a friend and team-mate of Engers more than fifteen years earlier, and now 1978 proved to be a historic winning year for them both. In fact Woodburn's career as a super-vet was only just beginning, for in 1979 he won the 12-hour championship, and in doing so he finally took apart John Watson's record for the distance, which had been on the shelf for ten years. Yet Woodburn's mark of 285.5 lasted only a couple of weeks before Pete Wells pushed it up to 286.8. In 1980 Woodburn moved still further up the distance scale with his first attempt at a 24. He succeeded magnificently, taking the national title with a ride of 505 miles, less than two miles short of Cromack's record. The amazing thing was that he had ridden the 12-hour championship on the previous weekend, and finished second; without that 12 in his legs, surely he would have taken the record that day. In 1981 his target was an unprecedented double: the 12-hour and the 24-hour championships, this time with a decent interval of four weeks between. His success in this unique challenge

provided the motivation for his End-to-End record attempt in 1981, for no rider in the country was more likely to achieve it than Woodburn. But he was destined to disappointment: although he did not realise it, Woodburn was ill when he started the attempt, he never really got on terms with his schedule, and he finally climbed off after 600 miles. In a second atempt the following year however there were no mishaps, and he smashed the record by the huge margin of 96 minutes, with 1:21:3. This was the high-point of Woodburn's mile-eating career. In 1987 he was persuaded to try the ultimate long-distance challenge, the 1,000 miles, but his heart was not really in it, and he abandoned the attempt, returning to more normal racing challenges. In fact Woodburn finds it strange to be regarded purely as a distance man, for his aim in racing has always been to go as fast as possible, and the End-to-End target speed of 19 m.p.h. was in his view not really racing.

Woodburn was the second B.A.R. champion of the 1970s to take the End-to-End record, for Paul Carbutt in 1979 had trimmed 23 minutes from Dick Poole's time. Carbutt was a fine time-triallist and an accomplished roadman and Milk Race rider. He had been national champion at 50 miles, 100 miles and 12 hours, and he had topped the B.A.R. competition in 1977. But nothing really suggested him as a logical contender for the End-to-End record, for he had never even ridden a 24. In the event he put up a heroic display, for after starting well, he began to suffer badly on the second day, and collapsed completely with heat exhaustion in the Scottish borders. After a brief period when he was virtually unconscious, he summoned the will to continue, and somehow regained his strength and went on to his narrow victory. There was a good deal of controversy about this ride, for the opening of the Forth Road Bridge meant a significant shortening of the route, and there were those who argued that Poole's record had not truly been broken. Carbutt's courageous riding went a long way to deflect these criticisms, and his record was ratified. Carbutt later fell victim to an incurable illness and died tragically early.

Carbutt was not the only roadman to win the B.A.R. in the 1970s. In 1973 Ray Lewis did a Metcalfe, and took the title with three straight rides in three consecutive weekends. Earlier in the year he had crashed out of the Milk Race, and turned to the B.A.R. as a fresh challenge after that disappointment. His rides included the 12-hour championship, and Lewis's time-trialling experience undoubtedly helped him during his epic lone break in the final stage of the 1979 Milk Race. The man Lewis replaced as B.A.R. was Bob Porter, who headed the lists in 1972, and whose championship-winning 100 formed the basis of his victory. Porter's real ambition was to switch to road-racing, which he did in 1973 and at the end of 74 he turned professional for the Falcon team. It was not a happy experience however, and he soon left both the pro scene and the sport.

The dominant figure in the B.A.R. throughout the 70s was another rider whose talents and ambitions embraced both road-racing and time-trialling: Phil Griffiths, the man who set what was then an absolute record of five B.A.R. wins. Griffiths was a flamboyant character, a talker with views on everything, the natural focus of any team he was in, and to some an inspirer. To others he was a showman whose ego overshadowed his talents. His conversation was all verbal sparring, all needle, all wisecracking. Why did he do it - to unnerve his rivals, to boost his own confidence, or to compensate for all the big road-race wins which he wanted but which he so narrowly failed to achieve? When all the arguments about him are put aside, the fact remains that he was a brilliant time-triallist, who might have gained an even bigger place in the record books, had he not periodically abandoned the B.A.R. to seek glory in road-racing.

Griffiths's strongest distance was undoubtedly the 100, and his championship win in 1971 was the cornerstone of his first B.A.R. title. He would take the championship twice more, and break competition record three times, initially by rather small margins, but on the last occasion in 1979 he brought Taylor's time down by almost four minutes to 3:41:43. This ride was another of those quantum leaps which seem to occur in the history of the 100, and it was all the more remarkable because it was achieved on a day of near gale-force winds, when Griffiths had sat in the car debating whether it was even worth starting. He beat second man Pete Wells, famous for going fast on bad days, by 10 whole minutes, and it gained him a record average B.A.R. speed of 26.15 m.p.h. To Griffiths, as to so many others, the 12-hour was a race to be endured for the sake of the B.A.R., and he never topped 280 miles. Ian White, another great tester of the seventies, could never face a 12, even in 1973, the year in which he won both the 50 and the 100 championships, finishing well ahead of both Lewis and Porter. Griffiths was twice winner of the 50 championship however, while some of his best rides were arguably achieved when he up-dated some very tough R.R.A. records in 1977: the Cardiff-London, which still stands and was faster than the Woodburn-Patston tandem record; the London-Portsmouth and back; and perhaps best of all the London-Brighton and back, where Griffiths broke a great Les West record by three minutes, and set a mark which may never be beaten now, since modern traffic conditions have made this route impracticable for record attempts. Griffiths's five B.A.R. wins were spread over nine years, but he always believed that he could have won the title in the gap years too - a typically confident statement, but it may well be true, for after finishing fourth in 1970, it is a fact that he never took part in the competition without winning it, until he was finally deposed by Ian Cammish in 1980. By that time he was experiencing the back problems which put an end to his career. Griffiths will always be remembered as a controversial figure in the history of the sport: his image and his personality seem to stand out more clearly than his rides. This is a pity, for he made a huge contrbution to the sport, and more than anyone else in the 1970s, he bridged the gap between time-trialling and road-racing.

Phil Griffiths, master time-triallist with big road-racing ambitions.

Griffiths's successor as B.A.R. was a giant of the sport, a man who dominated middle-distance time-trialling as no one else has ever done, not even Ray Booty. Ian Cammish reigned over the B.A.R. distances throughout the 1980s, apparently winning at will and taking a unique total of nine B.A.R. titles. His domination was both exciting and boring at the same time: exciting because one could marvel at the speeds which only he could achieve, and boring because his superiority was so great that his victories became automatic and predictable. By comparison his rivals appeared to be midgets - which they certainly were not. Cammish had a tall, powerful, athletic physique, and looked a natural for any sport, but he was no prodigy as Webster had been, instead he progressed rather slowly, and was 22 before he figured in the B.A.R. tables. Like so many great B.A.R. riders, the 100 was his classic distance, and he became literally unbeatable at it. He won the championship no less than nine times, and in four stages between 1980 and 1983 he took ten minutes from Griffiths's record for the distance. On the last occasion his 3:31:53 blasted seven minutes off his own record time, the biggest margin ever in 100-mile history. Ordinary riders pondered long and hard on this, as they realised that it equated to riding a 21-minute 10, not once but ten times over, non-stop. It was this kind of calculation that put Cammish into a dimension of his own. He beat some very fine riders that day, half a dozen of them under four hours, but obviously they were in another race and another world altogether to the one that Cammish now inhabited. 1983 was his miracle year, for in the space of six weeks he broke the 50 record too, with the first 30 m.p.h. ride, and naturally won both the 50 and the 100 championships. Seven years later Cammish fixed his sights on Booty's straight-out 100 record, on the shelf for 34 years at 3:28:40, and he pulverised it with 3:16:56. Even this he felt was not the limit and in 1993 he took it down to 3:11:11. In the same year he seized the R.R.A. 25 and 50 records in a single, miraculous ride, going through the 25 in 41:22, and finishing the 50 in 1:24: 32.

How did he do it? This was the question everyone asked, but there were no clear answers. Subject to scientific physiological testing, Cammish was shown to have excellent heart and lung capacity, but nothing that was exceptional among athletes. His dedication to the sport however was complete, for throughout his racing career he worked for a living, and would train in the early morning before work, during his lunch hour, and again after work. He didn't go in for interval training, but for sustained tempo training, which was like other men's racing, for he reeled off twenty-two minute 10s in his lunch-break as a matter of routine. Even his winter training would include regular timed 50s at around 2:5. Yes, but how could you reach the level where that was possible, people asked, and the true answers were psychological. There was first an addiction to speed on the bike, a delight in fast riding as an end in itself; and this was accompanied by an apparent immunity to pain. The two went hand in hand: he enjoyed going fast, and because he enjoyed it, it didn't hurt. In a way it made sense, but it didn't help other riders, because they just weren't built that way. He admitted that he hadn't suffered during some of his fastest rides: cruising at almost 30 m.p.h., he couldn't get the pedals round any faster, but he wasn't suffering.

Yet, like Beryl Burton, Cammish did have his weaknesses. One was the team time trial, where he should have excelled, but his selection for the event in the 1984 Olympics proved a very unhappy experience. He could not adapt himself to group training sessions, and although he travelled to Los Angeles, his form was not great and he withdrew from the squad. On paper, Cammish could have ridden the 100 kilometre distance alone fast enough to win a medal, and the cycling public was baffled about what had really gone wrong. His other Achilles heel was the 12-hour race, in which he confessed to hav-

Ian Cammish on his way to his record 100 of 3:31:53

ing taken some terrible bendings. He came closest to the record in 1983, with 284 miles, but that was still three miles short, and he never won the 12 championship. The problem was that he simply could not pace himself correctly. He would hurtle through the first 150 miles in about five and a half hours, then suffer torments until the finish. He was incapable of backing off from his optimum speed of 27 m.p.h. He had to ride at that speed, and then simply hang on - or climb off shattered. It was perhaps reassuring to know that he had these weaknesses: if he had not, he would have appeared to be little short of a god in the time-trialling world in which he reigned supreme.

The one man to challenge this invincibility and make Cammish look human was Glenn Longland, whose great strength was Cammish's weakness - the 12-hour. He won the championship five times over a period of eleven years, and he raised the competition record three times, becoming the first to take it above 290 miles in 1986. That was the year in which he defeated Cammish for the B.A.R., recording faster times at all three distances, with a massive 25-mile advantage in the 12-hour. It was sweet revenge for Longland who had already trailed behind Cammish in second place for five successive years. Cammish, having won a record six titles in a row, had for once lost his motivation and edge, and he acknowledged that no one deserved the win more than Longland. With Cammish back to

Glen Longland, 12-hour miracle man, the first to top 300 miles in 1991.

his best again in 1987, Longland was destined to return to second place, but he knew he was a far better 12-hour rider than Cammish, and he proved it by taking the record that Cammish could never aspire to: the first 300-mile 12. This was a target which Longland had himself brought closer, but it still required fully nine miles to be added to his record, a daunting prospect which would call for ideal conditions. Longland got those conditions in September 1991, in his local event, the Poole Wheelers 12, which he had already won a dozen times in his career. Keeping his gears down in the 90s Longland cruised through the first 100 in 3:52; the second 100 took 4:02, leaving him to ride the final 100 in 4:05. Riding a perfectly judged race - without a speedometer - he made it to glory by just 100 yards, with a final distance of 300.068 miles, and no one else was within twenty miles of him. This long-distance record really meant something to every club rider who had ever felt the satisfaction of beating the hour for a 25, for Longland had strung together no less than a dozen sub-hour rides. It was an astonishing measure of progress in time-trialling speeds: thirty years before, still only one rider had ever beaten four hours for the 100; by 1991 several might have been capable of riding 200 miles in eight hours; but the prospect of reeling off three sub-four-hour 100s in succession was something that only Longland could have done, and he knew it. There were high hopes that Longland was the man who would finally up-date the 24-hour figures, but although he did win the championship in 1994, Longland never did mount a serious challenge to Cromack's long-standing record.

All records, awesome though they may be when they are established, are there to be broken, and the 1990s brought two vital new elements into time-trialling - the aerodynamic design revolution and a new era of scientific training. Both of these were closely associated with Chris Boardman, for although he invented neither of them, he became the perfect test-pilot for them. The way had been prepared to some extent when roadman Pete Longbottom quite unexpectedly became the man to wipe Engers's name off of the 25 record. In 1990 he took eleven seconds from Engers's 1978 time, with the help of a low-profile bike and disc wheel, but without tri-bars, which were not yet legal in R.T.T.C. events. It is a measure of Engers's ride that all the aerodynamic experiments to that date had not brought anyone very close to his twelve-year-old record. Likewise Cammish's astonishing 100 record was achieved on a transitional bike, with a low-profile front end, but no disk wheels and no aero bars, very different to the bikes of the 90s.

Gary Dighton smashed the 25 record in 1991, and came nearest to Cammish's 100 record with his 3:32 in 1990.

One year after Longbottom, first John Pritchard and then Gary Dighton, now using tri-bars, both blew the 25 record apart in the same race with 48:28 and 48:07 respectively. It was Dighton too who came closest to Cammish's 100 record with his 3:32:56 in 1990, but the record survived for six more years. With his short-distance brilliance and superbly aerodynamic position, it was Chris Boardman who took the 25 record into the next century with his 47:19 and then finally 45:57, achieved on a 110 fixed gear, the first competition record to be broken on fixed for well over thirty years. Before this last ride, Boardman had clocked a 17-minute 10 in a private trial which could not be recognised as a record. Boardman's natural talents had been honed by the coaching of Peter Keen, a former junior champion turned sports scientist, who developed a wholly new language of physical effort and achievement. Keen analysed with minute precision what happened to an athlete as he trained, how his physiology improved and how these improvements could be measured through pulse rate, lung capacity and power output. Boardman was the subject of these new methods, pushing himself to higher and higher sustained speeds, while consciously monitoring what happening. It was immensely influential because of the sensational times which Boardman achieved, but although it may all have sounded very clinical and mechanical, it wasn't really because Boardman's innate talents were the crucial ingredient. He responded perfectly to this

approach in a way that his great rival Graeme Obree apparently did not. After the early 90s, no ambitious time-triallist could ignore the Keen-Boardman language of effort and power output. Stuart Dangerfield has brought the 10 record down to 18:19, but this is still outside Boardman's unofficial time, while Boardman's 25 record has now survived as long as Engers's did, resisting weekly assaults by Dangerfield, Michael Hutchinson and all the other current champions.

The man who re-wrote the middle-distance records in 1996, Andy Wilkinson, was a north Wirral man like Boardman, but he was not initially a fan of scientific speed-training, grinding out 500 miles-a-week schedules instead. Perhaps this explained his transition from being a first-category roadman in the late 80s (he was 21st in the 1987 Milk Race) to long-distance record-breaker, hitting the headlines with his End-to-End record ride in 1990. Although the margin by which Wilkinson broke Woodburn's figures was the narrowest ever, this result conceals one of the most courageous End-to-End rides ever recorded. For the final one hundred miles, Wilko knew that he was running exactly even with Woodburn, sometimes a few seconds up, sometimes a few seconds down. In the last stages of exhaustion and almost falling asleep on his bike, he battled on to take the record by just 58 seconds. Wilko then became involved in aerodynamic experiment, but his interest took the unusual direction of recumbents, and riding a three-wheeled enclosed machine designed by Mick Burrow, he set an almost unbelievable new End-to-End time of 1:17:5, four hours inside his own official record. The R.R.A. agonised over the problem, but decided against recognising the new time, because it would clearly mean that a line would have to be drawn under their entire record book, as every distance would soon fall to the recumbent.

The unique Andy Wilkinson, holder of every time-trial record from 50 miles to 24-hours, plus the End-to-End.

Wilkinson was not wildly disappointed, for he was always a man looking for a new challenge. He modernised his training methods, switched to an ultra-modern low-profile bike and targeted the B.A.R. distances for the first time in 1996, with sensational results. He took the title with competition records and championship wins at all three distances, a feat never achieved before even by the giants of cycling history, not even by Booty, Colden, Griffiths or Cammish. Cammish's 50 record had lasted for a decade before it was trimmed by Graeme Obree in 1993, but Wilkinson took it down to 1:37:26. The 100 record was even tougher, having withstood all attacks for thirteen years, until Wilko's 1996 time of 3:27:39 - more than half an hour faster than Booty's historic ride of thirty years before. Finally, Wilkinson became the second man to top 300 miles for the 12, and this was the most painful of all, for he added just 300 yards to Longland's total, with 300.2 miles. True to form, Wilkinson did not contest the B.A.R. again, but in the following year he added one further proof of his brilliance when he obliterated Roy Cromack's legendary 24-hour figures with his superb 525-miles ride. Wilkinson stood then in the unique position of holding every record from 50 miles to 24 hours, and the End-to-End record too for good measure. A maverick with talents never surpassed in British cycling, Wilko then scaled down his serious racing, and set about enjoying his riding again, with audax and mountain biking. Wilko's 1996 rides were in the tradition of Booty's in 1956, Colden's in 1962, the 1969 spree by Engers, Taylor, Watson and Cromack, and Cammish's in 1983: dramatic leaps in speed which put the records on the shelf for years to come.

Since's Wilko's miracle year, Kevin Dawson has broken the 50 and 100 record, and seems on the verge of beating even Cammish's record total of nine B.A.R. wins. Gethin Butler has taken more than an hour from the End-to-End time, but Wilko's 12-hour and 24-hour times survive, and there is speculation that the latter may last as long as Cromack's did, since 24-hour racing now attracts only a fraction of the support which it once did. Butler has come nearest with his 509 ride in 2000. Throughout the 1970s and 1980s the shadow of Cromack's record made most rides at this distance look rather weak, but no one who finishes a 24-hour race can be called weak, and the vast majority of modern cyclists are unquestionably afraid of it. It no longer fits in with modern cycling culture or our modern lifestyle. George Bettis, John Cahill and John Woodburn were all double champions at 24-hours, while in the 80s the rivalry between Stuart Jackson and Ian Dow resulted in the pair claiming seven titles between them.

Above: the aerodynamic styling revolution of the 1980s crossed over from track to road; but as early as 1985, Mick Burrow was advocating a rather different approach to frame-design, below.

Not only 24-hour riding, but the whole future of time-trialling is regularly debated and said to be under threat. There are issues of road safety, arguments about dragstrip courses, about the role of technology, and the relevance of time-trialling to international racing. Some of these arguments have a long history, but the fact is that time-trialling is still the simplest, most accessible form of bike racing in Britain, and thousands of riders continue to support it. The longer distances are certainly in gradual decline, and without entries from riders in their forties, fifties and even sixties, the start-sheets would be almost blank. The shorter distances however are still intensely competitive, and in an effort to guide riders away from dragstrip courses, the R.T.T.C. introduced the short-distance series championship in 1995, over short, hilly courses. This is now well established, but the B.A.R. still survives, despite persistent criticism that it is unfair, unsafe, misguided and irrelevant. Its appeal is perfectly simple: times over standard distances provide an absolute measure for comparing one ride with another, and riders will always want to make these comparisons and will always want to improve their times. That is what the whole history of time-trialling is about. Impatience with the B.A.R. and with time-trialling generally has a long pedigree, and the B.C.F. has periodically tried to assert its leadership of British cycling by proposing to absorb the R.T.T.C. with the aim of steering British cyclists away from the worship of time-trials. These attempts have always failed, and in 1987 the B.C.F. expressed its frustration by tearing up the joint agreement through which they had governed the sport for three decades. Exactly what the B.C.F. thought they could achieve is unclear, for time-trialling's strength has always been its democratic support by club riders. If people didn't want it, it would die a natural death. Everything changes, and not only have the records of Frank

Sandy Gilchrist, the man who won virtually everything in Scotland in the 1980s.

Southall and Ken Joy and Ray Booty been overtaken, but the whole world in which they were set has now vanished. Despite all the changes in modern cycling however, the 25 and the B.A.R. distances remain serious sporting challenges and powerful links with the past. Like so many such links, they would be easy to destroy but not so easy to replace.

Time-trialling in Scotland took a big leap forward in the 1980s, thanks to some outstanding riders who up-dated the record-book, which had been frozen since since the mid 1960s. The most prolific winner in Scottish cycling history was Sandy Gilchrist, dominant between 1970 and 1985, with 22 individual time-trial championships, 3 road-race championships, 7 B.A.R. championships, and an incredible string of 13 hill-climb cham-

Sandy Gilchrist, the man who won virtually everything in Scotland in the 1980s.

pionships, broken only by Robert Millar in 1977, in a race which Gilchrist was unable to ride. Had he been permitted to compete for R.T.T.C. championships, there is little doubt that he would have won medals there too, but he had to be content with being part of the victorious team time trial squad. He devoured victories, from half-mile hill-climb to 12-hour time-trials, and if his name was on any start-sheet then he was the automatic favourite. The Scottish B.A.R. winning speed had been stuck on 23 m.p.h. since 1954, until Gilchrist took it above 24 m.p.h. in 1982. He was in fact too successful for his own good, for his class and his record naturally bred a certain amount of resentment, and just as naturally he sought new fields to conquer outside Scotland. He joined English sponsored clubs - first GS Strada and then Manchester Wheelers, he competed in English races, and he won international selection for B.C.F. teams, much to the annoyance of the Scottish team selectors. 1982 was probably his most brilliant year, when he made a clean sweep of all the time-trial championships from 25 miles to 12 hours, and took both the B.A.R. and the hill-climb, yet he was left out of the Scottish team for the Commonwealth Games because of political conflicts with the S.C.U. selectors. However Gilchrist had the last word in that particular battle when he was appointed national road manager in 1987, replacing the man who had passed him over. Cycling was even more of a minority sport in Scotland than in England, and Gilchrist embodied all the problems of the gifted rider who had to decide whether to be content to be a local champion, or to seek bigger challenges.

Exactly contemporary with Gilchrist was Dave Hannah, the other Scots rider who made a considerable impact on the English scene. Less versatile than Gilchrist, Hannah had more pure speed, and in the period from 1979 to 1989 he took the Scottish 25 record down from 55:32 to 52:59, pushed the 50 record down to 1:49:38, and, in perhaps the greatest of all his rides, became the first Scot to ride the 100 in under four hours in Scotland when he recorded a magnificent 3:57:48 in July 1984 on the Glasgow course; in achieving this Hannah deprived Gilchrist of one of his lifelong ambitions. Over a 15-year period

Hannah took the Scottish 25 title no less than 9 times, and the 50 title 7 times. He was no lover of 12s, but he rode a few, enough to give him two Scottish B.A.R. titles. One of the interesting things about Hannah is that he achieved faster times at every distance when he travelled south to race in England, a clear proof that competition drives up standards. One is left wondering what Gilchrist or Hannah would have achieved if they had based themselves permanently in the south.

In 1979 the S.C.U. was persuaded to set up a middle-distance B.A.R., which included a 25 and excluded the 12. Periodic calls for such a move in England had always been unsuccessful, but the S.C.U. decided to run it alongside the traditional competition, which still included the 12. The short version was tailor-made for Hannah, who won it 8 times in the 1980s, and equally so for his successor, Dave Gibson, in the 1990s. Gibson had been a junior road-race champion,

Dave Hannah, the first sub-four-hour 100 man north of the border.

and he came late to time-trialling, but with devastating effect, for he took 9 victories in the middle-distance B.A.R., to add to his many 25 and 50 championship wins. Women's time-trial records in Scotland had been even longer on the shelf, before first Sarah Phillips and then Andrea Pogson gave them a more modern look, with Pogson, who happens to be English, the first woman in Scotland under two hours for the 50. Both Phillips and Pogson won four Scottish B.A.R. titles in the 1990s. Sarah Phillips was later the victim of an road accident while she was out training, and the injuries she received tragically cut short her racing career. The S.C.U.'s independence had some interesting results: tri-bars were introduced a year earlier than in England, and helmets were made compulsory.

Scotland has produced a steady stream of riders with class and dedication, but the sport there has always been numerically weak, so the riders were without the structure and the incentive to develop their full potential, unless they moved south or went abroad. This was as true in road-racing as in time-trialling, where a talented, masterful rider like Willie Gibb, B.A.R. in 1987, could come in and out of the sport over a period of twenty years and still win the national road title, as he did in 1980, 1984, 1996 and 2000. Gibb was an exact contemporary of Robert Millar, in the same school and the same club, and there was little between them, but Gibb developed a successful career in the electronics industry, only returning to racing every few years to torment his younger rivals.

Track Racing

The track has always been both the most intimate and the most spectacular form of racing, yet year after year people have lamented the decline of track racing. Central to this complaint was probably the decline in top-level sprinting since the days when Harris had confronted the top European professionals before his home crowds. The big sprint, the high-speed shoulder-to-shoulder battle, had once been the high-point of any track meeting, but Harris's dominance had given way to the Lloyd Binch syndrome: the spectacle of a rider who could win mulitple national championships but who could never win glory on the international stage. This pattern was repeated by Ernie Crutchlow, the Coventry rider who was rather lightly built for a sprinter, but who took four successive sprint titles from 1970 to 1973, and who came back as professional at the end of the decade to win again. Crutchlow was also a successful tandemist, and partnered by Geoff Cooke he took gold in the Commonwealth Games tandem sprint in 1974. It was the relative weakness in the sprinting scene which tempted Harris to make his sensational comeback to win the professional championship at the age of 54.

Crutchlow's last amateur win was in the inaugural year of the national track championships at Leicester, an innovation which many people believed had harmed track racing by removing some of the status and the excitement from regional meets. The local leagues at tracks like Portsmouth, Welwyn, Cardiff, Reading or Salford remained healthy enough, but it was true that the championship week at Leicester seemed to absorb most of the public attention. There is also no question that events on the international stage affected the general perception of track racing: the dominance of the East Europeans seemed to place our riders on a distinctly lower plane, while one Japanese sprinter, Koicho Nakano, single-handedly extinguished the European pro sprinting tradition with his amazing string of ten world championships between 1977 and 1986. Nakano was never seen in Europe except for the championships. This Japanese master was honest enough to admit that the top East European amateurs would probably beat him. "I'm only human" he said, perhaps with a touch of irony.

It was the pursuit which replaced the sprint as the centre of attention in the eyes of many fans, and half a dozen riders between 1970 and 1990 continued to build Britain's superb tradition in this event. No rider had more brilliant

Ian Hallam, star pursuiter and king of the British tracks for almost a decade.

record at national level than Ian Hallam, the tall, lean, instantly recognisable king of the British track. He was six time pursuit champion from 1969-1974, but this was only the core of his prolific medal-winning career: with multiple victories too in the kilo, the Madison and the 20 kilometre race, he amassed some sixteen national track titles, before turning professional and adding still more in both the pursuit and the sprint. He was twice Commonwealth Games pursuit champion, in 1970 and again in 1974, he took the silver medal in the world championships in Leicester in 1970, and he was a key figure in the team pursuit squads which won the Olympic bronze medal in 1972 and retained it in 1976. This was the squad which technically won the gold medal in the 1973 world championships in Spain, but which settled for the silver. In a famous incident, the German team, clear leaders in the final lap, were brought down by a careless official on the track and could not finish. No other decision was possible but to declare Britain the winners, but the team generously refused the honours, and Germany became champions after all. In recognition of his unique record and of his sportsmanship and popularity, Hallam was awarded the

Tony Doyle progressed from amateur pursuiting to reach the top in the exacting world of continental 6-day racing, as well as taking two world championships.

MBE in 1978. Hallam raced succesfully as a pro roadman for five years, and his stature made it all the more bizarre that he became embroiled in a bitter controversy with the PCA about a disputed decision in a road race, in which he had refused to accept the verdict of the judges. The dispute dragged on for almost a year, and overshadowed the closing phase of a fine career. Hallam's reign as king of the pursuit was brought to an end by Steve Heffernan, a smaller, punchier rider who took the title twice in 1975 and 1976 before turning professional and winning it twice more, and adding a bronze medal in the world championships of 1977.

Heffernan's departure to the pro ranks left the way clear for a new amateur pursuiter who would become one of Britain's greatest ever trackmen: Tony Doyle. Doyle had come up through the fast-pedalling, fixed-wheel tradition of south-London time-trialling, and in a medium-gear 25 he once recorded a phenomenal 56:30. He won three successive pursuit titles from 1977 to 1979 before his momentous season in 1980, when his career suddenly changed direction. He was the natural first choice for the Olympic pursuit event in Moscow, but at the last minute his place was given to his fellow team pursuiter, Sean Yates. Both Yates and the British team went out in the quarter-finals, and Doyle was incensed by the decision, stating that he had postponed turning pro for a year purely to wait for the Olympics. At the national championships, immediately after the Olympics, Doyle rode the pursuit as a professional, and easily disposed of all his opponents, while Yates won the amateur title. Just two weeks later in Besancon, Doyle was crowned world pursuit champion; rarely can a rejected rider have proved his point so emphatically. At the age of 22 an entirely new career now opened up for Doyle, as he set his sights on the gru-

*Colin Sturgess,
national and world
champion pursuiter,
who overshadowed
Chris Boardman for
several years, but
whose later road
career was less happy.*

elling but lucrative world of the European sixes. He made his debut at the London six in 1980, but this was to be the last of that series, so all his later victories were scored abroad. Simpson had won a six-day race in 1965, and after three years' apprenticeship, Doyle became the second Briton to do so in 1983 in Dortmund, partnered by Australian Danny Clark. It was with Clark that Doyle would achieve most of his grand total 23 six-day victories. This part of his career was to some extent hidden from British cycling fans - it was a remote and alien world - but he was seen on British roads throughout the summer, winning the Girvan stage-race twice, and missing victory in the 1984 Sealink International by one second. Not surprisingly, the six-day world had turned Doyle into a tough, aggressive rider who gave nothing away to anyone, and who was no stranger to controversial finishes. There was always a degree of needle between him and Yates, and when Yates himself had turned professional he inflicted two defeats on Doyle in the national pursuit title races of 1982 and 1983. A more serious disappointment was Doyle's inability to defend his world championship title in 1981, having crashed just before the event. Thereafter his way to the gold medal was too often blocked by the Frenchman Bondue or the Dane Oersted, and he collected no less than three world's silver medals in the 1980s. His year of triumph was 1986, when he finally regained the rainbow jersey in Colorado, with revenge over Oersted. He also won the British pro title three times in succession between 1986 and 1988, taking his revenge on Yates in the process.

The six-day circuit exacted a heavy price in terms of crashes and the serious injuries which Doyle sustained, and which finally forced his retirement in 1992. But perhaps even these physical stresses were less traumatic than the events in which Doyle found himself after his retirement. Late in 1995 he decided to stand for the presidency of the B.C.F., expressing the widespread feelings of frustration that the Federation was remote from its members, and promising a new era. He won the election, but within weeks of his victory he was in conflict with the existing board, who in effect refused to work with him. Legal action followed from both sides, and cyclists watched with amazement and fury as their officials plunged the organisation into a state of civil war. Doyle resigned his post in April 1996, but the crisis dragged on for months, and eventually resulted in the entire management being swept away. At the time the full story of what was going on was obscured by reporting restrictions due to the legal actions, and even in the years since then, the full truth has never been told; but it was undoubtedly the worst crisis in the history of the B.C.F., bringing threats from the Sports Council to end its vital funding.

After the Doyle-Yates era, the amateur pursuit title was won twice each by Shaun

Wallace and Darryl Webster, and throughout most of the 1980s Webster was a constant member of the all-conquering Manchester Wheelers team pursuit squad, which won the national championship no less than nine time in succession. Before Webster joined the pro ranks, he was defeated not by his Wheelers team-mate, the young Chris Boardman, but by Colin Sturgess, whose brief career would see him crowned as Britain's fourth world pursuit champion of the post-war era. In fact Sturgess's career was not really brief, as he had been racing since he was eight years old - in South Africa where he grew up - and this was the source of his precocious talents, and also of his early demise. He first hit the headlines as winner of the national junior pursuit title in 1985, defeating none other than Chris Boardman, and adding victory in the kilo championship too. In the following year, while still a junior, he took the silver medal in the Commonwealth Games in Edinburgh. He retained his junior title in 1986, and by 1987 he disposed of both Boardman and Webster in the senior championship. He repeated his win over Boardman in 1988, and it certainly seemed then that Sturgess was the man of the future, and not Boardman, whom Eddie Soens had described as the best cycling talent he had seen since

Chris Boardman, uniquely talented test-pilot for the new bikes and the new training methods of the 1990s.

Norman Sheil. Sturgess was fourth in the pursuit in the Seoul Olympics, and there was much controversy when he turned pro at the end of that year, aged only 20, and disappointment at the loss of a potential Olympic champion four years ahead. But Sturgess could not wait, and his decision seemed to be vindicated at the world championships in Lyon, when he won gold, convincingly beating Dean Woods of Australia, with Doyle trailing back in seventh place. Sturgess remained unbeatable on the home tracks, but of course he did not come up against Boardman now that he was approaching his best, and professional pursuiters in Britain were thin on the ground. He had meanwhile been road racing with a number of continental teams, but his career now seemed to lose direction. He was disqualified from the 1990 Milk Race for taking a tow after he had been dropped from the bunch. He changed teams each year for three successive years, but was unable to break into the six-day circuit. The highlight for him in the early 90s was the bronze medal in the 1991 world's pursuit, and after a brief spell in a South African team, Sturgess announced that he was quitting the sport at the age of 23. His career has strange parallels with a number of other British riders, such as Graham Webb or Cyril Peacock, who won world championships, and who then lost their way in the professional sport. In Sturgess's case he was surely burned out before his time, having been racing more or less seriously since the age of 12, and his career faltered just as that of his junior rival, Boardman, was blossoming.

The really fascinating thing about Boardman's progress in these few years was the way he was continually able to raise his speed from one threshold to the next. He had taken the national title in 1989, but had lost it through illness to Simon Lillistone in 1990.

*Trevor Gadd steers
Steve Cronshaw.
Gadd swept all before
him in the sprint
events in 1977 and
1978.*

A time between 4:45 and 4:55 was then the target speed at this championship level. Yet at the 1990 world's in Japan Boardman went much faster still, recording a best-ever time of 4:36 to reach the last eight before being eliminated. Lillistone too produced a personal best of 4:42. The final was won by the Russian Berzin in 4:33, so Boardman considered that he was on target towards a possible world medal. In 1991 he travelled confidently to the world's in Stuttgart again as national champion, a 4:44 ride having given him the title; for good measure he had broken the 5,000 metres world record too with a time of 5:47. In the competition in Stuttgart Boardman recorded another dramatic improvement to 4:31, but he was left reeling by the way times had been taken to another level altogether by his rivals, so that he reached only the last eight, and the final was won by Lehmann of Germany in 4:25. The bikes, the clothing, the tracks - everything was getting smoother and faster, but Boardman had to ponder long and hard before accepting the challenge of finding yet more speed - and not mere fractions of a second. This speed shock had been looming for some years: already at the 1984 Olympics, the individual pursuit winner, American Steve Hegg, had ridden faster than the British team pursuit squad, and the gap between British track speed and the rest of the world was a huge physical and psychological problem.

It is a matter of history that, with help from coach Peter Keen and bike designer Mick Burrow, Boardman solved that problem magnificently, improving to 4:24, and catching Lehmann in the 1992 Olympic final. That speed equated to four kilos at 1:6, and it's worth remembering that when Trevor Gadd was sweeping all before him in 1978, he won the national kilo championship with a time of 1:8. This was Britain's first Olympic cycling gold medal since 1920, and it was greeted as a fitting climax to years of technical experiment and physiological progress. Except that it wasn't really the climax, for in 1993 Graeme Obree, from a completely different background, with completely different training methods, and a completely different bike of his own idiosyncratic design, was able first to match Boardman's speed and then defeat him at the world championships. The rivalry between these two riders in the pursuit and in their attacks on the hour record made cycling history in the mid 1990s. Obree was an individualist who defied all the conventions, he had no teachers and no followers. The contrast in their style and approach to competition made good newspaper copy, but the truth is that these two both possessed an outstanding athletic make-up, and they each chose their own special path to the top. In 1996 Boardman brought the four-kilometre time down to 4:11 in winning his world title, a time which would have been beyond the reach of any team pursuit squad in the world at the Seoul Olympics in 1988.

Pursuiting - both individual and team - had gradually become the central spectacle of the track, but a number of riders had also put some of the fire and glamour back into sprinting. There was Trevor Gadd who stormed to six championship gold medals in the two years 1977 and 1978 - winning the sprint, the kilo and the tandem with Steve Cronshaw. Gadd was by far the most exciting sprinter seen for some time in Britain, but he was hugely disappointed to collect just one silver medal at the 1978 Commonwealth Games in Edmonton. Afterwards he quit the sport, complaining of total lack of support for riders at the international level - no financial or technical support and no coaching. What he had achieved he had done entirely alone he claimed, and yet when he went abroad to ride for Britain he found himself accused of failure. Then there was Paul McHugh, the tiny, power-packed pupil of Eddie Soens, who at the age of 17 sensationally won the national title with a time of 10.8, and who went on to hold the sprint championship for three years from 1984 to 1986. McHugh continued his career as a professional and claimed four more titles, but he recognised that pro sprinting in this country, indeed all pro track racing, was dying, and that the future must lie in open competition. In the meantime English fans were taken aback when Eddie Alexander from Edinburgh won the amateur title twice, and took fourth place in the Seoul Olympics. When open racing came to the track in 1993, it was another Scot, Stuart Brydon, who disposed of McHugh and all the other competitors. It was a sign of the revolution in track coaching that had been going on in Edinburgh, and a pointer to the future national and international tirumphs of the Scottish sprinters. The City of Edinburgh Racing Team had been formed in the mid 80s by coach Alan Nisbet with the specific aim of raising track standards, and soon any Scots rider with track ambitions gravitated to Meadowbank. The training was not quite as scientific as it later became under Peter Keen, but it was highly effective, and it laid the foundations of the later achievements of Craig MacLean and Chris Hoy.

Paul McHugh, seven times national sprint champion, first as an amateur then as a professional.

Women's Racing

The Beryl Burton era in time-trialling ended officially at the close of 1983 with her 25th successive B.A.R. victory, but from 1979 onwards she would occassionally not contest a championship, giving her old rivals Shirley Killingbeck and June Pitchford the chance to claim a title. It was Pitchford was stepped up to first place in the B.A.R. competition in 1984, an astonishing 23 years after first getting into the top six, and with an average speed that was faster than Beryl's in her final year. Pitchford went on to win the B.A.R. for three years in succession, and when she retired with recurring back problems, she was followed in 1987 by Margaret Allen, another veteran who had raced with Beryl in the Morley C.C. twenty years earlier, and then stopped riding for ten years. Allen won again in 1989, but only after a prolonged battle against Sue Golder, a 42-year old rider from New Zealand who spent two summer months racing in England. Golder was at the top of the table throughout the summer, and Allen only dislodged her in the last race of the season. In doing so she defused an unusual problem for the time-trialling community, for no one really knew whether an overseas rider could or should be crowned as a British time-trial champion; Allen's last-minute victory solved a thorny diplomatic puzzle. Allen was involved in another last-minute drama in 1989: she arrived six minutes late for her start in the final, crucial event, and lost her chance of winning her third B.A.R. title. Her vanquisher was the first of a new generation of younger riders, Sue Wright. Although she was almost 30, Wright was not one of those who had spent years in the shadow of Beryl Burton, and in 1991 she became the first to break a Burton competition record, the 30, with her time of 1:7:24. Wright, who topped the B.A.R. again in 1992, was also the first City stockbroker to win a women's cycling

Sue Wright, twice women's B.A.R. and first record-breaker of the post-Burton era.

championship, an interesting pointer to the social changes in the cycling world of the 1980s. She was edged out of the B.A.R. in 1990 by Elaine Ward, whose winning margin was one of the narrowest ever recorded: 0.009 m.p.h. Ward was a member of a traditional cycling family, and she partnered her father Paddy to an R.R.A. mixed tandem 25 record of 46:33.

Beryl did not contest the B.A.R. after 1983, but she did not relinquish her grip on the shorter distances without a fight, and it was here that she suffered her first defeats in the early 1980s. If anyone was going to beat her over 10 and 25 miles it would surely be Mandy Jones, whose brilliant road-racing talent had given her a world championship bronze medal at the age of 18. Mandy took the 10 championship from Beryl in 1982 and 1983, the 25 championship in 1983 and 1985, and the 50 championship in 1982, while in 1984 it was the turn of Barbra Collins to edge out Beryl by just one second for the 10-mile title. Beryl came back from these defeats and took both the 25 and th 50 in 1986,

which was her last championship-winning year. When she had given up her road-racing career, Mandy herself won the B.A.R. in 1991, taking the 25 and 50 championships along the way. It is noticeable that, with the exception of the 30-mile, none of these riders had really threatened the Burton legacy of competition records, in spite of all the technical advances in training and equipment during the 1980s. This situation was about to change with the arrival of riders like Maxine Johnson, Yvonne McGregor, Jenny Derham and Jill Reames.

In 1993 both McGregor and Johnson broke the 10 record, with Johnson leaving it at 20:38. In the same year McGregor became the second woman to go inside four hours

Jill Reames, fastest-ever woman B.A.R. in 1997 with 27 m.p.h.

for the 100, although her 3:58:31 left Beryl's record still standing, and a further three seasons were to pass before her great middle-distance records fell at last. Beryl's tragic death occured in May 1996, so she never witnessed the events of that summer, when McGregor really took the 25 record apart in 1996 with her ride of 51:50. Jenny Derham took exactly two minutes from the Burton 50 record, with 1:49:31, and most sensationally of all Sharon Lowther at last broke the 100 record with 3:54:38, minutes before Derham came home in the same event with 3:53:04. Beryl's 1968 ride of 3:55:05 had at last been overtaken after 28 years. Not surprisingly Derham won the B.A.R., again setting a record average speed faster than Beryl's. Derham was 27 years old, had a young family, and had come from nowhere in cycling terms in just two years. Her secret was that she had been a runner, and had run middle-distance events on road and track for ten years. She had pro-

Mandy Jones, time-trial champion, track champion and world road champion, the most veratile woman rider since Beryl Burton.

gressed from running to duathlon to cycling, a pattern that was becoming increasingly common, and running still played a role in her training.

Derham had taken women's time-trialling speeds to new heights, but only a year later the standard was raised even higher when her 50 record was broken and the women's B.A.R. average was taken over 27 m.p.h. for the first time by Jill Reames. In complete contrast to Derham, Reames had been a junior champion and an international rider alongside Mandy Jones in the early 80s, before taking ten years out of the sport. Reames took the 50 record down to 1:47:48 and she remained supreme at that distance, winning the championship four times in five years. She had missed out on the ideal conditions in that 100 in September 1996, but she took three 100-mile championships and won the B.A.R. for the second time in 1999. McGregor concentrated on her brilliant track career, and on riding the shorter-distance time-trials, winning six pursuit championships, four 25-mile championships and four 10s. By the year 2000, women's racing had completely emerged from the Beryl Burton era, with only her 12-hour record left standing. In the field of straight-out records, the Eileen Sheridan era had yielded a little earlier: Sue Wright up-dated the 50 and 100 records in dramatic fashion, with rides of 1:36:46 for the 50 and and 3:50:39 for the 100. Pauline Strong took another minute from that 100 time, and then went for many of the longer-distance records, culminating in her End-to-End time of 2:6:49 in 1990, a full 36 years after Eileen's ride. In 2001 Lynne Taylor reduced this to 2:5:48, a marvellous ride in very tough conditions. Nevertheless a few of Eileen's place-to-place records still survive, modern traffic conditions having made them unattractive as targets.

Having won the national road-race championship a dozen times, Beryl had largely turned her back on the bunches by the mid seventies. She was tired of the negative racing, where all too often the whole field would wait for her to attack and then sit in until the sprint. This impression was confirmed by the high number of women's road races which ended in a bunch sprint, the championship races being especially prone to these tactics. There was a structural problem in women's road-racing, namely that there was only one category, and given the great spread of ability found in any field, there was little that many of the riders could do except to sit in. The same few riders dominated all the results in the later seventies: Carol Barton, Denise Burton, Catherine and Margaret Swinnerton, Brenda Atkinson, Julie Earnshaw and Faith Murray. This pattern was emphatically broken in 1981 when Mandy Jones won the championship race after a lone attack that took her seven minutes clear of her pursuers. Having a relatively weak sprint, Mandy's style was to attack for victory long before the finish. She had already taken a bronze medal in the 1980 world championships, and at 19 she was clearly the most exciting new prospect in women's racing for many years. She underlined her class by breaking the women's hour record in 1981, adding almost two kilometres to the old figures. In 1982 on the track she won her third national pursuit title and set a new women's 5,000 metre world record of 6:41. In time trials she rode a 55-minute 25, and she beat Beryl Burton in the 50 championship. All this was a foretaste of what was to come in the world championships at Goodwood, when she rode away from the rest of the field to take the gold medal alone, in a style worthy of Beryl herself. In the following year she again dominated the national road race with a solo win, but in the world's event she was unable this

Lisa Brambani, four times road-race champion in the late 1980s.

time to escape from the lead group, and took fourth place. At the end of that season the cycling world was stunned to learn that she was retiring from racing, at the age of 21. She had never had a career and had devoted herself entirely to cycling for six years. Having achieved so much already, she wanted to start a family and a business, and start living a more normal life. In fact after a season out, she did come back to racing, although to the less pressurised sphere of time-trialling. With its youthful brilliance and its early end, her career seemed closer to the careers of top-level swimmers or gymnasts, who live entirely for their sport at a very early age, and only then set about building a normal adult life for themselves. Her career underlines once again how extraordinary was Beryl Burton's lifetime commitment to competition. Mandy too had complained that her rivals now raced very negatively against her, and this increased her feeling that there was probably nowhere further for her to go in English racing.

Had she stayed in road racing for a little longer, she might have found greater challenges and greater opportunites, for the world of women's racing was about to change rather dramatically. Women's cycling was introduced into the Olympics for the first time in 1984, and in the same year the Tour de France Feminin became a major target for international riders. Olympic recognition meant more to the world at large than cycling world championships, so that state aid and commercial sponsorship would soon follow, and within a few years mountain-biking arrived, which would be a women's sport from the first. In the Tour Feminin the most consistent British rider over a number of years was Clare Greenwood, who never won the national road race title, but who was a top-ten finisher in the two-week stage race on more than one occasion. In the late 1980s the unbeatable figure in women's road-racing was Lisa Brambani, winner of four successive national titles, able to sprint or win alone, and able to beat Mandy Jones to several 10-mile championships. One of her best results was to finish 5th in the 1987 world championship race, and she lost the 1990 Commonwealth Games race by a whisker. She travelled to road races throughout Europe and would spend part of each year in the United States, racing for a sponsored team. Like Mandy she achieved her success at a very young age, and like her she too retired very young and for similar reasons. By a strange coincidence Brambani's successor, Marie Purvis, was also to become a four-times winner of the national road championship. Purvis was a native of the Isle of Man, in the tradition of Millie Robinson, Peter Buckley and Steve Joughin, and unlike Jones and Brambani, success came to her only when she was over 30. In 1993 she became the first British rider to win a stage in the Tour Feminin, taking a major Alpine stage and finishing 6th overall.

In the early 1990s several pieces of history were made in women's cycling. In a handicap race in March 1991, Julie Hill and Sharon Beech took first and second, leaving the men to pick up the lower placings - the first such victory in an open road race. In the same year, Pauline Strong and Caroline Alexander signed professional contracts with Raleigh, Strong to attack road records, and Alexander to ride moutain-bike races. These were the first women professional cyclists in Britain since Eileen Sheridan's years with Hercules in the early 1950s. In the climate of the time, Raleigh were no longer interested in running a professional road team, and it made better commercial sense for them to form a multi-discipline team to cover all the spheres of the bike market. Their decision to sign women as professionals also shows the widening social base of competitive cycling in the 1990s. Alexander would go on to win several national off-road titles, and she would be joined by other women who switched from top-level road or track racing, such as Sally Dawes.

On the track as on the road there were a handful of girls who accumulated national titles year after year, but who displayed all the classic symptoms of the Lloyd Binch syndrome. Faith Murray won no less than six successive sprint championships between 1972 and 1977, then Brenda Atkinson won four, and Louise Jones another six. But there was a kind of unspoken exchange rate, in which one world's medal was worth four or five domestic medals. A less prolific winner at home than these was Sally Hodge, but Hodge gained greater renown when she won the newly instituted women's points event at the 1988 world championships. In a baffling sequel, Hodge was never actually awarded a medal, the officials claiming that the event was a demonstration - whatever that meant. The range of track events continued to proliferate far beyond the classic sprints and pursuits, and the international track teams became bigger. Sports subsidies and media attention made the chase for medals more intense, and the modern velodrome became a very different place from the traditional track. Riders like Murray, Atkinson, and Louise Jones entertained the crowds at Leicester for many years and become national figures in their sport. They had won the highest possible honours in their own country, and written themselves into the record books, but the glory of international medals eluded them. Whether that mattered or not depends on one's scale of values.

The Bike Business

From the 1970s to the 1990s Condor shared in all the many revolutions which overtook the sport and the bike trade. The business reaped the rewards of the growth in cycling, and it became more prosperous than it had ever been in the Spartan days of the 50s and 60s. They moved to larger premises in 1980 but still in Gray's Inn Road; they brought out new designs, and they moved into mountain biking; but they always knew that the key to their success was their carefully established name, their involvement with the sport, and their commitment to giving good service to serious road cyclists. They guarded their reputation, never grew too big, never opened distant branches, and never spread their name too thin. Their association with some top riders, even in the years after the Condor-Mackeson team had dissolved, gave them continuing publicity. The Skol Sixes of the 1970s, where Tony Gowland rode in the Condor colours, sometimes with the great Belgian Patrick Sercu and sometimes with the Australian Don Allan, were vital meeting-points for the sport where a huge amount of business was done. With the Bilton team, Condor entered the reinvigorated professional racing scene in the 80s, and then they joined the move to sponsored clubs. Monty's skill as a mechanic meant that he was in demand each year to man the service car in many big races - the Milk Race in the late 1970s and early 80s, the Sealink Inter national and the Peace Race. This was unpaid, and it was a major sacrifice of time and energy, but it had great publicity spin-off and it kept Condor at the heart of cycle sport.

The original and distinctive frame designs with the hand-cut lugs were still being made - in the shop window they were the crown jewels that caught the eye, and they

Monty and Grant moving into the second shop at 144 Gray's Inn Road in 1980.

*Monty Young with
Gerrie Taylor and the
seervice car in the 1979
Milk Race.*

appealed to some of Condor's celebrity customers, like Mick Jagger, who was then a cycling fan and a regular at the Skol Sixes, in fact Jagger had witnessed Moser's historic hour record at Mexico in January 1984. Jagger bought several machines, and he introduced Eric Clapton to Condor, and Clapton too ordered a hand-built frame in 1972 that was a work of art; at the time it broke new ground in prices at £247 for a complete campag-equipped machine, which would just about buy a carbon fork now. Condor also had a nice line in gold-plated frames, which were over the top for most British tastes, but which they took to trade shows in America, and they always sold. They also developed a range of very different streamlined frames, lugless with ultra-modern geometry and finishes. Although they always guarded their identity as a family business and a single specialist shop, they took every opportunity to put their name around, whether by giving up weeks of their time on Milk Race service duty, sponsoring cyclists setting off to ride to India, or lending bikes to the media for photo-sessions or films. In any shopping guide to London, Condor appeared as the shop for the connoisseur, alongside Hatchards for books, Moss Bros for suits, Stanfords for maps, and Dunhill for pipes and tobacco. Their bikes won several design awards - from the Sunday Telegraph and from the prestigous Conran Foundation, who featured a Condor machine in their *Good Design Guide* of 1985.

Change can easily kill a traditional business, but it can sometimes breathe new life into it, and this is certainly what happened to Condor in the 1980s, with the design revolution which hit the bike industry, and the environmental revolution which spread throughout western society. Bike design had been virtually static for decades, in fact cyclists always used to believe that traditional wisdom built up over the years was a guarantee of good design. With the sole exception of the Moulton, experimentation was directed entirely at reducing weight, and this led to the craze in the 1970s for drilling out the frame and components to save weight. With the advent of computer-aided design and wind-tunnel testing, this was revealed to be a complete fallacy, because the turbulence created around the drillings negated any possible advantage from the weight-saving. The lesson was learned, and by 1980 the search for smooth, polished, aerodynamic forms was under way. Tubes became oval, cables were routed inside frames, front brakes were mounted behind the fork crown, drink bottles were flattened, and so on. Then suddenly

A unique aero tandem built for Vic Haines; it was a steel tubeset, overlaid with carbon fins to a design by Mick Burrow.

at the world championships in 1981, a new generation of bikes appeared, with small front wheels, sloping top-tubes and upturned handlebars. Aerodynamic modelling had been applied to the bike as a whole rather than to its components, and these "funny bikes" were the result. A second leap forward came when Moser unveiled the radical new bike which he used for his hour record in 1984, with its disk wheels. For the rest of the decade, for pure speed in track events or time-trials, this was the fashion, and cyclists throughout Britain set out to re-equip themselves. When the riders added aero helmets and skinsuits, the whole image of the cyclist changed so that they almost resembled science-fiction robots; journalists christened this development the age of the cycling mutant. Riders would take press photographs of European trackmen into frame-building shops, and demand an identical machine - and they got it. Even at the time however, doubting voices were raised about these designs, arguing that this was not the way to go; among these voices was the former 25 record holder Mick Burrow, who advocated a completely new look at the frame, and who was already working on a prototype of the monocoque shell that would eventually become the Lotus bike ridden by Chris Boardman. With hindsight it seems obvious that although these early aerodynamic designs may have appeared radical, the position of the rider on the bike was essentially unchanged.

Aerodynamic design however was only a part of a wider revolution in attitudes to cycling hardware, and we moved suddenly into an age of non-stop innovation, where machines and equipment were highly-prized precisely because they were new. This was in complete contrast to the old idea that what had been tested and proved for years must be the best. Science was applied to the bicycle, to clothing, and to training aids, so that

"What the best-dressed cyclist is wearing", from the Telegraph, April 1996. The bike was the lugless 853 Baracchi, the last newly-designed steel-framed Condor, before the move into alumimium and carbon.

WHAT THE BEST-DRESSED

CYCLIST
IS WEARING

From royalty to ragamuffin, cycling is one of this nation's most popular outdoor pursuits. But once on your bike, kit is crucial to overall performance. We climb on the saddle and explore the cyclist's world

FROM the midst of Britain's 4 million cyclists comes a cure of hardened individuals who, come rain or shine, manoeuvre their contraptions of aerodynamic steel at speeds of up to 65 miles per hour.

Recent developments in clothing fabrics have got the serious cyclist doing wheelies with excitement. Sports designers over the past decade have been experimenting with how to make a good thing even better. The important factors of balance and grip led them to develop a synthetic version of leather called Lorica, which is lightweight, non-chafing, water resistant and doesn't rot.

Lorica repels water whether it's perspiration or rain and helps prevent blistering, a chief problem of life on the open road. As a bonus, it can be machine-washed. Other new inventions include gel-filled foam pads on palms and soles for shock-absorbing. 'Quick release' shoes are important in the event of a tumble where strapped-in feet could get trapped.

High-tech performance fabric Coolmax has infiltrated the cyclist's lair. This lightweight polyester product can be combined with Lycra to smooth around bodily contours, leaving no gaps for wind pockets which slow you down. Silicon leg-gripper panels on shorts stop them riding up and anti-bacterial padded inserts on the backside help absorb shocks on bumpy terrain.

Aerodynamic fin-tail helmets are worth their lightweight in gold. The most expensive models are panelled for supreme ventilation. The Air Piranha label wins outright, coming up to every level of British and European standards.

As with any speed sport where more than smoke can get in your eyes, protection is crucial to overall performance. Briko's polycarbonate goggles are light, impossible to scratch and come with interchangeable lenses for different racing conditions.

The bike for champions, according to Grant Young, a partner at retailers Condor Cycles, is the Reynolds 853 Baracchi. Made from light steel tubing it grips the road and has a finely-tuned record groupset (the componentry making up the brakes, gears, brake levers etc). The inbuilt cordless computer has eight functions, including monitoring average and top speed and distance, as well as a 24-hour clock.

Racing cyclists have no need of a bicycle repair kit because the service car is never too far behind, but a plastic bottle filled with an energy drink is a permitted luxury.

HELMET: Aerodynamic Air Piranha racing helmet extra small to extra large in red, black or silver, £99.99, by the Specialized Bicycle Component Inquiries 01372 740 084

GOGGLES: ZEN HPS protective polycarbonate cycling goggles (anti-scratch), one size, assorted interchangeable lenses and colours to suit riding environment (i.e. sunlight or dark nightlight), £68.99, by BRIKO. Inquiries 01435 863 615

TOP: Coolmax/Lycra Condor team jersey, with Campagnolo logo, s-xxl, £34.99, by END inquiries 01606 497 749

GLOVES: Palm Springs cycling glove in synthetic leather with Gelfoam grip, small to extra large, in purple/black, red/black, grey/black, £19.99, by Specialized Bicycle Component Co. (see helmet)

BICYCLE: Custom-built Condor 853 Baracchi racing cycle, made of Reynolds 853 steel tubing, with Campagnolo record groupset, Katoye cordless computer, Vittoria open quarter CX 19 tyres and handmade wheels. colours to order. £2,289

SHORTS: Coolmax cycling shorts, small to extra-large, black only, £39.99, by ENDURA (see top)

SOCKS: Racing socks in acrylic/

SHOES: Quick-release racing shoe, made

between 1980 and 1985 we saw the arrival of computer speedos, turbo trainers, hard-shell helmets, clipless pedals, aluminium frames, deep V-section rims, and lycra clothing. The last stretched and moved with the body, it felt great, it slipped through the wind, and it could be printed in bright designs and team colours. After initial resistance by the British racing authorities, disk wheels and tri-bars became legal in the 1990s, and then they too were added to the list of now-essential components.

And simultaneously there came the mountain bike revolution, developed in America and reaching Britain in 1983. At first no one here was sure if it was just a passing fad; BMX had arrived in 1980, but serious cyclists looked down their noses at it, as being little better than the other youth craze of the age - skateboarding. But mountain biking was here to stay: it appealed to the back-to-nature, escapist ideals of the 80s, so that the city-dweller pedalling through Epping Forest or Richmond Park somehow imagined himself in the Rocky Mountains. The most unpredictable thing of all was the way mountain bikes were found to be ideal for city cycling, with their fat tyres, wide range of gears and relaxed riding position. Like the Moultons twenty years earlier, their novel image attracted huge numbers of buyers who had not thought of themselves as cyclists before. Bicycle sales in the UK boomed: in 1979 they topped one million for the first time, and by 1989 they were at two million, with 20% of those mountain bikes. The serious side of off-road sport developed rapidly, with the first official world championships held in America in 1990, and the first British championships in the following year. Traditional roadies remained unmoved by the mountain-bike craze, but they were a dwindling minority. Some established cyclo-cross stars like Tim Gould crossed over to MTB and became champions in the new discipline. When Alex Moulton bought back the rights to re-launch his new Moulton in 1983, the new bikes acquired a small cult following, but the design could never become a mass-maket success again because it had been outmanoevred by the mountain- bike movement.

The constant innovation in the design of mountain bikes reinforced still further the drive towards change in road-bikes: every features was scrutinised, there were no longer any design dogmas that said that any given component must be like this or like that. Radical new designs for the road frame proliferated: there was the Kirk Precision, made of magnesium, not in tubes but in a pressed girder-like structure, with no down-tube, resembling the old Paris Galibier. Another bike to dispense with the down-tube was the Slingshot, which used a spring-loaded steel wire instead. Most astonishing of all perhaps was the Zipp carbon, which consisted only of a downtube and chainstay in one piece, with a saddle suspended from it on an out-riding arm. In the excitement over new designs and new materials, the old mystique of ordering a custom-built frame died rapidly. No one now cared about frame angles or even sizes; all that mattered was novelty and modernity of design. Likewise brakes, gears, pedals, stems, wheels - everything was looked at afresh. This new approach was of course just one aspect of the rage for innovation in design and technology that was sweeping through every aspect of our social lives.

The mountain-bike revolution was the basis for the astonishing rise of the American bike industry,

The bicycle in fashion: in the 80s London seemed full of girls in knee-length pedal-pushers.

Condor entered the mountain bike market in 1985 with their "Countryman" model.

with high-quality brands like Marin, Trek, Canondale, Specialised, Scott and Giant springing up, and soon diversifying into road bikes - at a time when British bike manufacturing seemed to be dying. The Americans had the money and they had the innovative drive to change the way bikes were perceived, built and used. These American bike-makers quickly began testing new frame materials - aluminium, titanium and carbon-fibre - forcing their European rivals to do the same. The manufacture was increasingly sub-contracted to factories in the Far East, with only the assembly being carried on at home. Steel tube manufacturers responded by devising lighter and lighter materials, but the tide of fashion was against them.

This new high-tech, high-competition, high-cost environment was not one in which the small, traditional frame-builder could survive with his steel-brazing and his cottage-industry approach. In 1997 Condor took the crucial decision to move into aluminium frames, and five years later into carbon-fibre, and the new generation of frames are now custom-built in Italy. Had this decision not been taken, Condor would have survived as a bike shop, but not as a bike-builder: whatever the virtues or defects of the steel frame, the market-place had decided that the future lay elsewhere. By the late 1990s the single-shop craft frame-builder was an extinct species. The market was now a global one, both in the demands of fash-

Some of Condor's customers were better known outside the cycling world.

ion, and in the economics of supply. This was the culmination of the long process of internationalisation which had begun to work in the British bike trade in the 1950s, when road-racing fashions arrived here. For those who love the retro look, Condor are still happy to build a curly-lugged, chrome-ended steel frame in their own workshop, but it cannot last much longer.

The crucial decision to completely up-date the frame-building was taken by Grant Young. Grant had entered the business unofficially at the age of about ten, when every school-free day and every Saturday would find him helping in the shop and learning bike mechanics from Monty. He joined officially at fifteen in 1972, and was managing jointly by the early 80s, when he also took over from Monty on Milk Race service duty. He took a couple of years sab-

Rob Hayles, of the Team Haverhill-Condor squad, rides an experimental bike with a single-bladed fork, 1994.

batical in the mid-1980s to broaden his horizons, and when he returned to the shop he was staggered by the changes in bike technology, in clothing and in the whole market, now filled with design-conscious customers. Many small companies, faced with the technical changes of the 90s, would have opted out of the market, and the decline in steel frame-building could easily have seen the end of the Condor name. Grant considered however that this would have badly weakened the business. He believed that they had the knowledge and the market position to move into aluminium and carbon fibre. True, the frames are no longer built by a man in goggles with a brazing torch in a back room behind the shop, but they are still custom-built to Condor's own designs and to the customer's individual specification.

The other twin factors which fed the cycling boom of the 1980s were the ecological and health revolutions. By the late 70s, medical science had established a clear link between exercise and health: a sedentary lifestyle led to overweight and heart disease. It seems blindingly obvious to us now, but it wasn't then, any more than the tobacco-cancer link had been obvious a generation earlier. This insight led to the jogging boom, and the diet-and-exercise culture of the 1980s. In this context, cycling need no longer be seen as a second-best form of transport or as an eccentric hobby, instead it was a sign that you cared about your health, your appearance and your life. Bikes and bike clothing now featured in fashion shoots, with models draped over the handlebars, wearing flashy lycra skinsuits. The other effect of the new health consciousness was to bring older riders into cycling, perhasp for the first time, perhaps coming back after twenty years out of the

The team pursuit squad for the 1988 Seoul Olympics: Simon Lillistone of Team Haverhill on the right, with Boardman, Sword and Coull.

sport, and they tended to be people with a good deal of money to spend. Years ago young kids would gaze into Condor's window - I was one of them - and wonder how long it would take to save their pennies for one of those exquisite frames, priced at £19 or more. But for a middle-aged company director to invest £1000 or so in his hobby and his health was nothing. This was fortunate as the new designs and the new components all had one thing in common: they were a good deal more expensive than the old ones. An ultra-modern bicycle became as desirable as a set of golf clubs or skis. The rise of triathlon encouraged the link between the endurance sports, and it became common for athletes to cross over from running to cycling, which carried far less risk of stress injuries. Yvonne McGregor for example was first a road-runner who switched to cycling after persistent injuries of this kind.

And it was not just personal health which now came under the spotlight, but the health of the planet. The energy crisis, oil spills, atmospheric pollution, acid rain, chemical farming, the decimation of wildlife - all these things were recognised as the consequences of industrial greed. In 1979 Jim Lovelock published his highly original book *Gaia: a New Look at Life on Earth,* which argued that the earth was a self-sustaining natural organism whose balance mankind was now disturbing or even destroying. This book became the bible of the green movement, and it influenced the thinking of millions of people. Our cities and a good deal of our countryside had been ruined by traffic, and the gifts which the car had once seemed to offer had now turned out to be poisoned ones. Once again the bicycle seemed to offer a simple, rational transport alternative, and pressure groups began to campaign for a new planning approach to encourage cycling. Cycling was no longer a marginal hobby, but part of a new attitude to the environment. It was a form of transport for the thinking man and woman, for the independent spirit. This was particularly true in London, where cycling became once again a serious form of transport; in 1980 a survey revealed 20,000 bicycles entering central London each day, and Condor was one of the very few central bike shops which these commuters could reach easily. The advent of the bicycle courier in London created a new breed of professional cyclists - for that is what they are - and another new customer base, especially for emergency service during their working day. At the other extreme more and more people took up serious adventure cycling, setting off to ride into Tibet, through the Rockies or up Kilimanjaro, and the books they wrote when they got back inspired hosts of imitators. The higher profile that cycling has come to enjoy, the recognition of its social and personal value, has at last begun to have an effect on our concepts of safety and responsibility. There are still far

Don Allan, Australian six-day star and Condor rider.

too many tragedies involving cyclists, but those who cause them are now more likely to be held to account. The idea that the death of a cyclist on the road is automatically an accident is at last vanishing, and so is the perception that cycling must necessarily be a working-class activity.

Condor participated in all these startling and unpredictable changes. Once again they outgrew their shop, but they knew better than to move away from Gray's Inn Road where they had become part of the landscape. Climb into a London taxi now and ask for Gray's Inn Road, and if you look ill the driver knows you want the dental hospital, if you look fit he knows you want Condor Cycles. The bike market has changed completely in the last two decades, and it is now a global industry. Change is so rapid that every year the manufacturer is expected to unveil his new range, like a fashion house, using ever-changing designs in an endless

A double celebration in 1998: Condor mark their 50th year in business, and the move into their third Gray's Inn Road shop. From left: Joe Waugh, Phil Liggett, Rosaline Young, Monty Young, Tracey Young, Martyn Roach, Grant Young.

search for speed and market advantage. Having determinedly moved into this market, Condor has succeeded in creating for itself a unique niche between the big factories and the craft workshop. Making around 2,000 frames per year, the business is big enough to invest in the newest technologies, but small enough to tailor every bike to its customer's demands. Its continuing success shows the immense value of quality name that has been carefully built up and protected over fifty years. The Condor name may be slightly less famous in England than Colnago or Bianchi, but only slightly.

It has been quite a journey from the tiny, badly-lit shop in post-war London selling clumsy black Hercules roadsters, through the years of crafting two or three hand-built frames a week, running professional teams, ervicing international races, sponsoring clubs, surviving austere times, and finally emerging into the boom days of the 1990s. Of the scores of enthusiast's bike shops that were to be found in London in the 1950s, all but a handful have vanished, while Condor is still flourishing. That is why the period from 1945 to 2000 can truly be described as the Condor years, not the Claud Butler years or the Holdsworth years or even the Raleigh years, because those companies, however distinguished their pedigree, have not adapted and survived. In its involvement with the sport and in its business history, Condor has been a microcosm of all the forces, positive and negative, acting within the world of British cycling.

Condor has survived for three reasons: first, it has remained a family business; this has meant independence, without accountants and strategists telling the Youngs they must re-structure and re-orientate their business - and then sailing into disaster. Second, it has continually adapted to the changing demands of the market, but selectively, not following every passing fashion. Third and most important of all, it has remained committed to bike racing. The Youngs have always understood that they must be a part of the

2005 Condor: the carbon-fibre Baracchi.

sport, that their interests and the interests of racing cyclists were identical. When the mountain-bike revolution swept through Britain, they never abandoned the road-bike as most shops did. The shop business always went hand in hand with the building of racing frames, and the quality of each half of the business guaranteed the other. The philosophy has never been to take the money and run, but to sell quality, and that philosophy has been vindicated. In Condor, the serious cyclist has always known that he is in a serious shop, where the staff speak the same language as the customer, and where quality of product and service is paramount. That committment could well be the key to the next fifty years of cycling history.

Monty Young seems to have been around for a long time in British cycling, but is it really this long ?

225

Postscript

I set out to write this book for three main reasons. Firstly, to show how one small family business played such a central role in the history of cycle sport in. Secondly, I wanted to record the world of British cycling over the last half century, because amateur sport is rooted in everyday life, and like most facets of everyday life, it is ephemeral. Each weekend's racing is soon over, and the sporting news of each season is soon forgotten. I wanted to recall some of the great riders of the past, and give them a permanent place in a written history of the sport. Thirdly, I wanted to explore the role of sport in society.

The fifty years covered by this book have seen a revolution in our attitudes to sport. In a world dominated by the media, sport has become a high-profile business, a route to wealth and fame, a spectacle, and a major component in the entertainment industry. Clearly this was not true a generation ago, when cyclists inhabited a very different world, when they trained and raced without thought of reward. The idea that taking part was its own reward was in fact the cornerstone of amateur sport, and I have written this book in praise of that outdated ideal. I do not share the belief that the sole measure of the strength of British cycling should be our success-rate in prestigious international competition. This seems to me to be a model of sport imported from the world of business, where you invest money and effort, and demand results to match. I would argue instead that the health of the sport should be judged by the number of riders out training and racing each weekend. It is great to win races, but cycling still enriches our lives, even when we are just taking part: if it did not, we would not do it.

To the spectator, cycling is not terribly glamorous or exciting, perhaps it is not even very interesting, but it is something better: it is a participation sport. It was the product of an era when people thought it was better to do something than to watch something. Cycling is active and challenging; it extends the boundaries of what we demand of ourselves, and it produces a maturer personality, and a sense of physical and mental well-being. Above all, cycling has value because its motivation has to come from within. Only by doing it can you appreciate it. In an age when everything is fed to us from the outside, when we are told what to do and feel, what to think and believe, cycling is a throwback to a time when people created their own culture, and when they discovered the world for themselves. Cycling is personal, physical and immediate: it takes you out into the streets or the country, into the wind and the cold, and brings you face to face with your environment. In the age of technology, of entertainment, and of passivity, it confronts you with something harder, simpler and more elemental.

Perhaps this is the answer to the question we are so often asked and which we find so hard to answer: why do you do this? Why do you want to ride for 50 miles or 100 miles or even more, and push yourself to your physical limits? The answer may be that the rest of our lives are so safe, so regulated, so cocooned, that we do it to assert our own freedom. When you launch yourself off from the start-line of a race, you are alone and you are committed. You have put your ego on the line, and you cannot be lazy or clever or evasive. The race is a challenge, an adventure, a journey outside the boundaries of everyday life. Mountaineers and explorers are probably seeking a similar escape, but the bike racer takes a less risky route to the same experience. You are trying to discover whether you have command over your own destiny, or whether you do only what everyone else does, never sticking your neck out, never taking up a challenge. So when we are drawn into cycling, we are chosing something that is difficult but mysteriously satisfying. It symbolises our freedom from the cheap, stereotyped values that fill our lives, and it takes us on a voyage of self-discovery.

I happen to believe that this is true above all in the old-fashioned and much-maligned world of time-trialling. The history of time-trialling has to be written in terms of the winning elite, the champions and the record-breakers, as I have done here. But the special strength of time-trialling is that it is not an elitist sport, but an egalitarian one. The ordinary club cyclist can ride alongside the champion, and although he may not ride as fast, he can ride just as hard. Within any time-trial there is not just one battle going on but dozens, because it is the battle with oneself. Any rider can score a personal victory in a time-trial merely by starting and finishing the race, and if it were not for the hundreds of ordinary participants, there would be no champions.

The theme of this book has been the internationalisation of British cycling, how the sport that was once insular, and amateur in the best sense, has been subject to political and commercial pressures which have altered its scale of values. This process of evolution was inevitable: we don't run our social or personal life, our businesses or our politics, as if we still lived in the Victorian age, and sport could not escape change either. Technology, money, exposure to influences from abroad, the power of the media, new social attitudes - all these things have changed the way we see cycling, what we expect from it and how we approach it. Yet something fundamental must remain the same: in spite of all the changes there is obviously continuity too, because we are still getting up early on Sunday mornings and lining up to race. In spite of everything, we are still linked to the cycling days of Ken Joy, Eileen Sheridan, Ray Booty, Bill Bradley and the rest, by the pleasure that we get from this demanding but addictive hobby. We are drawn to cycling because it seems to express something that cannot be expressed in any other way. I do not claim that this book has made that something any clearer, but I hope it has shown how strong and vital the British cycling tradition is.

The essential amateur: released from championship pressures, Booty has fun on his trike. Ray doesn't know it, but it's clear that he has just unshipped his chain, and will get a nasty shock when he starts pedalling again.

Bibliography

The basic source for British cycling history is of course the magazine *Cycling*, which has been published weekly since 1891. Year after year its editors and journalists have created a precious record of the sport's history, and my book could not have been written without their work to build on. The early history of the magazine was told in A.C.Armstrong's *Bouverie Street to Bowling Green Lane*, 1946, which describes the origin of the B.B.A.R competition. The monthly magazine *Coureur: Sporting Cyclist* ran from 1955 to 1968, and its successor *International Cycle Sport* from 1968 to 1984. Both were dedicated to bringing continental news to British readers, but they also published excellent reports on the home scene.

There is a small group of valuable books on the recent history of British cycling. The 50th anniversary of the R.T.T.C. was marked by the publication of Bernard Thompson's *Alpaca to Skinsuit*, 1988, a survey of time-trialling history, and in the same year the R.R.A.'s history was the subject of Roy Green's *100 Years of Cycling Road Records*. The inside story of the B.L.R.C. is told in Chas Messenger's *Ride and Be Damned* , 1998, while Messenger's earlier books such as *Cycling's Circus*, 1971, are full of reminiscences of the Milk Races of the 50s and 60s. Messenger also wrote a book about training, *Conquer the World*, 1968, which includes an early account of interval-training theory. Peter Clifford's *History of the Tour of Britain*, 1967, is a systematic history of the first fifteen years of the race. The journalist David Saunders brought together a number of interesting articles, mainly on road racing, in his *Cycling in the Sixties*, 1971. Gregory Bowden's *The Story of the Raleigh Cycle*, 1975, contains a great deal of social, industrial and sporting history. There is a brief history of the W.C.R.A. in the booklet *Rebel With A Cause*, 1999, by Stella Farrell, Eileen Gray and Joan Simmons.

There are half a dozen autobiographies of British cycling stars: Eileen Sheridan's *Wonder Wheels*, 1956; Reg Harris's *Two Wheels to the Top*, 1976; Hugh Porter's *Champion on Two Wheels*, 1975; Les West's *The West Way*, 1970; Barry Hoban's *Watching the Wheels Go Round*, 1981; Beryl Burton's *Personal Best*, 1986; and Malcolm Elliott's *Sprinter*, 1990; and the study of Boardman by Phil Liggett and Antony Bell, *The Fastest Man on Two Wheels*, 1994.

INDEX

Jackson, Harry 98, 146
Jackson, Stuart 201
Jacob, Alan 83-87
Jacobs, Elsie 67
Jagger, Mick 216, 220
Jensen, Knud, death of 108
Jeoffroy, Terry 79, 81
Johnson, Maxine 211
Jolly, Brian 118
Jones, Graham 169-171
Jones, Louise 214
Jones, Mandy 211, 212-213
Jones, Rita 150
Jones, Stan 37, 42
Joughin, Steve 169, 172-3
Jowers, Ron 36, 41, 48, 49
Joy, Ken 24, 50-51, 59
Keeler, Dave 47, 58, 61, 68
Keen, Peter 186, 199, 208
Keighley, Roy 63
Kelloggs criterium series 177
Kelloggs Tour of Britain 178
Kershaw, Joan 123
King, Bernard 39, 40, 46
King, Bill 36, 39
Kirby, Brian 131
Kirk, Andy 152
Krebs, Fred 38, 42, 46
Laidlaw, Ken 148, 153
Lambert, Keith 167
Lander, George 31
Lawrence, Steve 169-171
Lawrie, Bill 100
League International 185
League of Veteran Racing Cyclists (L.V.R.C.) 185
Legalisation of racing 78
Leicester, national track championships centralised at 144, 176, 204
Leicester, World Championships at 156
Letts and Parker, tandemists 26
Lewis, Colin 93-97
Lewis, Ray 163, 195
Lillistone, Simon 174, 207-8
Linden, Jimmy 148, 151
Liversedge, John 58
Llangollen-Wolverhampton race 28, 94-95
Lloyd, Dave 164-165, 190-192
London-Holyhead race 30, 81, 85, 86, 89, 101
Longbottom, Pete 199

Longland, Glen 198
Maitland, Bob 15, 30, 31, 37, 42, 51, 52, 63
Manchester Velodrome 184
Manchester Wheelers 174, 176, 206
Marriner, Charlie 27
Martin, Neil 180, 181-183
Mason, Wes 88, 102, 114
Massed-start racing 28 ff.
Matthews, Eric 140
Matthews, Pete 114
McCoy, Charly 124
McGhee, Andy 153
McGregor, Yvonne 211
McHugh, Paul 209
McLoughlin, Joey 179-180
McMillan, John 151
McNamara, Mike 122, 135
McNaught, Gordon 149, 151
McNeill, Dick 46
Meadowbank Velodrome 209
Meekins, Doug 133
Mernickle, Keith 142-143
Metcalfe, Arthur 94-95, 112-113, 134-135
Michaux, Marcel 37
Miles, Iris 65
Milk Race 40 ff., 110 ff., 159 ff.
Milk Race, end of 185
Millar, Joe 151
Millar, Robert 171-2, 178, 186
Mitchell, E.V. 148, 150-151
Mitchell, Glen 181-183
Mockridge, Russell 73, 144
Moody, Christine 140
Moody, Eric 133
Moore, Willi 129, 190
Morgan, Trevor 126-7
Moulton bicycle 77, 154-155, 219
Mountain biking 159, 218
Mummery, Joe 129
Munday, Eddie 57
Munford, Chris 36, 132
Murray, Faith 214
Mynott, Ron 24, 57
Nakano, Koicho 204
National Cyclist's Union (N.C.U.) 28 ff, 75
Needle and Young, tandemists 60
Newman, Alf 37
Nicholson, Vic 119, 154
Nickson, Bill 162